ETHICS IN **IT** OUTSOURCING

ETHICS IN **IT** OUTSOURCING

TANDY GOLD

CRC Press
Taylor & Francis Group
Boca Raton   London   New York

CRC Press is an imprint of the
Taylor & Francis Group, an **informa** business
AN AUERBACH BOOK

CRC Press
Taylor & Francis Group
6000 Broken Sound Parkway NW, Suite 300
Boca Raton, FL 33487-2742

First issued in paperback 2018

© 2012 by Taylor & Francis Group, LLC
CRC Press is an imprint of Taylor & Francis Group, an Informa business

No claim to original U.S. Government works

ISBN-13: 978-1-4398-5062-6 (hbk)
ISBN-13: 978-1-138-37444-7 (pbk)

Library of Congress Cataloging-in-Publication Data

Gold, Tandy.
　　Ethics in IT outsourcing / Tandy Gold.
　　　　p. cm. -- (Applied software engineering)
　　Includes bibliographical references and index.
　　ISBN 978-1-4398-5062-6 (hardback)
　　1. Information technology--Contracting out--Moral and ethical aspects. 2. Electronic data processing departments--Contracting out--Moral and ethical aspects. 3. Business ethics. 4. Engineering ethics. I. Title.

HD30.2.G636 2012
174'.4--dc23
　　　　　　　　　　　　　　　　　　　　　　　　　　　　　　　　　　2012005280

Visit the Taylor & Francis Web site at
http://www.taylorandfrancis.com

and the CRC Press Web site at
http://www.crcpress.com

For Dan, Bosh, Pun, Nique, and Wumpet

My Beloveds

Contents

When the minted gold in the vault smiles like the nightwatchman's
  daughter,
When warrantee deeds loaf in chairs opposite and are my friendly
  companions,
I intend to reach them my hand, and make as much of them as I do
  of men and women like you.

—Walt Whitman, A Song for Occupations

Chapter 1

Overview of Ethics in IT Outsourcing: An Oxymoron?

1.1 Building a Framework for Ethical Discussion

1.1.1 The Macro View: Follow the Money

The Supreme Court of the United States prevents a vote count for a Presidential election, and the federal government spends billions of taxpayer dollars propping up financial institutions that respond to this largess with higher consumer fees and even higher executive bonus pay-outs. Within such a cultural environment, do we beg the question of ethics, or does it simply become naïve?

Before we construct a model of IT outsourcing ethics during such challenging times, it may be instructive to first look at the seat of the law. Governmental law represents the ultimate source of recourse for the most blatant of ethical violations. Yet, as any historian knows, the history of United States government is not exactly an innocent one. In May 1856, while sitting at his desk at the senate, Massachusetts Senator Charles Sumner, an outspoken civil rights activist, was beaten by cane until bloody by Representative Preston Brooks, who returned to a hero's welcome in his home state of South Carolina. And on March 1, 1954, four Puerto Rican nationalists used automatic pistols to shoot 30 rounds from the visitor's balcony into the House of Representatives during a debate over an immigration bill. President Andrew Jackson, the force behind the death march of 1838–1839 in which 15,000 Cherokees were forced to leave their land and homes, ignored the Supreme Court ruling in *Worcester v. Georgia* (1832) that found that they could not be forcibly moved. President Jackson himself survived an attempt on his life when two point-blank pistols held by his would-be assassin misfired.

Today, many U.S. institutions appear to have violated the very positions of trust and power originally intended by their authority, including governmental, religious, and not the least, business entities. This is the backdrop in which the question of ethics in IT outsourcing must be grounded. IT outsourcing is just one of many ethical conundrums that generate great emotion, debate, and concern about fairness and equity in a world of the shrinking middle class and scarcity of well-paying jobs.

Oddly enough, the current environment of increasingly overt ethical violations occurs within the context of a U.S. business culture that demands, as a prerequisite for a meaningful professional career, a carefully nurtured public persona based upon a highly specific code of professional ethical conduct. This conduct is most often expressed in terms of building and documenting a professional reputation that reflects extreme loyalty and accountability in the form of achievement of objective job-related results. Within large IT corporate divisions, demonstration of the ability to execute within a complex organization and technical environment in a way that demonstrates personal integrity—in the form of dedicated, against-the-odds commitment to delivery of promised business results—is one of the strongest determinants of professional advancement.

Perhaps this paradox is to be expected—taking pride in fair play while simultaneously—and selectively—rewarding those who compromise their ethics. The key will be to honor and acknowledge both aspects of our collective national split personality. Americans are one and the same the most generous of donors to Haiti and almost completely oblivious to the simultaneous suffering in the Congo. We are both the enthralled audience of the environmentally conscious best-selling movie *Avatar*, and the voters who look the other way as yet another species becomes extinct or irreplaceable habitat is irretrievably compromised, depriving our children and grandchildren of their precious legacy.

1.2 Outsourcing Fundamentals: The Egoless IT Manager

We begin by defining our terms with as much precision and clarity as possible.

IT outsourcing is defined as a business transformational process that enables savings from IT (information technology) jobs that are moved to countries external to the United States, or "offshore." It is understood that, for the great majority of IT outsourcing programs, the outsourced jobs generally reside within large (Fortune 100 and above) firms. This is because the up-front transformational costs and transfer of knowledge generally (not always) make outsourcing a volume play. It is challenging for both the U.S.-based customer and the offshore outsourcing service provider to establish financial gains on relatively small numbers of outsourced IT positions. Small is generally defined as outsourcing fewer than 100 full-time equivalent (FTE) jobs at one time. This volume is for a variety of reasons, including program overhead costs that include the implementation of necessary updates in business processes, security management, communications, and IT methodology. These are some of the pre-requisites required for a successful shift to offshore outsourcing. The primary drivers behind IT outsourcing, within the context of this volume, are assumed to be about following the money. Immediate monetary savings from labor arbitrage is not the only driver behind outsourcing, but it is certainly one of the primary ones (Tandy Gold, Outsourcing Software Applications Offshore: Making it Work, CRC Press, 2004).

The analysis of offshore outsourcing in this earlier volume concludes that it is the strategic advantages of IT outsourcing that represent the true benefits over the long term. These benefits include widespread IT process formalization resulting in sustained competitive advantages that often outweigh the tactical cost savings—even as large as they are. It is unlikely that outsourcing as a discipline would have become a wide-spread phenomenon; however, without the simple fact that offshore IT workers receive roughly $25 per hour in compensation, rather than the $70 to $90 per hour their U.S. equivalents generally command. Note, however, that not all IT roles are good candidates for offshore outsourcing.

How widespread is offshore outsourcing? Note that *roles* as referenced herein are not equivalent to IT jobs. It is not uncommon for one U.S. IT worker to perform a variety of roles in a given job. For example, an individual's job may incorporate the roles of IT programmer, tester, quality assurance, maintenance programmer, and technical mentor. Large U.S. firms—again, the only ones large enough to offshore jobs because of the volume required to make it profitable as an IT delivery model—rarely offshore more than 10% of their IT organizations. This is for a variety of reasons including security and the need for certain roles to function near U.S.-based end users. In a given firm with an IT workforce of 1000, roughly 100 individuals will often work offshore. This is called the co-sourcing model. Co-sourcing refers to an offshore staffing model in which tactical roles such as programming are moved offshore, and strategic and customer facing roles remain onshore. The upshot of all of these factors is that the overall economic impact of off shoring jobs is often described as minimal by economists in their review of broad indicators. Offshore outsourcing has yet to be defined as a definitive contributor to current or past financial downturns. Later in this volume we will review research that, together with public opinion and popular newspapers, appear to contradict these findings. The inconclusive nature of the macroeconomic data is one of many gray areas related to an investigation of offshore outsourcing. Clearly there is no lack of thorny ethical questions that arising from the analyzing the offshore model.

Given this backdrop, what is generally the focus of IT ethics today? If you were to stop a Fortune 100 employee and ask about business ethics, how would he or she respond?

- First, business ethics in a large company environment generally comes under the heading of compliance. Corporate ethics frequently focuses upon addressing illegalities relative to discrimination based upon sex, ethnicity, sexual orientation, religion, or other personal factors. Examples of codes of compliance are the rules of accounting, hiring policies, tax regulations, and corporate by-laws.
- Second, corporate value statements reference the goals of integrity, honesty, and similar principles. These are of limited practical value if they are not modeled seriously by the firm's executive leadership. Enron probably had a robust corporate value statement. Enough said.
- Third, ethics refers to voluntary corporate ethical participation in programs such as Green IT, by which a firm's negative environmental impact or "footprint" is minimized.
- Finally, business ethics commonly refers to the active support of worthy causes and charities, along with similar measures of positive corporate citizenship.

These are all worthy expressions of business ethics. For the topic at hand, however, with a special focus on ethics in IT outsourcing, they may serve as means of confusion, or worse, of deliberate obfuscation.

1.3 Ethical Hypotheses: Guideposts on the Investigative Journey

As we start our journey, let's begin by establishing some hypotheses to test as guideposts along the way.

Hypothesis 1 — Discussions of ethics are rarely clear cut and straightforward, reflecting our national inconsistencies. All dialogue takes place within the context of subtle, varying shades of gray.

We start our investigation with the realization that we ultimately may end up with more questions than answers, and that the answers we uncover may be somewhat less than definitive. Identifying cause and effect for macroeconomics has never been without debate, and is often laden with rhetoric supporting a specific viewpoint. In Chapter 6, we explore the macroeconomic environment further, and create an ethical framework for IT outsourcing at the level of the broad economy.

Hypothesis 2 — The central ethical issue in IT outsourcing at a macro level is the transfer of corporate labor dollars overseas and the resulting disenfranchisement of U.S.-based workers who are economically impacted through job losses.

As any member of large business in corporate America knows, ethical considerations usually stop short of the dollar. The same company that raises fees 30% without warning, understanding completely that this will negatively affect their poorest, most desperate customers, may see this new business policy as purely financial—the normal course of business undertaken for the benefit of stockholders and employees. This same firm may hold itself proudly as completely ethical because, during the same time period, it launched a Green energy program, issued a new corporate value statement, remained completely in compliance with all human resources laws and regulations, and even contributed millions of dollars to a favorite charity.

How does one apply ethical values as an individual within a corporate environment (the micro level of ethical inquiry)? This can be a challenging question. Even with the broad shades of gray we are painting here, bringing in personal principles relating to ethics gets uncomfortably close to religious beliefs that represent discriminatory compliance factors protected by law in the workplace. Yet ethical principles that are not applied on a personal level are devoid of true expression and power.

When I attended graduate school for Computer Information Systems, I was taught about a principle called the "egoless programmer." It was understood that a programmer, as the author of computer code, could choose to deliberately confuse his or her IT peers in a misguided attempt to become more important. A programmer could achieve this by writing such poorly written and complex code that he or she literally became the only person who could understand and maintain it. In my many years of consulting at large firms, this scenario is not far-fetched. Literally every large company I worked with retains some portion of program code that is untouchable because it could break and cannot be fixed. The original author's are long gone, and updating the code represents too much of a risk.

The egoless worker is a valid concept as applied to business in general. Within this framework, the egoless IT worker utilizes their power and authority in the workplace to align with the business goals at hand, in the broadest sense, rather than sacrifice those for self aggrandizement.

Despite its apparent simplicity, the egoless worker can be a relatively subtle concept. For example, for those who cannot tolerate even positive change, displaying aversion to new concepts and ideas may be a not-so-subtle way of ensuring the status quo prevails.

Hypothesis 3 — Egoless decision making is an effective ethical framework at the personal or micro level of ethics.

In Chapter 5, we explore micro ethics further and create a personal decision-making ethical framework as it relates to IT outsourcing.

1.4 The Internet: A New Level of Personal and Public Transparency

A discussion of ethics would not be complete without the latest, rather unexpected, ethical equalizer and enforcer—the omnipresent, and at times seemingly omniscient, Internet. A growing public awareness, fueled by the rapid spread of on-line information such as social networking sites, makes it harder and harder for any individual or firm to hide much of anything. Within today's rapid spread of information, it is not uncommon for the viewers of the latest video post of a high school locker room incident to have actual visual experience of the event prior to formal notification of school authorities.

The moral seems to be that somewhere, somehow, the secret will out. Perhaps later rather than sooner, perhaps incompletely rather than with clarity, the isolated facts come together to paint the picture.

What we have not come to terms with as an individual, business community or society is how profoundly the Internet holds us all to a higher level of accountability. The vague knowledge of racial profiling is not equivalent to a video of a policeman wielding a club on an un-armed African American. The former may be tolerated, the latter reviled, and the individuals involved face the specific consequences of their actions in new ways.

We are learning to conduct ourselves within the context of this greater accountability. It has not quite penetrated the national consciousness and understanding that wherever we are there is more than likely also a camera, a program that can access our email, or another program that provides an electronic or paper trail of our spending and therefore our physical whereabouts. As we increasingly understand that even our biology leaves a DNA trail that can be utilized to redress the innocent, our large businesses are increasingly subject to a kind of scrutiny, skepticism, and accountability that moves well beyond such standards as Generally Accepted Accounting Principles (GAAP).

The level of corporate as well as personal ethical accountability has been upped tremendously by that technological innovation called the Internet. The corporate watch word- "don't write anything in email that you would not want printed in a newspaper," is now replaced with "don't do anything in public that you would not want videotaped and distributed on the internet."

Hypothesis 4 — in our maniacally plugged-in, video-gone-wild world, the truth will out.

1.4.1 The New Level of Internet Fueled Transparency Reveals the Ethical Underpinnings of Business

Associated with this widespread ethical transparency is a frequent question—one that corporations find themselves ill-equipped to address. At what cost do we support a particular profit? Who benefits and who pays? Do we profit at the cost of the environment, of an endangered species, of world climate changes, of anguish and poverty, and if so, how are those costs measured? Is a company that knowingly polluted and made sick an entire town accountable? If so, how can this be repaid?

This is where the new power of accountability and an associated level of new moral standards begin to appear. In the movie *Capitalism: A Love Story,* noted whistleblower Michael Moore shows a family being evicted from a four-generation farm by a bank. There is a knock on the door, there are tears. A retirement-aged worker says, "I could make the payments at $ 1700, but not at $ 2700." We see a $1,000 check from the bank to the family—the pay-off to vacate the home in good condition—and the ultimate insult. "What we are witnessing" says Mr. Moore in a voice-over "is a robbery."

When salt-of-the-earth, hard-working people are victims of upstanding businesses out to earn an "honest profit" within the bounds of the legal system and are treated with gross unfairness for all to witness, what is the impact? Is there another level of accountability?

Hypothesis 5 — whether large firms (and the individuals who represent them) are prepared or not, the general public will judge them within a broader sense of ethics, not the narrow sense of profit motive. The Internet brings to our homes the emotional impact of these business models. The results are seen, felt, and heard—no longer a faceless statistic on a spreadsheet.

1.5 The Molar (Corporate) View: Worker as Expense Precludes Effective Pro-Active Resource Management and Development

Offshore outsourcing brings with it a perception of ethical concerns and visibility regarding management and worker relationships, fairness, and equity. It is not a stretch to say that the structure of today's very large firm is not optimized to deal with the ethical shades of gray that more and more frequently arise regarding various business models and practices. What is the background canvas upon which these relationships occur? While we live in a democracy, the daily work experience of a typical U.S. worker is more akin to life in a monarchy or perhaps an oligarchy. Most workers report to one or more absolute authorities in the form of their direct manager.

The manager's authority, according to job-related social networking sites and documented research, is often experienced as arbitrary, capricious, and changeable. (Dr. Stephen Hartman, School of Management, New York Institute of Technology's summarization of organizational behavior theory can be found at http://iris.nyit. edu/~shartman/mba0299/120_0299.htm). Worker performance management processes rarely emphasize coaching or ongoing dialogue to maximize worker productivity. More frequently the performance evaluation process represents an after-the-fact accounting and rating that is tied directly to bonuses or raises. It is not unusual for a management team to receive a great deal of pressure to limit severely the number of top-rated employees. Managers are often forced to fit their employee assessments into predefined percentages driven by budgetary requirements. For example, each manager is allowed no more than 10% top rated workers, no more than 15% above average, and so on.

The view of employee performance as static leads to the ultimate cost—the need for an employee to leave a firm altogether to obtain real opportunities for growth. For many workers, this is the only option to overcome the personal rut created by corporate inertia.

Much of this can be traced to the real motivating structure behind employee behavior (other than an individual's desire to do good work for its own sake). This is the set of formal measured goals that constitute the basis of—job performance appraisal. Very, very rarely does a corporate reward structure motivate managers to develop their employees beyond their current roles.

Executive teams are constantly pressured to cut operating costs, and employees tend to be viewed primarily as expenses to be minimized. As market competition and pressures increase, employee labor expense is less about maximizing return on investment and more about generating more work from less. Employees are viewed as a commodity, and the goal is simply to obtain the maximum work-load via whatever is necessary—longer work hours, higher productivity, and, of course, labor arbitrage via offshore outsourcing.

Given that most large firms lack sufficient IT resources to perform the required work in most large firms, the emphasis is rather on keeping the direct team close and focusing them on the tactical work at hand in a kind of endlessly cycling mad rush. While, of course, at some level this is what workers are there to do, there is a cost to the organization for keeping employee contributions relatively static year after year, focusing on one hurdle after another without any kind of longer term view.

The corporate opportunity cost of minimizing employee development is extremely high. As employees are forced to leave to achieve growth, their knowledge and experience also walk out the door. Although the cost of hiring and on-boarding of resources is frequently documented—the classic human resources concept—the actual policies and procedures relating to employee development do not generally reflect those realities, As a result, it is the next firm that benefits from the years of experience garnered by the departing employee. One of the strange cultural quirks of U.S. corporate life is that the annual budget, strategic management and prioritization of capital equipment—now often a fraction of the firm's employee and human resources expenditure—still gets the lion share of executive focus. Until the performance measures of management teams incent employee resource development as much as tracking and monitoring IT projects, the draconian disconnect between the real cost of people management and the business processes behind them will continue.

Some firms overtly use fear to manage workers, believing in the stick rather than the carrot. Unfortunately, IT workers in such situations tend to pass their disillusionment into their work, their relationships with clients, or both. It is difficult for anyone to maintain a loyal, caring, and focused professional presence when feeling threatened or minimized daily on the job.

The very structure of large firms presents challenges. The tendency to view employees through the narrow lens of expense management leads to mismatched employee management processes and policies, and the general employee hoarding that is part of a business culture that is chronically understaffed. Large corporate silos tend to exacerbate this unrealistic, tactical view of personnel.

A group of 60 IT workers in one department that does not have the opportunity to significantly develop their skills over time may be viewed as an unfortunate tactical necessity—especially if they are succeeding in their project delivery. Multiply that same group by a dozen divisions, and suddenly the existence of 720 IT professionals who are unable to grow and develop represents a huge missed opportunity of strategic significance.

Not very long ago, business intelligence—the ability to understand and respond to customers' needs and preferences through data analysis—represented the hottest growth trend and strategic opportunity in information technology. Those companies that invested in business intelligence technology were able to grow and blossom. Other firms who did not make that investment were swallowed whole.

Workforce development may well be the next strategic imperative. As large numbers of baby boomers retire and specialized IT skills become more difficult to obtain, the U.S. may indeed experience what is hard to conceptualize with the high unemployment rates of late: a shift from an employer to an employee driven market for highly skilled workers. That this shift is occurring within a framework of high unemployment does not lessen the challenge of finding replacements for those leaving highly skilled roles.

In Chapter 2, we look at high level workforce trends and the necessity of mutual commitment to ethical conduct by both IT workers and their employers.

Hypothesis 6 — Strategic workforce development (aligning skills development with market needs, opportunity, and global availability) may become the next strategic IT imperative. Firms that master the concept thrive; those that don't, die. In short, strategic workforce development is one of the key competencies to invest in via funding from offshore largess.

1.6   Change Management: A Limited Framework for Enabling Ethical Change

If the de facto human resource departmental focus on legal compliance ignores the true cost of resource management by enabling static, tactical management of IT and other workers, it is also true that most large firms come closest to addressing the ethical issues of IT outsourcing via the discipline of change management. The limitations of change management illustrate the gaps in addressing ethical issues within a broad organizational context.

Change management is often tapped to help implement strategic initiatives, such as offshore outsourcing, that require an emotional as well as business journey. Most businesses work hard to focus on the objective components of work, but initiating outsourcing often means ignoring the emotional component at the peril of program success.

Actively embracing change is not a typical human reaction, and change management programs focus on addressing that reality. Many change management programs include such activities as stakeholder analysis; establishing internal change agents; defining targeted and tailored communications, and similar components designed to overtly support change as it relates to individual acceptance.

Offshore outsourcing is not a comfortable implementation for most IT organizations. Newspapers sell papers by presenting a "sky is falling" scenario with little context for the natural limitations of the program, and emotions tend to run extremely high due to the uncertainty such programs generate. If clear and honest communication is not emphasized through change management or similar programs, it is not uncommon to lose top performers and a great deal of valuable knowledge in the process of launching the initial offshore program.

The foundation of most change management methodologies is based upon stakeholder analysis. The goal is to help stakeholders achieve alignment with the change by identifying the benefits of change within their particular set of responsibilities, but offshore outsourcing may present little in the way of immediate benefit to IT workers within the scope of their particular roles or job. What is most difficult for IT workers is the apparent loss of long-term, productive, business relationships that served as the bases for successful achievement in their work, sometimes years in development. It is difficult not to see these changes as a loss of control. It is not unusual for an employee's major role to move from directly doing work to supervising others doing the same work. The new resources responsible are remotely located and are from a different culture, In "high touch" business cultures where the team member is located down the next corridor or floor, it is big jump to be relegated to phone calls to faceless groups half a world away.

The pressures to deliver (and measures of performance) remain the same, but the level of formality in documenting work roles, responsibilities, status, and execution must be increased across the board. The unwritten rules of work delivery—most business processes are chock-full of them—become obsolete as the shared time zones across the team may be only a few hours per day, so even direct phone communication is time limited.

Often there is little recognition of these significant skill requirement shifts at the ground operational level, and IT workers may just show up one day with completely different roles. They are suddenly supervising, mentoring, and coaching others without the benefit of additional training or skills development in these areas.

Those who have natural faculties make the shift, but others have difficulty learning these skills without formal support, and many are unable to adjust.

If executed correctly, change management can be of tremendous help. The discipline generally incorporates a communication plan that, hopefully, includes a strategic vision of staffing that delineates how additional offshore program financial returns will be invested in the firm to make it stronger. The areas of growth for U.S.-based roles onshore include IT strategy, program and project management. Shifting the focus from tactical savings from labor arbitrage to the strategic opportunity the financial returns present enables loyal IT workers to envision a future in which they can—ironically—finally find opportunities to grow their skills to benefit the organization.

Under the broad heading of change management, which ideally encompasses comprehensive communications and training along with business and technical process assessment and re-engineering, diverse silos within the organization can consolidate and align. This realignments may create even more significant strategic savings in the long term.

One aspect of these savings, for example, relates to the potential for centralized management for multiple independent IT contractors. Prior to offshore outsourcing, it is not uncommon for each IT department, based on its own specific needs, to manage vendors on an individual basis, contract by contract. This means of course, lost opportunities for savings via economies of scale for onshore consultants, large on-boarding costs, and few opportunities for knowledge transfer when each individual contract ends.

Despite the many advantages of change management, with the potential to provide many strategic benefits by addressing broad issues of resistance to change, targeted communications, and business process re-engineering, the focus of the discipline remains limited. The primary focus of change management is upon making a transition to the new mode of execution. Change management as a discipline does not incorporate tools to evaluate how and where to balance the ethical implications of change. This book will hopefully provide a framework for discussion and analysis of these concerns.

Hypothesis 7 — Change management, while invaluable in navigating the challenging waters of successful offshore program initiation, is not an effective model to evaluate the ethical implications—if any—of the change in question.

1.7 Analytical Methodology of Ethics: Validation of Personal Observation

As it relates to profit-seeking entities with specific monetary commitments to shareholders, the concept of business ethics tends to be somewhat elastic. Several authors have explicitly stated that the corporation is not an ethical entity, as outlined in

Chapter 2. Are ethical considerations irrelevant? Is the role of the firm to bend to whatever ethical considerations that may accrue in the pursuit of profit for shareholders?

This book references three levels of inquiry into these questions. In Chapter 5, we look at the micro or ethical questions at the level of the individual. In Chapter 6, we consider the question of ethics on a molar level, relating to a corporation as whole. Finally, we discuss the macro or large scale ethics of economics in Chapter 7.

The methodology of inquiry will deeply tap into and validate the personal view. In the classic analytical book *Working,* Studs Terrell (1974, The New Press) published a series of interviews from workers across a wide variety of professions. In this fascinating study, one of the most memorable interview portraits was of a bricklayer who viewed his contribution as a noble art, and remembered with regret every brick that didn't quite meet his personal standards of artistic merit. What is clear from classics such as these is that personal anecdotes represent a valuable and perhaps the only means of exploring these questions.

Ethical decisions are ultimately acted upon at the personal level, and even as they relate to corporate decisions, they are by their very nature subjective. In this book, similar to the social analysis performed by Studs Terkel and other social scientists, the realm of personal experience is a valid component of the picture exploring ethics in offshore outsourcing.

Hypothesis 8 — Personal history, experience and observations are valid avenues for exploration in the realm of ethics and ethical conduct.

1.8 Historical and Academic Context: Is a Corporation a Moral Entity?

Now that we've thoroughly committed to an exploration of the subjective as part of this exercise, it will be helpful to provide a historical context. In this summary, I am indebted to the *Stanford Encyclopedia of Philosophy* (plato.stanford.edu) authored by Alexei Marcoux (reprinted with permission).

Business ethics is defined as the "applied ethics discipline that addresses the moral features of commercial activity" [1]. Marcoux makes the observation that the panoply of topics under this heading, from legal compliance to studies of beliefs and attitudes, varies so considerably in content that they "often seem to have little in common other than the conviction . . . that whatever each is pursuing *is* business ethics" [2].

Marcoux cites ancient texts that include moral guidelines for commercial activity, including the Code of Hammurabi (ca. 1700 B.C.), Aristotle's *Politics* (ca. 300 B.C.), the *Talmud*, and even the Ten Commandments. As an academic discipline, business ethics develops as a more robust topic of study in the 1960s. Ironically, today many of the endowed chairs of business ethics are founded in response to ethical breaches, as when John Shad gave Harvard $30 million to start a business ethics program in 1987 in response to an insider trading scandal. [3].

Recent literature (Tom Donaldson, Patricia Werhane) views business ethics as an answer to the primary question: "Is the corporation is a moral agent?" [4]. Peter French argues that corporations are indeed moral agents since they possess the needed ingredients or corporate internal decision structures (CID) for such a status. The CIDs are comprised of an organization chart outlining decision authority and rules, such as those in articles of incorporation or by-laws. These CIDs define whether a decision by that authority is a personal decision, or a corporate [5]. French believes that these structures create "moral agency" in the corporation via corporate actions, intentions, and aims.

Manual Velasquez (1983) disagrees with this conclusion, stating that "attributing moral agency to corporations opens the door to intuitively implausible concept that a corporation can be morally responsible for something no natural person connected with it is responsible for" [6].

A second area of inquiry under the broad topic of modern business ethics involves defining how and for whom a corporation is governed [6]. This question is posed as a means of providing an answer to the underlying question related to the following well-known article. This article, entitled "The Social Responsibility of Business Is to Increase Its Profits" by Milton Friedman, was published in the *New York Times Magazine* in 1970 and is one of the earliest contributions to recent business ethics debate.

Interestingly, Marcoux describes an emerging point of philosophical agreement that rests on the central perception of how many "exit opportunities" or alternative employment opportunities are available to workers—in other words, how robust the employment market is in general and as translated into alternative job opportunities [7]. One group conceptualizes workers as an interrelated group of contractors—the "firm-contract" analogy that likens workers to shareholders. The second views the firm as a political entity and the workers akin to citizens—analogous to stakeholders.

The firm-contract analogy emphasizes a wide array of alternative opportunities in a thriving employment market. The firm-state proponents emphasize the cost of exit opportunities to justify voice rights of workers (i.e., workers must be provided voices to stay satisfied and avoid the cost of early exits).

Marcoux observes that "the virtually exclusive focus on the large, publically traded corporation is...strange" [7]. He observes that the narrow view of this debate "leaves out those workers who don't have a viable exit choice even though disgruntled, and also ignores the disagreements among the ownership class."

The key underlying principles of the worker–manager relationship in the United States are the *at-will* and *just cause* [8]. Absent a specific overriding contract, the at-will employment terms governs the employment relationship as a default contract. Under an at-will arrangement, employment may be terminated by either party without notice, as long as the termination does not violate the law (racial discrimination, whistle-blower recrimination, etc.). Werhane (1985) argues that arbitrary dismissal, as sanctioned by at-will employment terms, in and of itself is disrespectful of an employee's personhood [9] and states that workers should be provided a good reason for termination.

Maitland (1989) and others cite the at-will doctrine as leading to stagnation. In Europe, the prevalence of mandatory just-cause employment rules is viewed by some as a "significant disincentive" to job creation and entrepreneurship. Stated another way, the harder it is to fire workers, it is also harder to hire [10]. Proponents of at-will employment advocate it as a direct means of providing a vibrant labor market that enables an equal voice in the corporate world.

Solomon and Hanson (1991) [11] distinguish three levels of business ethics that we will utilize and analyze in this book as applied to IT outsourcing. Examples of macro, molar, and micro ethical questions are illustrated in Table 1.1. In Chapter 2, we explore the current research on all three levels of ethical scope in detail.

1.9 Summary

Our first chapter outlines our method of inquiry and the questions we shall explore. Underlying these is a set of hypothesis that is reasonable and will begin the inquiry process, although it is anticipated the analysis of these initial questions will lead to the unexpected. Our eight hypotheses are summarized below:

1. Ethics discussions are conducted in shades of gray, never in absolutes.
2. Disenfranchisement of U.S. workers is the central ethical issue in IT outsourcing at the macroeconomic (macro) level.
3. Egoless decision making can be a guiding framework of personal business ethics.
4. The truth will out.
5. The U.S. public is aware of ethical violations by large firms, and judges accordingly.
6. Strategic global workforce planning and development is the next IT imperative—the key strategy to implement to remain competitive.
7. Change management as currently structured does not effectively address ethical questions.
8. Personal history and experience represent legitimate data points in exploring ethics.

Some of the questions we are left to explore are:

- Is business activity always ethical, no matter how questionable, because it is a means of defraying personal and community poverty?
- Does membership in a larger business landscape, by its very nature, require ethical compromises from all participants?

Table 1.1   Sample Ethical Questions Relating to Micro, Molar, and Macro Levels of Inquiry

Level	Financial Equity	Transparency and Communication	Compliance	Business Model Fairness and Integrity
Micro or individual	Are ethical and strict legal compliance practices followed in equity compensation (monetary recognition and rewards) of my team members?	Do communications to my team reflect transparency and honesty?	Is my team in compliance?	Can my team members feel good about their roles as individuals representing a fair model of the company's business?
Molar or corporate	Does the company conduct business (selling and buying) at fair market values?	Does the company communicate as honestly and transparently as possible in its role of corporate citizen and member of the community?	Is the company in compliance?	Does the company's business model reflect basic ethical principles as interpreted by persons of integrity?
Macro or business world	Are the normative business practices ethical?	Does the industry environment encourage open and honest communication?	Are the laws and regulations requiring compliance appropriate, updated to reflect advances in technology, and clear and well enforced?	Does the national industry advocate basic ethical precepts such as "first do no harm"?

■ Is economic security a prerequisite for an ethical lifestyle? In other words, can one live ethically in desperate poverty?

■ If one is rescued from desperate poverty by an ethically questionable business, is that business now ethical?

These are the rather subtle dilemmas this volume invites you to explore.

References

General: Tandy Gold, *Outsourcing Software Applications Offshore: Making it Work*, 2004, Boca Raton, FL: CRC Press.

[1] Alexei Marcoux, The Center for Ethics and Entrepreneurship, August 2011. www.ethicsandentrepreneurship.org

[2] Alexei Marcoux, *Business Ethics Gone Wrong: Individual Liberty, Free Markets and Peace.* The Cato Institute, August 2011 (originally published July 24, 2000). www.cato.org

[3] Mark Borkowski, Business Ethics???, *Toronto Free Press*, October 11, 2006. www.torontofreepress.com/

[4] David T. Risser, Collective Moral Responsibility, In *Internet Encyclopedia of Philosophy*, December 14, 2009. www.iep.utm.edu/colletci/

[5] Peter A. French, The Corporation as a Moral Person, *American Philosophical Quarterly*, 16 (3), 1979, 207–215. University of Illinois Press on behalf of North American Philosophical Publications. www.jstor.org/stable/20009760

[6] Manual Velasquez, Why Corporations are not Morally Responsible for Anything They Do, *Business and Professional Ethics Journal*, 2 (4), 1983. http://philpapers.org.rec.velaow

[7] Alexei Marcoux, Business Ethics. In *The Stanford Encyclopedia of Philosophy*, Zalta, Edward N., Ed., Fall 2008. http://plato.stanford.edu/archives/fall2008/entries/ethics-business/

[8] Anonymous. Employment at Will. In *The Free Dictionary by Farlex*, August 2011. http://legal-dictionary.thefreedictionary.com/Employment+at+will

[9] Patricia Hogue Werhane, *Persons, Rights, and Corporations*, 1985, New York: Prentice Hall.

[10] Anonymous. What they Don't Know Won't Hurt Them: Defending Employment-At-Will in Light of Findings that Employees Believe They Possess Just Cause Protection, *Berkeley Journal of Employment and Labor Law*, 23, Winter, 307, 2002. http://lawbrain.com/wiki/employment_at_will

[11] Robert C. Solomon and Kristine Hanson, *It's Good Business*, 1985, New York: Atheneum.

[12] George Bernard Shaw, *Major Barbara*, 1st World Library, 1st ed., Sept. 2004.

Appendix: Looking at Business Ethics through the Lens of Popular Culture and Literature

Perhaps literature can add clarity—or pose more questions—than the current, rather narrow published debate on business ethics. One of the more droll and entertaining commentaries was provided by the playwright George Bernard Shaw—himself no stranger to the struggles of making ends meet as the son of a lower-middle class clerk.

The play is *Major Barbara* [12], and it describes the homecoming of an estranged father to his now-grown children—two daughters, and a son. The long-absent father and breadwinner is the head of a munitions factory. One daughter and the titular character is an erudite, intelligent, and pious member of the Salvation Army; she is followed about by her intelligent and sweet fiancé. The son, a mama's boy, is astonished and disgusted to learn upon his father's return after many years that his comfortable childhood home has been financed by his father's munitions factory.

At the beginning of the play, the father arranges to trade visits with the daughter. He will visit her Salvation Army if she will return the favor and visit his munitions factory. On the day of the visit to the Salvation Army, Major Barbara is disillusioned when her supervisor is willing to take money from her wealthy, death-dealing father and considers the arrangement the equivalent of "selling her soul."

When his progeny visit the munitions factory, the father reveals an eden-like existence: beautiful homes, churches, schools, manicured lawns. He also relates to Barbara and her fiancé the firm's recent elation upon learning that its latest bomb killed twice as many as expected in a recent skirmish.

In the end, Major Barbara is restored to her faith by viewing the munitions factory as so many souls to save; her educated, gentle philosopher boyfriend wins the negotiations to inherit the running of the munitions factory, and the son declares himself "prodigiously proud" of the beautiful life his father created.

Some of the dialogue is very funny and very real. When the topic turns to personal beliefs and personal salvation, father states his beliefs defiantly: "There are two things necessary to salvation . . . money and gunpowder."

He is asked, "Is there any place . . . for honor, justice, truth, love, mercy, and so forth?" and answers, "Yes; they are the graces and luxuries of a rich, strong and safe life . . . I saved [Barbara's] soul from the seven deadly sins . . . Food, clothing, heat, rent, taxes, respectability, and children." He continues to explain how he never needs to "bully" a worker because each worker is bullied already by the worker hierarchy above him, each snubbing the next, resulting in a "colossal profit" for him.

Finally, the father describes his daughter's Salvation Army as a form of bribery: bread for souls. He holds to Major Barbara that saving the souls of his well-housed, well-fed employees is cleaner work.

What is fascinating about Shaw's juxtaposition of characters is how very blurry the lines demarcating the ethical and unethical are revealed. Almost no part of the ethical conundrum of business is left untouched.

- ■ Is faith-based charity a form of coercion?
- ■ Are the sacrifices of some, e.g., the deaths produced by the munitions factory, necessary for the economic welfare of others?

This volume invites you to explore these subtle issues.

Chapter 2

The Cost of Ethical Compromise: An Overview of Current and Historical Research and Business Practices

"There is no such thing as a minor lapse of integrity."

Tom Peters

2.1 Today, We are Confused

A quick search of the Internet on the topic of ethics in outsourcing illustrates a range of opinions from "this is irrelevant" to the active hiring of a professional of deep experience for the purpose of enterprise-wide leadership:

- A veteran IT journalist states that outsourcing as a business tool has nothing to do with ethics: "You're acting as the agent of your employer, an amoral (not immoral) entity. You're increasing shareholder value, a goal with no intrinsic moral substance. ... For every human being you lay off, another gets a job. Going offshore is morally neutral. ... Your responsibility [is] to use the best tool for each job" [1].

■ A broad review from the Bergen County (New Jersey) chapter of the American Ethical Society notes the concern that "the gainers have some moral obligation to the losers" and "the process seems unstoppable" [2].

■ A letter to the editor of the New York Times chastises the publication for using underpaid "outsourced" freelance writers. A written response from the editor states that the newspaper could not afford to hire everyone it published, and minimizing the use of freelance writers would deprive the freelancers of a writing forum that helps them find work elsewhere [3].

■ A large financial services firm advertises for a director of business ethics [4].

Let's apply our "follow the money" guideline to explore these contradictions.

2.2   Macro Level Costs of Ethical Compromise

Let's start by looking at the cost of ethical compromise at the macro economic level. When debates at the macro level concern offshore outsourcing, they center upon whether jobs in the United States need to be protected.

This book is not about macroeconomics; and if it were, it is worthy of note that little agreement about outsourcing exists even in that professional sphere. Some believe that outsourcing—not just IT outsourcing, but the steady migration of work overseas across manufacturing and other industries that constitute the American business legacy—contributes to the robust economic growth enjoyed by the U.S. for many years.

One of the most credible "outsourcing as pro-economy" groups is the ITAA (Information Technology Association of America). ITAA published a study titled "The Impact of Offshore IT Software and Services Outsourcing on the U.S. Economy and the IT Industry" in 2005 [5]. This study estimated, optimistically, that the total potential savings from the use of offshore outsourcing would grow to $20.9 billion. These dollars in turn could be utilized to spur both new investments in new IT projects and the additional jobs they would bring. Contributors to this study were Nobel Prize winning economist Dr. Lawrence R. Klein and Dr. Nariman Behravesh, Global Insight's chief economist. "The U.S. IT work force will continue to grow," says ITAA President Harris Miller.

The study concludes that the positive economic mechanisms of worldwide sourcing of IT software and services ultimately reduces U.S. inflation, supports increased U.S. productivity, contributes positively to U.S. gross domestic product (GDP), and increases demand for U.S exports: "Worldwide sourcing of IT ... increases total employment in the United States. ... The economy will create 516,000 jobs over the next five years ... with global sourcing but only 490,000 without it. ... Global sourcing actually adds to the take-home pay of average U.S. workers," the study concludes [6].

Of course other economists, just as educated and wise, espouse the opposite view. Robert Reich, who presided as U.S. Labor Secretary during one of the most sustained economic booms in recent history, expresses the concern that jobs are lost, perhaps permanently. Reich outlines a negative cycle in which U.S. workers must adjust to lower salaries due to competition from overseas. This ultimately results in less overall national expendable income, and the extension and deepening of our national economic recessions. "Many companies have ... cut their payrolls for good. ... Technologies have made [overseas] workers ... just about as productive as Americans. ... So let's be clear: The goal isn't just more jobs. It's more jobs with good wages. Which means the fix isn't just temporary measures ... but permanent new investments in the productivity of Americans" [7].

As outlined in Chapter 1, supporters of the at-will doctrine note that it fundamentally provides more worker choices and freedom when supported by a robust labor market. The underlying issue in that debate, of course, centers on the role of public policy in determining wages and the impacts of that policy. For example, David Millon (1998) [8] argues that requiring employers to provide a just cause for dismissal will enable prospective employees to bargain for higher wages if hired as exceptions to the at-will doctrine.

What is interesting is that these considerations have not registered a key variable—impending dramatic shifts in the availability of labor. If job and labor availability lie at the center of much of this debate, we are in an interesting time [9]. Certainly baby boomers represent a huge, one-time influx of labor, and the economy now faces the departure of very large numbers of workers in the U.S. Depending upon the assumptions regarding population growth as a whole, these workforce population changes can be represented anywhere from a steep decline to a relative flat rate of growth as compared to the workforce growth trends in other countries. This relatively flat or declining rate of growth is particularly significant as compared to the overall world workforce population growth data shown in Figure 2.1 and Figure 2.2 [10].

Between 2020 and 2030, the decline in the rate of growth in the U.S. labor force is dramatic and sharp. The implications extend beyond social security and pensions because many employees will be required to work later and longer to support the ones who retired earlier. Clearly, the skilled labor force in the U.S. and other Western countries is going to decline precipitously between 2010 and 2030, and any ethical challenges in offshore outsourcing must be evaluated within this context.

What is more, this population shift is not simply a U.S. trend—it is global. Increasingly, as large firms grow across multiple geographic zones, and international mergers and acquisitions proliferate, these global labor force implications become more significant. These global shifts are illustrated by research from the Stanford

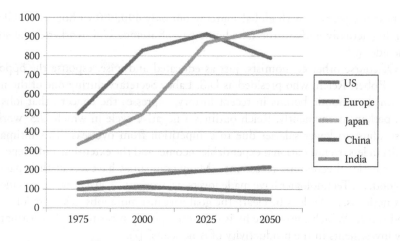

Figure 2.1 Workforce aging population trends for selected countries. (*Source:* United Nations Department of Economic and Social Affairs Population Division, World Population Ageing, 1950–2050. http://www.un.org/esa/population/publications/worldageing19502050/index.htm)

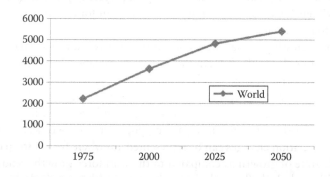

Figure 2.2 Worldwide workforce aging population trends worldwide. (*Source:* United Nations Department of Economic and Social Affairs Population Division, World Population Ageing, 1950–2050. http://www.un.org/esa/population/publications/worldageing19502050/index.htm)

Center on Longevity [11] in Figure 2.3. If employee empowerment is at the heart of the matter, as the at-will proponents suggest, public policy related to the availability of workers within the rapidly shifting variables reflected by offshore outsourcing and sudden, dramatic workforce reductions are central factors to be evaluated.

Richard B. Freeman, an economist specializing in this area at Harvard University, posits that globalization will have a major impact on the "impending shortage," as he calls the upcoming baby boomer-related workforce reduction. He estimates that the size of the available global workforce has roughly doubled with

Chart 7	Only the youngest countries will see continued workforce growth. The United States is an exception.				

	Working-age Population (in millions)			Percent Change in Working-age Population	
	Level	Absolute Change		● 2005–30 ● 2030–50	
	2005	2005–30	2030–50		
Uganda	13.9	19.8	24.6		
Afghanistan	12.7	16.5	20.7		
DRC	29.5	36.4	49.8		
Pakistan	93.2	64.8	38.8	Continued growth	
India	703.8	324.6	88.0		
Vietnam	55.1	20.8	0.4		
Mexico	66.1	20.3	−4.2		
United States	200.7	27.9	19.8	Moderate growth,	
China	928.7	40.8	−109.8	then slowing or shrinking	
United Kingdom	39.7	0.9	0.4		
South Korea	34.4	−3.1	−8.3		
Italy	38.9	−3.9	−5.4		
Germany	55.3	−8.1	−5.6	Shrinking	
Japan	84.9	−15.7	−16.9		
Russia	102.4	−19.4	−17.0		

Note: Working age = 15–64   −40% −20% 0% 20% 40% 60% 80% 100% 120% 140% 160%

Figure 2.3   Workforce growth slows dramatically in the "First World." (Source: Stanford Center on Longevity. With permission.)

the entry of China, India and the ex-Soviet bloc. This glut, he believes, will result in lower wages and less overall worker empowerment and leverage in the U.S. [11]

Hypothesis 1 — Global corporations, as driven by profits and not ethics, are working actively to anticipate and balance the impending increases in the cost of Western labor through offshore outsourcing and other means.

Hypothesis 2 — One "valve" or "spigot" that directly impacts that cost is encouraging the ease of access, cross-cultural integration, training, and availability of the ever-growing, plentiful, and technically astute Eastern workforce.

The Beveridge curve (Figure 2.4A), published by the U.S. Bureau of Labor Statistics, shows the relationship between unemployment (horizontal axis) and the job vacancy rate (vertical axis). In other words, it illustrates a "job mismatch" on a macro level [12]. The general expectation is that as the number of job openings increases, the number of workers in extended unemployment lowers. What has economists puzzled of late (still true as of 2011) is the so-called "jobless recovery" in which the lower right corner shows an increase in job availability that exerts minimal impact on unemployment. In other words, based on these data, the level of job openings for the second quarter or 2010 were about the same as in 2003 (approximately 3,250,000 openings), but the number unemployed in 2003 was 9,000,000 compared with 15,000,000 in 2010—a 60% increase!

The downward dotted line show a dramatic decrease in the number of job openings mapped against increasing numbers of unemployed between 2000 and 2010. Dave Altig, a contributor to *The Wall Street Journal*, believes the latest Beveridge mismatch describes non-labor related improvements:

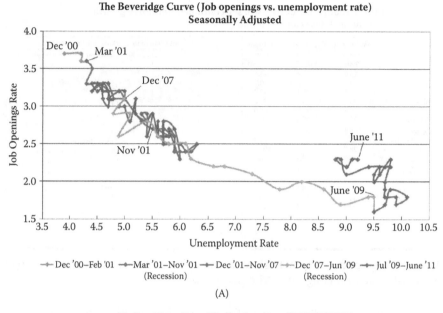

The Beveridge Curve (Job openings vs. unemployment rate)
Seasonally Adjusted

—◆—Dec '00–Feb '01 —◆—Mar '01–Nov '01 —◆—Dec '01–Nov '07 —◆—Dec '07–Jun '09 —◆—Jul '09–June '11
(Recession)   (Recession)

(A)

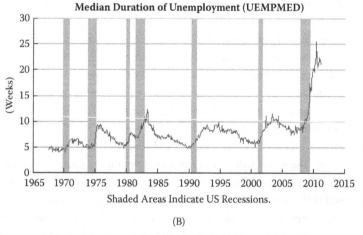

Median Duration of Unemployment (UEMPMED)

Shaded Areas Indicate US Recessions.

(B)

Figure 2.4 (A) Beveridge curve. (*Source:* U.S. Bureau of Labor Statistics) (B) Median duration of unemployment, 1965–2011. (*Source:* Federal Reserve Bank of St. Louis, http://research.stlouisfed.org/fred2/series/UEMPMED)

[The]... productivity gains realized in the United States through-out the recession and early recovery reflect upgrades in business pro-cesses.... [This] shift in required skills has been concentrated within individual industries and businesses... [not] captured by our most straightforward measures of structural change [13].

A companion graph prepared by the Federal Reserve Bank of St. Louis (Figure 2.4B) shows the medium duration of unemployment since 1965. The number of individuals at risk to become permanently unemployed as a result of long-duration employment is at an all-time high [14]–[16].

Looking at macro trends by industry since 2007, the largest losses or reversals of positive growth have been in professional and business services, leisure and hospitality, financials, information, retail, and construction [17]. Manufacturing reveals a steady decline for the duration [17] and serves as a good bellwether for analyzing IT outsourcing as the older cousin of the trend. At the same time, employee compensation is at a record low vis-à-vis both corporate profits and gross national product (Figure 2.6). Figure 2.7 illustrates U.S. unemployment trends developed from interactive unemployment charting data available from the Bureau of Labor Statistics (http://data.bls.gov/pdq/SurveyOutputServlet). Figure 2.8 plots mass layoffs across all industries since 1990, as also tracked by the Bureau of Labor Statistics [18]. These graphs establish a chilling picture summarized as follows:

- The total number of job openings fluctuates, although they fluctuate. When they are increasing, however, they do not reduce the number of chronically long-term unemployed (Figure 2.3). This suggests a fundamental gap between the skills of those looking for jobs and the available jobs.
- The number of unemployed is at a near-record high and the unemployed on average are without jobs three times longer than during any period in recorded history. The implication is that those unemployed more than 24 months will face major barriers in rejoining the job force (Figure 2.5).
- The depth, length, and seriousness of the recession are longer and deeper than ever (Figure 2.5), as measured by comparing the rate of recovery of the current recession with other recessions since 1940.

Relative employee compensation has remained flat or been reduced, while GDP and corporate profits show dramatic recoveries that are not translating into greater employment or higher wages (hopefully this is merely a lag). How much of this pain is caused by moving jobs offshore? According to International Monetary Fund data as analyzed by the Hackett group [19], roughly one third of job losses since 2000 can be attributed to offshore outsourcing. Over time, the offshore percentage has increased from roughly 10% in 2000, through 25% from 2003 to 2009, to 33% from 2009 to the present. While the total number of jobs lost due to outsourcing has increased over time, other factors turn out to be much more significant, despite the fact they do not sell newspapers and are not generally mentioned in the press. Automation and the associated increases in efficiency and productivity are responsible for the great majority of the reduction in skilled job openings in the U.S [19]. This theme surfaces consistently—productivity gains overshadow outsourcing as a root cause of the reduction in the overall number of skilled U.S. jobs. This is true

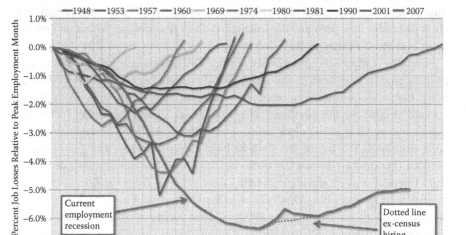

Figure 2.5 Recovery trend measured as percent job losses versus peak over time. (*Source:* www.calculated riskblog.com. With permission.)

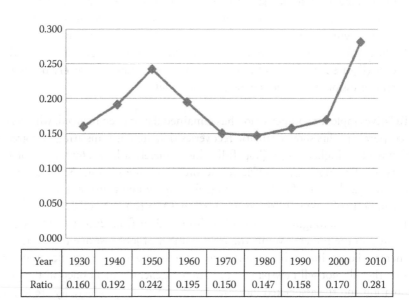

Year	1930	1940	1950	1960	1970	1980	1990	2000	2010
Ratio	0.160	0.192	0.242	0.195	0.150	0.147	0.158	0.170	0.281

Figure 2.6 Ratio of corporate profits versus wages. (*Source:* U.S. Bureau of Economic Analysis.)

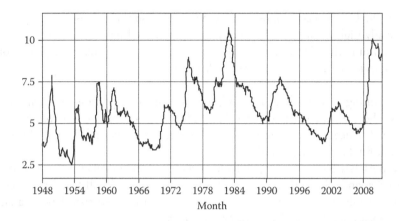

Figure 2.7 U.S. unemployment since 1990. (*Source:* **Martin Neil Baily, paper presented at Scholars Strategy Network Conference, Cambridge, MA, September 3, 2010. With permission.)**

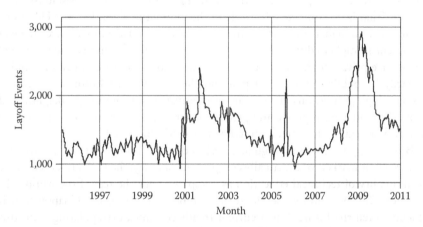

Figure 2.8 Mass layoff events across industries since 1990. (*Source:* **Bruce J. Bergman,** *Monthly Labor Review,* **September 2008. With permission.)**

across all robust research on outsourcing, and is reflective in extensive research on the long history of moving U.S. manufacturing work overseas.

The data paint a picture of the deep disenfranchisement of many U.S. workers. Some of the more interesting ethical questions are:

■ If the offshore trend creates winning economies in formerly relatively stagnant nations such as India, are those individuals impacted by the economy less deserving than U.S. citizens? In other words, is the economic well-being of a family in India less important than the well-being of a family in the U.S.?

■ If the U.S. protected jobs from going overseas so that wages remained artificially high in the global marketplace, would the higher prices over the long run hurt the U.S. economy? For example, would U.S.-based large corporations leave the U.S. completely to keep prices low?

When looking specifically at IT job losses, it is again important to emphasize—against the grain of what we have been educated to believe—that productivity gains made a deeper dent than offshore movement in the loss of IT jobs. This leads us to our final macro hypothesis.

Hypothesis 3 — Some IT skills (e.g., global change management) will be in greater demand while others (e.g., COBOL programming) will face less demand. This trend will become more pronounced as global firms shift their labor management policies to reflect global workforce realities.

Clearly, the country that "wins" in the long run is able to provide a highly educated, relatively low cost work force. What are the ethical implications of these macro trends? We will explore the significance of these compelling trends in detail in Chapter 7, but one specific intuitive finding has been definitively established by research. That is, to compete effectively in the international market, the U.S. must ensure access to higher education as measured by the relative national percentage of enrollment in higher education. Note that although this finding is often assumed to reference private higher education, such education in most countries is funded primarily by public monies. In Japan and the few Western European countries that have high proportions of enrollments in private institutions (e.g., Belgium and the Netherlands), both public and private higher education institutions are almost entirely financed by the state, as noted by the World Bank [20].

Broader opportunities for high quality, low cost education will be mandatory for the U.S. labor market to realistically compete. As of today, the U.S. ranks extremely low in quality of technical education as compared with the rest of the world [21]; see Figure 2.9. We will look again at these important findings in Chapter 8. It is difficult to tell the future, but if current trends continue, extrapolating from this decade to the next (2020 to 2030), this is what we can anticipate:

■ Highly skilled roles continue to be harder to fill. As baby boomers retire, their jobs are moved overseas, filled via a proactive employer-sponsored training programs, or both.
■ More countries compete for programmer jobs. South America, led by Brazil, increasingly garners larger numbers of offshore jobs from the over-tapped labor market in India. However, India is still the leader by far, maintaining over 70% of the market due to existing long-term offshore contractual relationships.
■ U.S. unemployment tapers off but remains relatively high as the total number of individuals seeking employment is reduced by the aging of the baby boomers. However, most individuals without extensive training find it difficult to

obtain jobs that provide livable wages, Unemployment will remain high, along with a high number of unfilled jobs. The gap between the poorest and richest continues to widen.

■ Consumer market as well as technical leadership are likely to move to China, based on its educational achievements, current investments in infrastructure, and the sheer size of its up and coming consumer market.

■ The U.S. is divided increasingly into wealthy and poor classes, and the middle class continues to shrink. Those who have access to higher education are more likely to be able to move into highly skilled jobs where demand can sustain both job growth and substantial salaries. This will enable a small middle class to survive. The U.S. is unfortunately on the path to re-enact the Gilded Age, during which legions of the poor work to support the very wealthy few.

Given the importance of education outlined above, where does the U.S. currently place? Unfortunately, despite the opportunities provided by our and relatively mature infrastructure and wealth, we rank firmly in the mediocre middle. The U.S. consistently performs only average in international testing of reading, math and science skills. The Program for International Student Assessment (PISA) is translated into each country's language, and is subject to the review and approval of each country's educational leaders to help minimize cultural bias.

In the U.S., about 4,500 randomly chosen students participate annually in the test. 500 points represents the average grade for each of the three tests (mathematics,

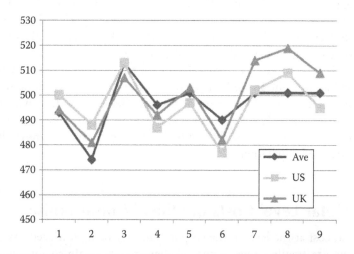

Figure 2.9   Percentage shares of enrollments in private colleges and universities. (*Source:* World Bank, OECD Programme for International Student Assessment, 1994.)

science, and reading) [21]. In late 2010, the U.S. placed 30th in mathematics; China, Singapore, Hong Kong, South Korea, and Taiwan topped the list. In science, China is the leader in test scores, followed by Finland, Hong Kong, Singapore, and Japan The U.S. placed 20th in the sciences, and 17th in reading [21].

Both sets of U.S. scores are dismal, and have been for many years. Like the HDI index that we will explore in Chapter 8, this result puts U.S. education slightly below average—somewhere between Portugal and Kenya. In an odd but significant mirroring of the split in the job market, U.S. education experts point out that the U.S. score reflects the combined tendency to have many top performers and many bottom performers to skew the average. Unless we improve both our scores and the learning opportunities within in the U.S. we will continue to lessen our competitive standing internationally.

Another factor is that top students in China, Australia, and other high performing countries are often recruited into teaching, with a direct focus on investment of educational resources. Few of the brightest U.S. students enter the education field because of the relatively low wages and status accrued by such jobs. As echoed by many, remuneration of U.S. teachers must be addressed before we can compete effectively in global education.

Unsurprisingly, recent evident indicates that socioeconomic factors largely determine PISA performance by U.S. students. There is a high correlation between parent education levels and student scores [22]. Hanushek and Woessmann found that if countries want to improve their GDP, they must improve the quality of education. There is a roughly 15-year lag, but the increase is statistically significant. The graphed result is remarkably linear [23]. Statistical modeling of average U.S. PISA scores suggests the high likelihood of a significant decrease in GDP over the next 15 to 20 years. The implications of the research are striking. If the U.S. could turn the current trend around to a positive outcome, a 25% increase in PISA test scores would bring an aggregate GDP gain of $115 trillion.

Figure 2.10 illustrates the remarkably direct relationship between income and educational attainment at the individual level in the U.S. Even those who completed some college but did not earn degrees did better than those with no postsecondary education [24]. Clearly, ethics at the macro level encompasses the ethics of educational opportunity and the continuing focus on economic growth based on a highly educated population.

2.2 Molar Level Costs of Ethical Compromise

The ethical cost at the level of the corporation may be high indeed. As personal reputations are fragile—once damaged they may be maimed forever—so too the reflection of corporate misdeeds can be searing. Perhaps one of the factors impacting some large bank stock prices (Figure 2.11) is the public reaction to the bailout.

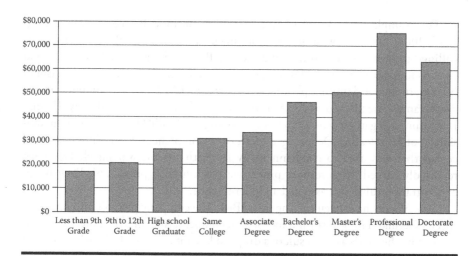

Figure 2.10   Earnings versus educational attainment.

If the base relationship between business practitioners is the handshake and the word of each individual, corporate alignment with ethical behavior can sometimes be a conundrum. Corporations are profit-driven entities, yet they exist within a complex web of communities and political systems, pictured so beautifully by Shaw in *Major Barbara* (Appendix, Chapter 1). It is tempting to draw a line in the sand and state unequivocally that a business is a nonethical entity, but when the line in the sand is relatively extreme, it is difficult to support that position.

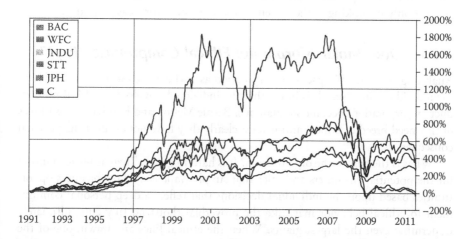

Figure 2.11   Large bank stock prices versus Dow data before and after bailout.

For example, Jack Beatty ("Hitler's Willing Business Partners," *The Atlantic*, April 2001, http://www.theatlantic.com/magazine/archive/2001/04/hitler-apos-s-willing-business-partners/3146/) and Edwin Black [25] developed evidence that IBM technology was involved in supporting the chilling, data-driven fanaticism of Nazi Germany. A damning photograph shows an IBM Hollerith computer in the death camps; members of the U.S. Department of Commerce, headed by Thomas J. Watson, are gathered in a circle in a photograph with Hitler. A German subsidiary of IBM called Dehomag undertook a comprehensive machine-tabulated census that was used to condemn many to death. As the war raged, Dehomag reportedly earned extraordinary profits via black market prices [26]. Each major concentration camp was assigned a Hollerith code.

Several suits have been filed against IBM. The company paid $3 million into a special German Holocaust fund focused on compensating forced laborers and others hurt by the Nazis as the result of a dropped lawsuit in April 2001; IBM admitted no guilt.

This book is not focused upon gathering evidence or making decisive judgments in this area. Indeed, in the spirit of full disclosure and as a former IBM employee, I was directly involved in IBM's "Re-inventing Education" program by which it donated millions of dollars in technology and services to many schools around the country—one of many generous investments IBM makes annually to the broader U.S. community.

This case illustrates, however, how thin the veil between the profit motive and the service of evil may ultimate become, and hopefully results in our collectively rethinking the ultimate neutrality of the work ethic. The typical statement "I was watching only the bottom line" becomes chilling indeed in the wake of extreme ethical concerns. Clearly, no company should participate in certain actions even to earn profits. It is a paradox that sometimes we can evaluate and understand what is at stake only by looking at the extreme situation—the worst case scenario.

2.2.1 Does Molar (Corporate) Ethical Compromise "Pay?"

Analyzing the ethical impact of a corporation as a whole leads us now inevitably to the individuals involved. It is ironic that the individuals involved in ethical misconduct by corporations become so infamous. Bernie Madoff and Ken Lay are examples of this need breed of ethical anti-heroes; clearly they have not escaped the personal consequences.

What is the cost to the organization? It is hard to gauge. There is no accounting for the potential customers and sales that simply walk away. Lost business opportunities based upon the individual decisions that reflect a deep personal commitment to ethical behavior may, like the proverbial thousand tiny cuts, ultimately undermine even the largest giants. When the ethical lines are drawn, one of the biggest costs of being on the wrong side of the line is the distasteful necessity of being grouped with one's similarly ethically compromised peers. When the table is set, I want to be seated with those known for integrity, not with those known for pursuing profit at any price.

Are today's large banks—the ones that gambled away their safety nets through derivatives and other forms of legal poker, received taxpayer bailout money, and returned the favor by voting themselves even bigger individual bonuses—hurting? Again, it is hard to imagine that the ethically straight and narrow would voluntarily to maintain such relationships. In reality, some corporations are caught and "pay the piper"; others never do. Measuring our ethical actions in terms of a worst-case scenario—the corporate equivalent of never writing anything in an email that we would not want published in a newspaper—would seem to be the true guidepost. The reality is that many like Madoff and Lay who performed such actions paid the price as individuals even though they seemingly acted on behalf of the corporation. The example of Nazi Germany creates a vivid scenario. Corporations clearly act within a larger, societal, ethical context, whether or not they choose to acknowledge it. Just as clearly, corporations can support good or evil. They can harm and kill or nurture and support the good of humanity as interpreted by the broadest of measures.

A company president was sharing his story of an ethical awakening. He ran a carpet company that routinely polluted. When he learned of the devastating consequences of his company's policies, he came to a realization that he was a "pirate." Intentionally or not, he robbed and plundered. As you go about your daily activities and take on leadership in any context, question yourself. What is the price of your profit? When you are gone, what is your legacy? How would you like to meet your grandchildren as adults and explain your actions?

Assessing my personal experience across many years of Fortune 100 executive interface, I personally find that the destructive drive often results from personal ego. This is a need, perhaps based upon insecurity or a breathtaking level of self-absorption, to win at all costs. But "win" here is defined very narrowly. Those with the intelligence to "win" on a major scale (destroying irreplaceable natural resources, creating a food distribution system and policies that allows millions of innocent children go hungry in a land of plenty) do not extend the "winning" to their own offspring. For who wants to live in such a world?

This sad scenario is accurately depicted in the *Back to the Future* movie in which Biff reigns supreme in a land not fit for anyone, even his own loved ones. This price, however, is something that the Biff-like executives are willing to pay. Surrounded by a false yet toxic cocoon of luxury, such executives have little motivation in terms of personal comfort after the first zillion is achieved. It is hard not to believe that these individuals who wreak such havoc for future generations, with so little regard for the quality of life of their own descendants, won't also experience their own self-reckoning as the cocoon falls away even for them.

There is a curious dichotomy between the reality of large corporate life and the popular view of these large firms. Business people are often imbued in the popular imagination with a kind of ethical stature that they may not earn in actuality. The banking industry, historically perceived as a bastion of security, safety, and maturity in popular culture, is certainly viewed differently today. It is my experience that most large firms intend to execute ethically but that ethical framework is hampered by an incredibly narrow focus on short-term profits at any cost. As a result, the public image ascribes the business person with a level of balanced pragmatism that is often undeserved.

The real determinant of behavior within the typical Fortune 500 firm is the measure of success—including written evaluations and goals—of the individual worker. These measures drive the behavior of workers who need their jobs to stay financially afloat. The extent to which they compromise their own personal ethics or ideals may vary on a case-by-case basis, but the reference point is often so narrow that larger issues are simply not relevant.

This is how the beautiful woods are run over by parking lots, the last nesting places of species are destroyed, and compromises in quality affect our general health and well-being across many industries. There simply is no measure within the corporate entity to underscore the huge relative impacts of such decisions. All that remains is the framework of an individual worker trying to achieve a quarterly budget.

At the most extreme end of the spectrum, you may ultimately see members of the U.S. Chamber of Commerce sitting down with a modern personification of evil, sipping tea and ostensibly talking about efficiency.

What is important to realize is that the departmental bifurcation that is of necessity a feature of large corporations—the typical paper-stamping hierarchy that is at once necessary and ridiculous—foments and supports both the destructive narrow focus and the out-of-control ego. Human resources departments create guidelines for performance that often bear no relation to day-to-day jobs, and thus create a kind of desperation for a typical worker just trying to get through the day. Neither human resources nor the employee's manager has authority to make these measures more realistic; the employee falls through the cracks, and yet another sale is made that destroys a unique resource, compromises our health, or drains the national treasury and requires a bailout.

The rare whistleblower who bucks this trend often must deal with the resulting ridicule along with social and financial disenfranchisement. I am convinced that in the corporate life of every employee, he or she faces at least one moment—perhaps many—when a choice must be made between doing the right thing and losing his or her livelihood. The lack of an ethical framework within our business culture, as clearly illustrated in current events across our world economy, is threatening our very lives. We are at risk without an ethical guidepost that allows us to say, "Stop! This is worth more than a 10% increase in the numbers for this quarter." We pretend that corporate life represents a mythical objective reality that is self policing, while we are slowly but surely discovering that large corporations are chock full of the same error-prone, politically suffocating, and essentially illogical human relationships and structures that we have experienced in other institutions, starting with the first school we attended when we were very small.

What does seem clear, in support of our early hypothesis, is that in the land of the Internet, few secrets remain. Just as tonight's nightly news shows a snapshot of a thief caught on a hidden camera, the sheer speed, breadth, and reach of the Internet make every company inherently responsible for the ethics of its business model. That the so-called corporate ethical model may be comprised of a hodge-podge of mismatched employee incentives and half-baked, weak "corporate values" does not matter when the damage is done. The opportunity is gone, and the negative picture may be indelibly printed in the public mind. This is the high cost of ignoring the molar ethical construct.

Many firms that behave ethically at home but somehow feel it is acceptable to compromise overseas continue to come to light; they have no place to hide. On the positive side, firms that go out of their way to encompass ethical behavior are often cherished in the public view. Nonprofit groups such as Habitat for Humanity and the growing number of investors interested in the creation and support of stock portfolios comprised of ethically aware firms underline this as a growing trend.

While it may appear on the surface that large firms with their almost unlimited resources, deep governmental ties and influences, and global reach, are above the law and pay no consequences, recent events provide another view. The Murdoch scandal that disbanded one of the oldest tabloid newspapers in the United Kingdom serves as one example. When we look at firms in the past and the individuals who built fortunes from them, we can perhaps see more clearly. The men who created the great fortunes of the preindustrial and industrial ages did so at great cost to the quality of lives of many workers including, the victims of child and slave labor. Their financing of great public works such as charities, hospitals, and libraries is commendable but does not obviate the ethical compromises they made to build their wealth. Hopefully the future of the corporation will incorporate the awareness that individuals driven to amass and maintain these great fortunes did not escape the unrelenting eye of historical truth, so that the great driver that is public opinion will minimize the abuse of future workers.

2.3 Micro Level: Cost of Ethical Compromise for Individuals

Unlike the topics relating to ethics of the business community (macro) and the corporation (molar), the ethics of individual behavior represents a well-worn path and involves some aspects that appear uncomfortably close to religious or culturally-based beliefs. But working within the framework outlined above, only a rare member of the corporate world would not feel ethically compromised at sometime in his or her career, perhaps even daily. Digital Equipment Corporation was an example of a company that excelled in addressing the ethical framework of its own business model. We explore the impacts on individuals of working within the safety net of an overtly ethical company in Chapter 7, "Recalibrating the Reality."

The central theme of micro or individual ethics in the workplace relates to the misuse of power. While active dialog surrounds the question of the corporation as moral agent, there is no dispute about individuals as moral agents. Despite a wide diversity of opinion, the close proximity of the work environment generally reveals true character. At many moments of the work day, choices must be made regarding the use of power to benefit the many or the few.

Sources of workplace power vary and arise from direct authority or indirect influence, present or past relationships, professional results and reputation, specialized professional knowledge, certification and experience, or all these factors. Of course, expression in the work place is executed privately between a few individuals, yet ironically it is true that an individual's personal character (the basis on which he or she views and wields power and sources of power) is almost immediately transparent within a large organization.

The daily cost of being recognized as one who misuses power is hard to overstate. My personal experience is there are always some individuals who utilize their power for expression of their ego. For example, the manager who collects talented workers but does not allow them to express their talents, or the worker who constantly tries to undermine supervisory authority. There are many subtle variations. It is also my personal experience after many years in the corporate world that those who routinely misuse power find it difficult to re-establish their power base once it is lost through the frequent shifts that occur so often in corporate life. I once held a solid leadership role with a large firm and earned an excellent salary. For six long months, I had absolutely nothing to do. I learned later that this was not atypical. My manager was a collector of talent but for whatever reason generally did not allow its expression. When eventually I left that position, I moved within the firm to one of the best professional opportunities and growth experiences of my career. I also learned that almost everyone viewed my former manager in an extremely negative light. Most of them said they never wanted to work for or with that individual again. Although it may appear naïve to some, it is my belief that this kind of impact will always limit and circle back to the person with that reputation. Ultimately one cannot be a leader and remain utterly self-focused.

Building a personal reputation of delivery is a prerequisite for a successful IT career. No one wants someone who delivers empty promises. So many of the global teams I lead face deadlines or have to fulfill promises that were once reasonable, even conservative, but quickly became very difficult due to intervening circumstances. Yet business results must be met in full, not in part, and personal reputations of integrity are central to the success of any kind of real professional IT leadership career. The challenge at micro level is not so much evaluating the importance of integrity, but evaluating where it intersects with the large ethical questions. If one is a loyal, hardworking member of a team that is ultimately destructive, does the micro ethical sense become essentially unethical? It is interesting that these questions are finally receiving sufficient focus to become part of popular culture.

The New York Times of July 24, 2011 [27] contained a discussion about the ethical implications of a worker moving to a country with a rigid governmental regime known for violations of human rights. Was this a personally ethical move? The open discussion responses ranged from yes, if one worked to right the wrongs of the regime (in essence "cancelling out" the compromises needed to get through the work day, even if not employed by the government), to yes, it would be an incredible experience to teach children to value human rights taken for granted in the U.S., to no, don't contribute to such countries at any level.

What was most significant about this newspaper "conversation" was the absence of a suggestion to "just take the job, focus on the work at hand, and ignore the broader ethical implications."

While the world of day-to-day ethics contains few absolutes, it is also abundantly clear that all of us are held accountable for our choices. Any action or lack of action on the part of an individual represents fair game for measuring the strength of character and commitment to ethics in his or her daily life.

2.4 Statistics, Facts and Views of the Ethics of Economic Distribution and Inequality

No book about ethics in outsourcing would be complete without an exploration of the rising rate of overall inequality of income in the United States. While the philosophy of economics is outside the purview of this book, it is important to understand the backdrop of the recent, rather extraordinary changes in the income gap between the wealthy and the poor. While collection techniques may cast pre-1981 data into doubt, it is clear that after 1981 the gap between rich and poor increased and widened rapidly over time [28]; see Figure 2.12. Furthermore, changes in data collection methodology suggest that pre-1993 and post-1992 estimates are not comparable, and create a data gap.

What drives this increased level of inequality? According to the U.S. Census Bureau's *Report on Income Inequality*, researchers tie the long-run increase in income inequality to changes in the U.S. labor market. The report cites a skills gap and mismatch between labor market demand and available skills. The consequent impact on working families is illustrated in Figure 2.13 and the increasing economic pressure on most U.S. working families is clear.

The U.S. Census Bureau conclude, "Changes in the labor market in the 1980s included a shift from goods-producing industries [that had] . . . provided high-wage opportunities for low-skilled workers to technical service industries (that disproportionately employ college graduates)" [29].

Perhaps the most disturbing aspect of this rise in inequality is the rate of childhood poverty and hunger in the United States. Americans pride themselves on equality of opportunity; we cherish our heritage of achieving success from the bottom. The rapidly growing specters of childhood hunger and need in the midst of our

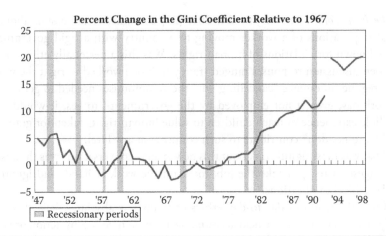

Figure 2.12 Changes in percentile ratios, 1967–1998. (*Source:* U.S. Census Bureau, Current Population Reports, June 2000.)

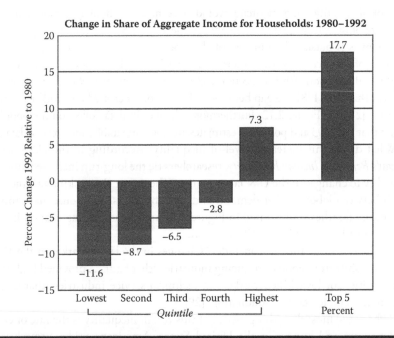

Figure 2.13 Percent changes in aggregate household income, 1980–1992. (*Source:* U.S. Department of Agriculture Economic Research Service.)

wealth represent an increasing ethical violation. According to the U.S. Department of Agriculture, food-insecure, low food security, and very low food security households are defined as follows:

■ **Food-insecure** — Households at times are uncertain of having or unable to acquire enough food to meet the needs of all their members because of insufficient money or other resources. Food-insecure households include those with low food security and very low food security; **14.5% (17.2 million)** U.S. households were food-insecure at some time during 2010 (Figure 2.14).

■ **Low food security** — These food-insecure households obtained enough food to avoid substantially disrupting their eating patterns or reducing food intake by using a variety of coping strategies such as eating less varied diets, participating in federal food assistance programs, or obtaining emergency food from community pantries; 9.1% **(10.9** million) U.S. households faced low food security in 2010.

■ **Very low food security** — Normal eating patterns of one or more household members were disrupted and food intake was reduced at times during the year because the family had insufficient money or other resources; 5.4% **(6.4 million)** U.S. households had very low food security at some time during 2010 (Figure 2.15).

According to the Food and Agriculture Organization of the United Nations (http://www.fao.org/), the world does produce enough food for everyone, even with ongoing increases in world population. Certainly this is true in the wealthy U.S. as

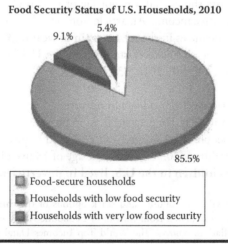

Figure 2.14 Food security status in U.S. In 2010, 14.5% of U.S. households experienced some level of food insecurity. (*Source:* U.S. Department of Agriculture. ***Food Security in the United States: Key Statistics and Graphics.*)**

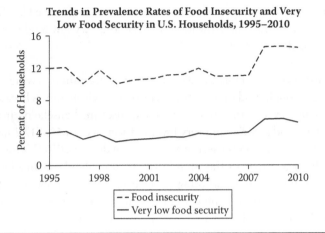

Figure 2.15 U.S. food security trends. (*Source:* **Food and Agricultural Organization of the United Nations.**)

well. Obtaining sufficient food requires income (ability to afford food), and of course effective distribution [30].

As illustrated in Figure 2.16, the percentage increase in median CEO income since 1990 outstripped corporate profits by almost 200%, while the average wage income for those remaining employed increased only marginally. In 1975, the top 0.1% of earner salaries comprised roughly 2.5% of the nation's income including capital gains, according to data collected by University of California economist Emmanuel Saez [31]. By 2008, that wage share quadrupled to 10.4%. Recent research by economists shows that a major factor in this change is the very large rise in corporate executive income. An article from *The Washington Post* on June 18, 2011* discussed discrepancies in the relative gain of wealth [32].

Let's look at hunger and poverty statistics in the U.S. based on U.S. Census Bureau data and posted in July 2011 [33]. In 2009:

■ 43.6 million people (14.3%) lived in poverty.
■ 8.8 million families (11.1% percent) lived in poverty.
■ 24.7 million people (12.9%) aged 18 to 64 lived in poverty.
■ 15.5 million children (20.7%) under the age of 18 lived in poverty; **one fifth or one in five children in the U.S. lived in poverty** [emphasis added].

---

* Based on analysis of salaries, bonuses, and stock options of the three highest-paid officers in the largest 50 firms calculated from Bureau of Economic Analysis data. All figures have been adjusted for inflation. *Sources:* The World Top Incomes Database and reports by Jon Bakija, Williams College; Adam Cole, U.S. Department of the Treasury; Bradley T. Heim, Indiana University; Carola Frydman, Massachusetts Institute of Technology's Sloan School of Management and NBER; Raven E. Molloy, Federal Reserve Board of Governors; Thomas Piketty, Ehess, Paris; Emmanuel Saez, University of California at Berkeley and NBER.

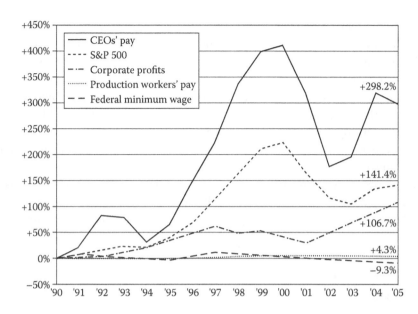

Figure 2.16 **Comparison of CEO pay, corporate profits, S&P 500 Index data, and worker pay, 1990–2005 (all figures adjusted for inflation). (***Source:* **Institute for Policy Studies and United for a Fair Economy, Executive Excess 2006, 13th Annual CEO Compensation Survey. With permission.)**

- 50.2 million Americans (33 million adults and 17.2 million children) lived in food-insecure households.
- 17.4 million households (14.7%) were food-insecure.
- 6.8 million households (5.7%) experienced very low food security.
- Households with children reported food insecurity at almost double the rate for households without children (21.3 versus 11.4%).
- Households that had higher rates of food insecurity than the national average included households with children (21.3%), especially households with children headed by single women (36.6%), single men (27.8%), black non-Hispanic households (24.9%), and Hispanic households (26.9%).

A good source of statistics on hunger in the United States can be found at www. whyhunger.org.

A rare and candid look at power in the United States* written by an anonymous investment manager who works with the very wealthy (top 0.5%), describes their privileges:

---

* http://sociology.ucsc.edu/whorulesamerica/power/investment_manager.html, a website created by Professor G. William Domhoff, Sociology Department, University of California at Santa Cruz.

"A highly complex and largely discrete set of laws and exemptions from laws has been put in place by those in the uppermost reaches of the U.S. financial system. It allows them to protect and increase their wealth and significantly affect the U.S. political and legislative processes. They have real power and real wealth. Ordinary citizens in the bottom 99.9% are largely not aware of these systems, do not understand how they work, are unlikely to participate in them, and have little likelihood of entering the top 0.5%, much less the top 0.1% (Figure 2.17). Moreover, those at the very top have no incentive whatsoever for revealing or changing the rules. I am not optimistic." [31]

How does U.S. executive pay compare to other nations? The data in Table 2.1 [34] were collected by Dr. Mark Kroll. While the ratios and relative formulas may vary slightly over time, the U.S. ratio is many times the ratios of other countries as

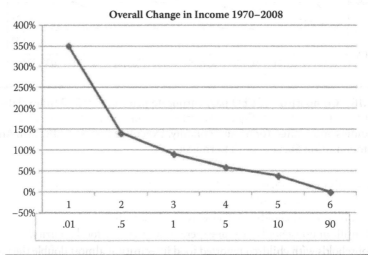

Relative Income Percentage (U.S.)	Number of People	Average Income	Overall Change in Income 1970–2008
Top 0.1%	150,000	$5.6 million	+350%
Top 0.5%	610,000	$870,000	+140%
Top 1%	760,000	$440,000	+90%
Top 5%	6 million	$210,000	+59%
Top 10%	7.6 million	$125,000	+38%
Bottom 90%	137 million	$31,000	−1%

Figure 2.17 Overall change of income level lessens as income decreases.

Table 2.1 Ratios of CEO Pay to Average Worker Pay

Country	Ratio
Japan	11 to 1
Germany	12 to 1
France	15 to 1
Italy	20 to 1
Canada	20 to 1
United Kingdom	22 to 1
Venezuela	50 to 1
United States	475 to 1

shown by these representative numbers. As shown in the table, the ratios of CEO pay to worker pay for those nations are at least 10 times (roughly) the ratios of other nations. Research from Cornell University shows an increasingly wide gap between CEO pay and average worker pay over time [34].

What are the costs of the widening gap between the richest and poorest, and the widening spread of childhood hunger in one of the richest countries of the world? Another way to pose the question is to evaluate the cost of the shrinking middle class [35]. If current economic trends do not change, the future United States will consist of very, very few wealthy surrounded by many, many poor.

In an exploration of the middle class by *Money Magazine*, the "only universally accepted definition of middle class is the oldest: neither rich nor poor. . . . The middle class has always been considered vital to a country's stability and growth." As far back as 350 B.C., Aristotle said that no democracy could last without middle class rule; the rich and the poor simply distrust each other too intensely to surrender the reins. In a study by the Organization for Economic Cooperation and Development (OECD), the U.S. had the third highest percentage of people living in poverty among the world's 28 leading nations, right after Mexico and Turkey.

If you are middle class in America, making 75% to 125% of the 2008 median (average) U.S. income of $50,000 ($37,500 to $62,500 in 2008), you too may somehow be forced to drop out of the middle class.

We can perhaps look at history—at times such as the feudal era when the wealthy few were surrounded by the myriad poor. It is hard to believe that the similar spread of ignorance, poverty, sickness, and unhappiness is the future of our proud American legacy. The wealthy too suffer, perhaps not from hunger, but in walled-off fortresses, facing limited mobility and constant fear of attack. The author joins many others in hoping that this dark vision of the future is somehow averted and that we are able to literally spread the wealth for the benefit of all.

2.5 Summary

The impact of IT offshore outsourcing (and outsourcing in general) is inconclusive, despite the many years of experience and the diverse U.S. industries that followed this trend. While there is clearly movement of jobs overseas as a result of outsourcing, studies show that the program returns create U.S-based jobs. A linear conclusion is therefore not possible. What does seem clear is that productivity gains eliminate more jobs than global outsourcing.

The U.S. is currently undergoing a unique set of economic circumstances that appear, at least on the surface and in the popular imagination, to be exacerbated by the movement of jobs overseas. These trends include deeper, more lasting troughs of recession and the consequent widening income gap. Of greater concern is the puzzling statistics that demonstrate that even as the demand for workers grows in some sectors, the long-term unemployment rate appears to be unaffected by this demand. This leads to the conclusion that the skills of available workers are increasingly mismatched with the skills required by open jobs. The overriding concern relates to the economically invisible—the group dropping from employed, to unemployed, to poverty. This group forms a growing, voiceless population of disenfranchised workers.

References

General: Kalyan Chakroaborty and William Remington, Offshoring of IT Services: The Impact on the U.S. Economy, *Journal of Computing Sciences in Colleges*, 20 (4), April 2005.

[1] Bob Lewis, Survival Guide: The Moral Compass. Corporations Aren't Moral Agents: Creating Interesting Dilemmas for Business Leaders, *InfoWorld*, March 22, 2002, updated April 3, 2003. http://www.infoworld.com/blogs/bob-lewis

[2] The American Ethical Union, The Ethical Culture Society of Bergen County, Ethical Dilemmas of Globalization. July 2010. http://www.ethicalfocus.org/platform/46-world-affairs/125-ethical-dilemmas-of-globalization

[3] *The New York Times.* Letter to the editor from Bob Schwarz, January 4, 2010. Response from Bill Keller, January 10, 2010. http://www.nytimes.com/2010/01/10/opinion/10pubed.html

[4] Director, Business Ethics, Company Confidential Job Posting, Monster.Com, Summer 2010.

[5] ITAA/Global Insight Study Finds IT Outsourcing Results in Net U.S. Job Growth, *HRO Today*, March 30, 2004. http://www.hrotoday.com/news/2755/itaaglobal-insight-study-finds-it-outsourcing-results-net-us-job-growth?id=523y

[6] ITAA/Global Insights Study Finds Global Sourcing of Software and IT Services Bolsters Domestic Employment and Wages across the Entire U.S. Economy, *Free Library by Farlex*, March 30, 2004. http://www.thefreelibrary.com/ITAA%2FGlobal+Insights+Study+Finds+Global+Sourcing+of+Software+and+IT...-a0114753040

[7] The Economic Reality that No One Wants to Talk about. Cross-posted from Robert Reich's blog, *The Huffington Post*, December 2, 2009. http://www.huffingtonpost.com/robert-reich/the-economic-reality-that_b_377167.html

[8] David Millon, Default Rules, Wealth Distribution, and Corporate Law Reform: Employment at Will Versus Job Security, University of Pennsylvania Law Review, 146, 1998, 975–1041.

[9] United Nations Department of Economic and Social Affairs, Population Division, Population Estimates and Projections Section, World Population Prospects: 2010 Revision Data Online, May 3, 2011. http://esa.un.org/unpd/wpp/index.htm

[10] Richard B. Freeman, Labor Market Imbalances: Shortages, Surpluses, or Fish Stories? Harvard University and NBERCentre for Economic Performance. Boston Federal Reserve Economic Conference on Global Imbalances: As Giants Evolve, Chatham, MA, June 14–16, 2006. http://flash.lakeheadu.ca/~mshannon/freeman_global_labour_imbalances.pdf

[11] Adele Hayutin, Global Aging: The New New Thing. The Big Picture of Population Change. Stanford Center on Longevity, Chart 7, Page 3, November 2007. http://longevity.stanford.edu/blog/2011/06/global-aging-the-new-new-thing-the-big-picture-of-population-change-in-asia/

[12] U.S. Bureau of Labor Statistics, Job Openings and Labor Turnover Survey Highlights, June 2011. http://www.bls.gov/web/jolts/jlt_labstatgraphs.pdf

[13] Dave Altig, A Curious Unemployment Picture Gets More Curious. Federal Reserve Bank of Atlanta Blog, July 16, 2010. http://macroblog.typepad.com/macroblog/2010/07/a-curious-unemployment-picture-gets-more-curious.html

[14] Federal Reserve Bank of St. Louis, Median Duration of Unemployment, updated September 2, 2011. http://research.stlouisfed.org/fred2/series/UEMPMED

[15] Percent Job Losses in Post-WWII Recessions, www.calculatedriskblog.com, http://cr4re.com/charts/charts.html#category=Employment&chart=EmployRecessAug2011.jpg

[16] http://www.bea.gov/index.htm; http://www.politifact.com/corporatewages/

[17] Martin Neil Baily, The Next Economy and the Growth Challenge for the United States, Presented at Scholars Strategy Network Conference, Cambridge, MA, September 30, 2010,Chart 11.http://www.brookings.edu/~/media/Files/rc/reports/2010/1001_next_economy_growth_baily/1001_next_economy_growth_baily.pdf

[18] Bruce J. Bergman, Extended Mass Layoffs after 2001: A Comparison of New York and the Nation, Monthly Labor Review, September 2008. http://www.bls.gov/opub/mlr/2008/09/art2exc.htm

[19] Michel Janssen, Honorio Padrón, and Erik Dorr, New Data: 2.8 Million Business-Support Jobs Eliminated since 2000; One Million More to Disappear by 2014, *Enterprise Strategy: Management*, November 15, 2010.

[20] World Bank, *Development in Practice: Higher Education. The Lessons of Experience*, May 1994. http://siteresources.worldbank.org/EDUCATION/Resources/278200-1099079877269/547664-1099079956815/HigherEd_lessons_En.pdf

[21] OECD Programme for International Student Assessment, http://www.pisa.oecd.org/pages/0,2987,en_32252351_32235731_1_1_1_1_1,00.html

[22] Simon Appleton, Paul Atherton, and Michael Bleaney, International School Test Scores, Economic Centre for Research in Economic Development and International Trade, University of Nottingham, August 2004. http://www.nottingham.ac.uk/credit/documents/papers/08-04.pdf

[23] Eric A. Hanushek and Ludger Woessmann, The High Cost of Low Educational Performance: The Long-Run Economic Impact of Improving PISA Outcomes, Programme for International Student Assessment, 2011. http://edpro.stanford.edu/hanushek/files_det.asp?FileId=263

[24] Jim Saxton, *Investment in Education: Private and Public Returns*, Joint Economic Committee Study, January 2000. http://www.house.gov/jec/educ.htm

[25] Edwin Black, Business is Business, *Letter from Washington*, 82 (7), April 2001. http://www.ibmandtheholocaust.com/articles/Hadassah200104/letter2.htm

[26] Edwin Black, *IBM and the Holocaust: The Strategic Alliance between Nazi Germany and America's Most Powerful Corporation*, New York: Crown/Random House 2001, http://www.jewishvirtuallibrary.org/jsource/Holocaust/IBM.html

[27] Ariel Kaminar, The Ethicist, Don't Ask, Do Tell? *The New York Times*. July 24, 2011.

[28] Arthur F. Jones Jr. and Daniel H. Weinberg, *Current Population Reports: The Changing Shape of the Nation's Income Distribution, 1947–1998*. U.S. Census Bureau, June 2000.

[29] U.S. Department of Agriculture, Food Security in the United States: Key Statistics and Graphics. http://www.ers.usda.gov/Briefing/FoodSecurity/stats_graphs.htm

[30] Food and Agriculture Organization of the United Nations. http://www.fao.org/

[31] G. William Domhoff, An Investment Manager's View on the Top 1%: Who Rules America, July 2011. http://sociology.ucsc.edu/whorulesamerica/power/investment_manager.html

[32] (Not) spreading the wealth, *The Washington Post*, June 18, 2011. http://www.washingtonpost.com/wp-srv/special/business/income-inequality/

[33] Food Security Learning Center. http://www.whyhunger.org/programs/fslcprogram.html

[34] Mark Kroll, CEO Pay Rates: U.S. vs. Foreign Nations, *Management*, 510, November 17, 2005. http://www.cab.latech.edu/~mkroll/510_papers/fall_05/group6.pdf

[35] John Alexander Burton and Christian E. Weller. Supersize This: How CEO Pay Took off while America's Middle Class Struggled, Center for American Progress, May 2005, p. 4. http://www.americanprogress.org/kf/ceo_pay_web_final.pdf [NOTE: This material was created by the Center for American Progress, www.americanprogress.org]

Appendix: Relevant Quotes

1. Bob Lewis. "Offshoring ethics: deciding whether or not to move work offshore should be a management methodology, not morality." InfoWorld Debate, April 4, 2003. http://www.infoworld.com/d/developer-world/offshoring-ethics-323

2. The American Ethical Union/The Ethical Culture Society of Bergen County. "Overall is this good or bad?... Some economists talk about a compensation principle.... If the gainers can compensate the losers, the economy gains.... The gainers [may] have some moral obligation to the losers. [The] process seems unstoppable.... It is not globalization ... but ... unfairness ... that is the moral and humanitarian problem." Ethical Dilemmas of Globalization Meeting, July 2010. http://www.ethicalfocus.org/platform/46-world-affairs/125-ethical-dilemmas-of-globalization

3. Letter to the Editor, *The New York Times*. "Publishers want to ... avoid financial responsibility for ... benefits like health care, vacations and retirement ... for regularly employed workers.... That's the real story. Don't bury it." January 4, 2010.

4. Response of Bill Keller, *The New York Times*. "We can't afford to put everyone ... on full-time.... [This] ... made me nostalgic for the old days, when there was a brighter line between right and wrong." January 10, 2010. http://www.nytimes.com/2010/01/10/opinion/10pubed.html

5. Job posting, Monster.com, 2010:

   > Director, Business Ethics: A core value ... is to be worthy of ... trust.... To further that value ... the Company maintains an Enterprise Business Ethics Office.
   >
   > Principal Responsibilities: Develop ... company-wide ethics training.... Facilitate a Business Ethics Advisory Council.... Create an ... ethics assessment which will result in action planning.... Provide guidance to employees.

Chapter 3

A Checklist for New Offshore Programs

"Ethics is the activity of man directed to secure the inner perfection of his own personality."

Albert Schweitzer

3.1 Alignment of Organizational Structures to Manage Ethical Decision Making Effectively

By the time is reported in the newspapers that a firm has engaged in unethical behavior, it is too late. Although a large corporation, like a discount furniture store that goes under every year only to reopen under another name, may appear to suffer no consequences for breaches of ethics in the large, it is hard to measure just how many opportunities are missed or how many deals are not brought to the table.

In the middle of my career, shortly after I published my first book on offshore outsourcing, I was approached by a country with a great deal of potential in the offshore field that wanted me to represent its interests in the U.S. This country was and still is known for serious ethical violations. Looking back, this offer represented one of my personal forks in the road. I knew it would be extremely financially rewarding, but I turned the offer down. I remember the ambassador's surprise at my response. Perhaps I was one of the first people he had met who could not be bought.

These small decisions such as walking away by deeply principled parties (of which I certainly hope I am one) represent the unmeasured costs of a core business culture unfettered by ethical principle. The most interesting business partners, the best and strongest employees—and their creativity and pride—go elsewhere. Employment of the best of the best is no longer a possibility, unless it is the best of the best as swindlers, cheaters, and liars. They will show up in abundance.

It is not realistic for most large firms to avoid IT offshore outsourcing completely in order to remain competitive, given the realities of the worldwide marketplace. Even if U.S. firms as a whole opted out tomorrow—an extremely unlike eventuality—it is hard to imagine that a self-enclosed bubble of falsely high wages across a global economy could survive for long. Then of course there is that small fact that industries have been moving labor offshore for decades—the very same years that the U.S. has been the strongest economic powerhouse in the world.

The ethics of outsourcing is, at its core, taking action to ensure that those caught in the unforeseen wave—those unable or unwilling to retool to meet the sudden, dramatic demands of new market forces—are provided the means to restructure their work lives. In such cases, a relatively small percentage of the year over year savings provided to displaced workers can mean an extraordinary difference to those individuals, families and communities.

This offshore checklist is hopefully just the start of a meaningful industry dialogue on how to go about minimizing not only negative public relations spin but the actual negative economic impact that IT offshore outsourcing can wreak.

3.1.1 Define IT Ethics Program Management Office (Ethics PMO)

Prior to empowering an organization to evaluate and make ethical decisions on behalf of IT offshore programs, an Ethics PMO must be defined. Key components, based closely on the typical IT program management office, should ring familiar to most IT professionals. The components of both types of PMO's include but are not limited to the following standardized processes:

- Overall methodology definition: how ethics principles are implemented and managed across the IT offshore program, including definition of the goals, prerequisites, deliverables, responsibilities, success criteria, metrics, and reporting associated with each step
- Scope management: diagrams or lists of items that "in" and "out" of scope.
- Requirements management: list of ethical areas to be addressed, and any needs specific to a particular department or section of the worker population.
- Organizational structure, roles and responsibilities: outline of program management hierarchy of decision making and responsibility as shown in a tool

such as a RACI diagram (responsible–accountable–consulted–informed); includes escalation management.

■ Communications management and reporting: description of the frequency, content, and responsibilities associated with program communications. Risk management: a risk register describing the potential risks and associated mitigation strategies.

■ Program expectations and norms: document setting the stage for expectations across all program stakeholders.

■ Budget management: description of how legitimate costs of IT ethics management are defined, approved, and managed

■ Return on investment (ROI) estimation and management: outline of anticipated and actual financial benefits of ethics management across the organization. Quality assurance: measurement of statistics that track the fulfillment of program goals.

■ Procurement management: guidelines for hiring and managing external resources as aspect of Ethics PMO.

■ Process change management: guidelines on how "before" and "after" ethics-related processes are developed, documented, approved, and managed.

■ Metrics management: standards for evaluating program success including deliverables acceptance and review.

Once this framework has been established, the next step is to prepare for executing the ethics program methodology. The following steps will generate the appropriate financial and employee skills decision framework to fund and execute a robust ethical alignment program on behalf of impacted employees.

1. Step One: Analyze Potential Impact
   Analyzing the financial impact on individuals and communities can serve as a guidepost to the level of investment that will be required.
2. Step Two: Research Most Effective Options for Impacted Workers
   Rather than hiding or spinning the situation, invest thought and dollars into helping worker re-entry into the marketplace to minimize the actual negative impacts on individuals and communities.
3. Step Three: Create Program-Specific Pragmatic Ethical Guidelines
   Based upon the research results, not a formula, define options to help those caught in the whirlwind to shift their skills to alternative ways to support themselves, their families, and their communities.
4. Step Four: Factor in Program Costs
   Following the steps above, calculate the cost of providing a soft landing to impacted individuals and the community. This cost needs to be included as part of the baseline financial requirements of an offshore IT program—from the start.

5. Step Five: Establish Community Communications

Pretending a firm is a closed entity that only acknowledges membership in a community to pursue tax breaks and infrastructure investments or support pet charities is not appropriate. Creation of a communication plan that acknowledges the community at large as a stakeholder in large-scale employment is simply recognizing a truth that must be part of any outsourcing program.

6. Step Six: Monitor Effectiveness of Ethical Investment

Be prepared to restructure and redress the project if metrics show that program goals are not being met.

7. Step Seven: Consider Expanding the PMO Reach

Utilize the Ethics PMO to create and enforce ethical constructs beyond IT outsourcing to all areas of the firm. Some guidelines for implementation of a robust ethical toolkit are explored below. Examples of major deliverables are discussed here and in Chapter 4.

3.1.2 Defining an Effective Ethics PMO

As IT professionals know, there is an entire body of literature on the IT execution PMO. The Ethics PMO is an untouched subject that can only be canvassed at a high level in this volume.

It is critical to empower the Ethics PMO with the required weight within the firm organizational structure. This is required for the PMO to be effective in evaluating, facilitating, and enforcing ethical decisions on behalf of IT offshore programs. Figure 3.1 illustrates the Ethics PMO high level methodology, and outlines the approach to establishing and defining a new Ethics PMO. The first step is to assess the requirements by department and by individual. This means identifying the individuals who would be impacted by an offshore program and assessing their skills and abilities, along with potential opportunities inside and outside the firm.

A shining example of a precursor to this concept, I met with a CIO of a New Jersey-based utility company who was able to negotiate outstanding new options for his former staff impacted by the offshore program. Most staff members were placed in jobs with the offshore company, which was chosen in part because it was growing rapidly and had a robust U.S.-based IT business. For most of his staff, this meant more money and the opportunity to develop higher value skills in the market place by exposure to the latest technologies. Those who were unwilling or unable to travel were able to keep onshore roles in their old jobs at the utility. Those near retirement received generous packages that enabled them to retire with no reduction in benefits. Only one person was unable to fit the above options and the CIO funded extended training to launch the employee in a completely different career.

Although no long-term data are available, I met with the CIO more than three years into the transition and all employees were content and benefitted materially

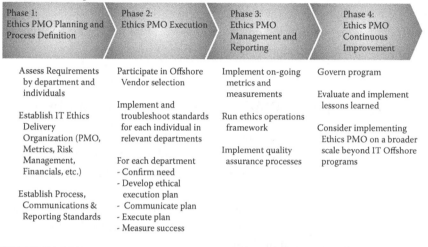

Ethics PMO Methodology

Goal of the Ethics PMO is to establish a framework of repeatable and measurable processes related to ethical practices for IT Offshore Programs, and achieve the desired benefits, effciency gains and long-term cost reductions for the organization within this framework.

Phase 1: Ethics PMO Planning and Process Definition	Phase 2: Ethics PMO Execution	Phase 3: Ethics PMO Management and Reporting	Phase 4: Ethics PMO Continuous Improvement
Assess Requirements by department and individuals	Participate in Offshore Vendor selection	Implement on-going metrics and measurements	Govern program
Establish IT Ethics Delivery Organization (PMO, Metrics, Risk Management, Financials, etc.)	Implement and troubleshoot standards for each individual in relevant departments	Run ethics operations framework	Evaluate and implement lessons learned
Establish Process, Communications & Reporting Standards	For each department - Confirm need - Develop ethical execution plan - Communicate plan - Execute plan - Measure success	Implement quality assurance processes	Consider implementing Ethics PMO on a broader scale beyond IT Offshore programs

Figure 3.1   Ethics PMO high level methodology.

from the offshore program. Clearly, the ability to create alternative employment options is highly dependent upon a multitude of factors, including:

1. The savings potential or return on investment of the offshore program over the long term. This determines the level of investment that is feasible in creating a soft landing for displaced workers.
2. The general robustness of the economy and the specific availability of jobs in the roles to be offshored. In general, it is best to assume that the economy will not be able to provide alternative jobs in the same field so that impacted employees will not become dependent upon income that does not materialize.
3. The particular needs and profiles of employees. A frequent assumption in offshore programs is that younger members of the organization can more easily retool to new roles inside or external to the organization. This may or may not be true. It is important not to allow assumptions based on employee profiles to determine the alternative opportunities. A top performing individual who filled the same role for over 10 years by providing reliable and excellent service over the years may easily make the transition into a new role.
4. Years of service in the organization. It is vital to be fair and equitable to individuals who are short of qualifying for retirement and provided many years of loyal service.

The most important factor is to include this analysis in the up-front design of an offshore program. Adjusting the offshore vendor selection process to include hiring of existing workers is often thrown in as a consideration, but not incorporated as a formal component of the evaluation criteria for offshore business partners. Incorporating the needs of the impacted employees into the vendor selection process is a best practice and an important role of the Ethics PMO.

3.2   Key to Ethics PMO Success: C-Level Standing

In parallel with determining requirements of departments and individuals, the Ethics PMO organization must be formed (Figure 3.2). Key to the success of the Ethics PMO is placing PMO members high enough in the organization—in other words, at as a peer with other C-level officers.

Early in the history of information technology, the strategic value of IT investments were often marginalized by its frequent placement under the chief financial officer or a similar organizational wing.

While this is a workable structure for some firms, this organizational placement is often problematic because the individuals who make decisions on IT investments tend to see them as overhead. Over time, the firms that view IT as overhead tend to fail miserably at keeping pace with the technology investments required to lead in the marketplace. As a result, as the industry developed over time, more and more

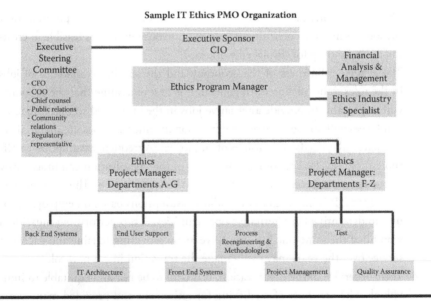

Figure 3.2   Ethics PMO organization.

firms created C-level roles in IT. Chief information officers and chief technology officers recognize IT investment as a strategic tool for growth in the marketplace.

Similarly, over time, the strategic investment in the reputation of the firm that the Ethics PMO represents will prove to be more than worthwhile. Unfortunately, like the firms of yesteryear that started too late investing in strategic IT technology, some firms have already sustained severe and long-lasting damage to their reputations. When a company is the butt of jokes on late night TV and in newspapers, the cost is incalculably high. We look in detail at the cutting edge role of the chief ethics officer in Chapter 7.

Another reason for establishing an Ethics PMO at the highest level in the organization is to empower it to address the rampant uncertainty across the ranks of the firm's middle management employees. These employees are at the heart of the operational execution and cannot afford to lose many cycles because of the period of deep uncertainty that accompanies the launch of a new offshore program.

This deep uncertainty tends to generate a great deal of emotion and stress at the beginning of an offshore program. Most employees cannot imagine a world in which they must suddenly be dependent upon the work of team members from a completely different culture located half a world away—team members they may never meet. Most IT jobs are challenging enough without that level of change, and stress is the typical (and understandable) reaction.

One of the well documented risks of IT offshore programs is losing the structural integrity of the IT delivery process to the extent that the customer experience is compromised. The inconsistencies of the broader organization—often held together by the delicate glue of long-standing human relationships built over time—can be fractured easily in a way that damages the customer relationship, and therefore the business as a whole, during the transition to offshore.

For example, a customer who can suddenly no longer utilize a favorite on-line shortcut to place a new order based upon past orders may "jump ship" in frustration. This is the kind of nightmare every firm wants to avoid. This kind of glitch could easily happen during the implementation of an offshore program, if, for example, code specifications that were normally worked upon in co-located teams are suddenly shifted offshore without the requisite detailed documentation.

Add to this deep uncertainty about change in daily execution of duties and pervasive overall uncertainties about careers and incomes—the result is often a very tense work environment. This is why, according best practices principles, direct involvement by very senior IT leadership is required to implement a company's first offshore program. The involvement sets the tone for what may be experienced as a time of political and business chaos, but also because in a very practical way it shows that the old organizational structure and decision-making authority are outmoded.

3.2.1 Empowerment of C-Level Ethics PMOs across Organizational Silos

Most large firms suffer from a very challenging problem in terms of their organizational structures. In order to hold together a level of professionalism required within vast interconnected web of matrix responsibilities, it is necessary to establish relatively deep silos. It is not unusual, for example, for an IT organization to have over 100 members and only at the very highest level is there a peer relationship with other internal senior level managers across different departmental disciplines.

While this allows a certain consistency of business culture as well as quality control within each discipline, it can make it very challenging to enable a robust ethics program, since there is often little understanding across the organization as to the nature of the work being performed in the other silos. The need for a relatively robust "cross-silo" business process re-engineering capability at all levels of the organization is another very important reason that the executive sponsorship of the Ethics PMO should be established firmly above the operational fray. For example, the process of assessing internal customer feedback may be very different if half the delivery team is located offshore. It may be necessary to establish a new role—offshore business liaison—to ensure that expectations and requirements are clarified. These roles must be designed so that Ethics PMO staff is above all other departments.

Specific to fair evaluations of individuals, it is important to establish a culture of objectivity that transcends internal departmental cultures. The higher the number of employees (as noted in Chapter 1, the numbers in large firms are high—usually a minimum of 100 workers), the more a firm owes fairness and accountability to its workers and the community.

3.3 Roles and Responsibilities of Ethics PMO Team

The roles and responsibilities of the Ethics PMO team members are depicted in a RACI diagram (Table 3.1). This matrix diagram outlines whether a given team member is responsible (R), accountable (A), consulted (C), or informed (I).

3.3.1 Team Members

Each member of the Ethics PMO shifts his or her roles and responsibilities as the PMO matures.

3.3.2 Executive Sponsor and Steering Committee

In the early stages, accountability for the PMO resides with the executive sponsor—ideally a chief ethics officer (CETO), or a CIO if the company has no CETO.

TABLE 3.1 RACI Diagram for Ethics PMO

Deliverables	Ethics Program Manager	Executive Sponsor	Executive Steering Committee	Financial Analyst	Ethics Industry Specialist	Ethics Project Managers	Ethics Team Members	Firm Employees	Community	Media
Phase 1: Ethics PMO Planning and Process Definition										
Project Charter Executive Summary	R	A	C	I	I	I	I			
High Level Ethics Program Project or Work Plan	R	A	C	I	I	I	I	I		
High Level Requirements Analysis	R	A	C	I	I	I	I			
Ethics PMO Initial Organization Chart	C	A/R	I	I	I	I	I			
Ethics PMO High Level Success Criteria	C	A/R	I	I	I	I	I			
High Level Program Risk Assessment	R	A	C	I	I	I	I			
High Level ROI / Budget	R	A	C	C	I	I	I			
Ethics PMO Initial Communications Plan and Meeting Structure	R	A	C	I	I	I	I	I	I	I

(continued)

TABLE 3.1   RACI Diagram for Ethics PMO (continued)

Deliverables	Ethics Program Manager	Executive Sponsor	Executive Steering Committee	Financial Analyst	Ethics Industry Specialist	Ethics Project Managers	Ethics Team Members	Firm Employees	Community	Media
Phase 2: Ethics PMO Execution										
Detailed Ethics Program Project Work Plan	A/R	C	C	C	C	C	I	I		
Detailed Requirements Documentation	A/R	C	C	C	C	C	I	I		
Final Ethics PMO Organization Chart	A/R	C	C	C	C	C	I	I		
Detailed Metrics by Department / group	A/R	C	C	C	C	C	I	I		
Detailed Communication Plan	A/R	C	C	C	C	C	I	I	I	I
Define Quality Assurance Processes	A/R	C	C	C	C	C	I			
Detailed Risk Assessment	A/R	C	C	C	C	C	C			
Detailed Budget / ROI	A	C	C	R	C	C	I	I		

TABLE 3.1 RACI Diagram for Ethics PMO (continued)

Deliverables	Ethics Program Manager	Executive Sponsor	Executive Steering Committee	Financial Analyst	Ethics Industry Specialist	Ethics Project Managers	Ethics Team Members	Firm Employees	Community	Media
Phase 3: Ethics PMO Management and Reporting										
Implement According to Detailed Project Plan	A	I	I	C	C	R	C	I		
Implement Quality Assurance Processes	A	I	I	I	C	R	I	I		
Implement Metrics	A	I	I	I	C	R	I			
Implement Risk Mitigation	A	I	I	I	C	R	I	I		
Implement Communications	A	I	I	I	C	R	I	I	I	I
"Revise Project Plan, QA Processes, Metrics as Needed based upon Departmental Discovery / Needs"	A/R	I	I	I	C	C	I	I		
Phase 4: Ethics PMO Continuous Improvement										
Evaluate Lessons Learned	A/R	I	I	I	C	C	I	I	I	I
Obtain Feedback	A/R	I	I	I	C	C	I	I	I	I
Implement Changes per Above	A/R	I	I	I	C	C	I	I	I	I

In the early stages, accountability for the PMO vision lies with the executive sponsors. They establish the vision, staffing, measures of success, and initial meeting and communications structure of the PMO.

The key is for the senior executives who comprise the steering committee to invest the time up front and agree on the vision and goals of the program, then provide sufficient budget, staff, and other resources to enable this vision. The importance of this executive vision and agreement cannot be overemphasized and is often overlooked, as busy executives focus upon operational execution. Later, when disagreements surface during execution, it becomes cumbersome and costly to retroactively clarify and shift goals and focus.

The executive sponsor and peer steering committee set the tone for the Ethics PMO and ensure that both content and process reflect the values of the firm. At this level the focus is often on return on investment (ROI). It is difficult to put a price on potential damage, but it can be achieved and is an important benchmark.

For example, while it may not be reasonable to invest 50% of the year-over-year savings in an Ethics PMO and the impacted employees, it may be reasonable to invest 10%. A look at the pre- and post- stock values of companies that did not make strategic investments in an Ethics PMO may be a good starting point for a financial estimation model.

If a competitor lost 20% of its business relating to negative press and customer dissatisfaction after an offshore implementation, the losses can be quantified and compared with the investment required to avoid those eventualities. It is almost always much less expensive to invest in avoiding negative publicity or customer dissatisfaction, than to try to clean up the mess later.

These purely financial assessments can establish a business case for investing in a soft landing for displaced workers, as part of the cost of doing business in offshore outsourcing. This investment can in turn be translated into a program and project plan, success criteria, and organizational matrix, and other operational deliverables for a "soft landing" program delivery.

Once the structure and membership are established above, the operational baton is passed to the ethics program manager, described below. The ethics program manager is both responsible and accountable for successful execution of the overall ethics program. As in most strategic initiatives, unforeseen questions and unexpected situations will arise. This underscores the initial, baseline importance of a common set of goals and vision across the executive team.

It is difficult to handle unforeseen events while simultaneously addressing gaps relating to a common long-term vision. Unfortunately, however, it is the rare executive team that does not succumb to the temptation to focus on the immediate tactical questions at the expense of creating the much more difficult mindshare relating to ideal future state and best path to achieve it.

3.3.3   Ethics Program Manager

The ethics program manager reports directly to the C-level steering committee, ideally headed by the chief ethics officer (CETO), CIO, or an equivalent. As illustrated in the RACI diagram, the program manager is responsible for execution of the program as a single point of communication and management, ultimately leading a team of project managers who represent the needs and interests of the various departments.

The ethics program manager's role is not atypical of the PMO role well documented in IT literature. The manager's primary function is to ensure that the program execution reflects the goals as set by the executive sponsor and the steering committee by creating and managing an effective, efficient operational program. He or she creates and enforces the operational deliverables based upon the guidance and leadership of the executive sponsor and steering committee across the four phases of the methodology.

3.3.4   Ethics Project Managers

Each ethics project manager applies the program guidelines, success criteria, and goals of the Ethics PMO to the needs of his or her specific department. After the level of investment is defined for the soft landing, it is time to analyze the particular needs of each individual impacted by the offshore program. If, per usual, the IT outsourcing project encompasses changes across multiple departments, it is likely that each department have some needs in common and others that are unique. The workers in some departments may be particularly hard hit to find alternative jobs via both external and internal opportunities; younger workers may be interested in extensive retraining, while more mature workers may require more options regarding near-retirement and purely monetary programs.

In addition, the ethical flavor may differ across departments, where the impact on loyal, long-term workers often resonate more heavily with other employees, the community, and even the media. Establishing a project manager to focus on the needs of a specific department essentially creates a formal organizational advocate in an environment that is changing so rapidly that the traditional sources of trust and connection rapidly become obsolete.

The ethics project manager is consulted in the development of overall program operational goals, but is responsible for creatively applying them to the needs of his or her specific department, and meeting the metrics and success criteria established by the program manager and steering committee.

3.3.5   Specialized Contributors and External Stakeholders

Specialists such as financial analysts and industry experts provide advice and counsel to the ethics program manager and steering committee based upon similar program experiences across other large firms.

Finally, it is important to include, as informed or interested parties, the often invisible stakeholders. These include the remaining firm employees, the community, the media, and the investment community. Some large firms become so self-referential they act as if there is no outside accountability. As we know from experience, this mentality can become very dangerous. As noted before, it is important for individuals as well as firms as a whole to maintain their conduct as if the world was watching—because it is. Creation of a communication plan that incorporates these broad stakeholders is a key success factor for program delivery and minimizes the dangerous human tendency to fill an information void with misinformation.

3.4 Setting Realistic Goals in Preparation for Executing Ethics PMO Methodology

3.4.1 Analyze Potential Impact

As described briefly above, analyzing the impact on individuals and communities can serve as a guidepost to determine the investment required. The goal of the Ethics PMO is to ensure that broader ethical principles are applied across the organization in a manner reflective of organizational values. How can this best be accomplished? The place to start is always with the details, listed below:

- How many workers are impacted? This is the financial analysis of labor arbitrage in reverse. How does the total number impact each worker? In other words, if 78 programming roles are moved offshore, will those workers be likely to find similar roles with similar pay? What is the impact to the community as a whole and the firm's reputation if the answer to that question is "no"?
- What are the local and national employment demand trends for impacted workers?
- What happened to other local or distant companies in the marketplace? Were they subjected to negative press or customer backlash? Were their stock prices and investments in positive community relations negatively affected?

It is true that this kind of analysis, and more importantly, these kinds of concerns are often deemed as outside the scope and the responsibility of the firm as a profit-making entity. It is a corollary of this book that a judicious and relatively small investment will serve to mitigate risks of community and media backlash, making a huge difference in individual lives as well as community well-being.

3.4.1.1 Research Most Effective Options for Impacted Workers

Rather than attempting to hide or spin an offshore project, how about investing some thought and dollars into helping workers re-enter the market place to minimize negative impact on individuals and communities? Let's revisit our classic example. The work of 100 IT workers at an average rate of $70 per hour will now shift offshore to individuals earning $20 per hour. A savings of $50 per hour translates to $200,000 savings per week based on a 40-hour week. This in turn calculates to $10 million per year over a 50-week work year or $50 million over 5 years.

Assuming a write-off of 10% year over year for business process re-engineering ($1 million); add another 10% write-off for the Ethics PMO to total $2 million. The year over year savings totals $8 million per year. The potential benefits that this 10%, $2 million investment means for displaced workers, their families and communities may be extremely far-reaching as translated into new training, near-retirement and other programs

It is important that all worker re-entry programs be measured by pragmatic success rates of the workers and not via a theoretical model. Some firms define their role as formally delivering the bad news to workers via a high priced placement firm: "Yes, there is nothing locally for you." The really valuable placement services involve looking at the long-term work potential of the individual worker across diverse opportunities and geographies. The goal is to identify marketable skills for the long term—those that exist, and those that can be developed due to a high level of both personal interest and ability.

3.4.1.2   Create Pragmatic Ethical Guidelines

Based on research rather than a formula, a company should invest in the development of options to help those caught in the whirlwind to shift their skills to alternative ways to support themselves, their families, and their communities. It is almost unheard of to publish success stories in this area because of the strict taboos and code of silence surrounding offshore program labor arbitrage. This head-in-the-sand approach is particularly damaging because it contributes to the general lack of research on the topic of what *does work* for worker repatriation.

One bright spot is the research on small business ownership and growth. There exists today a well defined body of realistic, grounded research on the critical success factors necessary for launching and growing a small business. Viewing the Ethics PMO as a mechanism for seed money to invest in the community and workers is not unlike the kinds of programs large firms often support in creating opportunities for women and minority owned small businesses.

Research focusing on individual job decisions and the viability of such decisions over the long term remains strangely absent. It is almost as if the impact of individual decisions such as where and how to be educated or where and how to work are not worth the research effort. If a worker succeeds, his story is interesting and well publicized. Those who fall off the employment path and the decisions that lead to that fall appear deeply uninteresting to researchers and the public alike. These individuals truly become invisible.

IT workers are not unintelligent and the threat of becoming invisible and forgotten despite past successes, investments in education and solid records of corporate contribution looms large. Often the ability to learn the most prized skills—those that are most highly desired in the marketplace of the moment—is construed as more a reward than salary raises, because these support job security for the future. One clear lesson we have learned from the dot-com bust-ups and downs of the IT marketplace is that no set of skills guarantees long-term career security. Creating a business environment that recognizes and supports those caught in the flux of market demands will often mean the difference between individuals and communities standing versus sinking—at relatively small cost to the business that so recently depended upon their good work effort.

3.4.1.3 Factor in the Cost

Based on the analysis above, the cost of providing a soft landing to individuals and the community should be factored into the IT offshore program from the start. Establishing the cost-of-worker-impact or a soft landing is very much a cost of doing business today. Some companies are quietly executing this; I know individuals receiving quite large payouts for relatively little tenure in an attempt to approximate these principles. Interestingly, these soft landing investments are as taboo for discussion as the job losses related to offshore programs, but they also are incredibly effective in preventing criticism from reaching the media, These investments seem to take the wind out of the sails of the negative press.

What must be weighed is the understanding that individuals comprise the community and the community in turn is part of a larger community, city, or state. We know of industries that left behind a wake of economic devastation not unlike a tornado. Housing was suddenly less valuable, schools upended, and little of the former town life remain in the wake of the job restructuring. The implication is that the firm owes nothing to these communities who just yesterday provided the educated staff and other infrastructure for marketplace performance.

It is in this light—acknowledgement of the individuals and communities that contributed to the growth of the firm—that an Ethics PMO can evaluate the investment and value of the soft landing. This is not generally acknowledged as part of business responsibility, which is often strangely one-sided. It is not unusual to ignore larger community interests unless they are utilized to lobby for various municipal or state advantages.

The typical public relations (PR) function is often disconnected from hard financial decisions and fiscal policy making, and often resides at the wrong level of the organization. The PR role is to influence and minimize negative press about larger community impact. An Ethics PMO can fill the gaps across the silos in the larger organization, first by establishing values and visions, goals, and policies from the top down, and then using them to proactively manage intercommunity relationships by establishing fair and ethical treatment of the individuals who constitute communities. The senior leaders of the Ethics PMO must decide the value of the company's contributions to its reputation in the larger community now and in the future, and invest that value in an Ethics PMO soft landing program.

3.4.1.4 Establish Community Communications

As noted above, creation of a communication plan that acknowledges the community at large as a stakeholder in large scale employment is simply recognizing a truth that must be part of any program. It is not unusual for large firms to struggle with communications throughout an IT outsourcing program. This can go to extremes based on a recent experience. I was hired to create a change management program for a large firm that was actually expanding and hiring. The offshore component involved no reduction in workforce.

The firm established a "no-communications" policy in the belief that communications established for this particular IT outsourcing program would have to be applied to future offshore programs that could include future workforce reductions. A carefully crafted communications plan was simply a check-mark on the project to-do list but the plan was never utilized. When the first wave of offshore workers arrived at the firm after minimum preparation and discussion, the workers were understandably confused and concerned. An exodus of top performers followed quickly.

This is an extreme example of the duck-and-cover de facto policy often adopted in the face of IT outsourcing programs. Most firms maintain very closely held communications, and the concept of sharing information at any level of transparency with the larger community is somewhat radical, and certainly unusual.

Ironically, at the moment I stopped to grab a cup of coffee in real time as I worked on this book, I found an article about this very topic. I will not mention company names because I cannot verify the facts. It appears that a very large communications company hired someone with whom it collaborated in an industry oversight regulatory role. A charity officer, responding to what appeared to be this ethically questionable activity, tweeted "OMG." The firm's communications representative responded by rescinding a recent grant for underprivileged children to attend summer camp. After the brouhaha settled, the large firm changed its decision and funded the camp but it was too late. The newspaper I read covered the story as "Today's Outrage." Ultimately, the charity decided not to accept money from such a questionable firm.

This case illustrates the classic communications rigidity that enables David to ultimately slay Goliath. One wonders how many of such missteps are required to put dents in sales and influence. I drive out of my way to avoid doing business with certain companies based on such stories. It is instructive to remember that ethical breaches are communicated literally at the speed of a tweet. Perhaps we need to coin the phrase "tweet-time OMG."

What does a communications policy to a community look like? It is not unlike the executive messages that ideally accompany a speech to the total company workforce outlining the vision for the future. Here are some key on-point messages:

- The firm must offshore some IT functions in order to remain competitive in the marketplace. Some jobs will be impacted. This is not an easy decision.
- Some key IT roles will remain for the long term, such as strategic, architecture, IT security, and customer-facing roles. Every effort will be made to shift impacted workers to these roles.
- Impacted workers unable or unwilling to shift to these roles will receive a significant investment in their futures. This investment will be garnered as a part of the business expense of the offshore program. This investment is made in recognition of the role these employees and the community at large played in the success of the firm over many years.
- This investment will be measured by the successful repatriation of these individuals in the workforce or early retirement and results will be reported to the community.
- As an even stronger firm, we look forward to continuing participation in the welfare of the community and believe that in the long run this IT outsourcing program will enable that strength and participation.

Following this initial message, as an illustration of corporate effectiveness and problem-solving, the firm can provide the statistics of employee repatriation. These can include, for example, the percentage of employees who launched their own businesses, were retrained for other roles, or chose and were able to participate in early retirement. The key is to illustrate the facts, including the reality of the business marketplace, while also demonstrating the investment in individuals and the community without violating privacy guidelines. This is highly achievable and serves to bring a grounded reality to the facts of the program and to avoid the typical, rumor-fueled, and emotionally charged assumptions that often accompany IT offshore programs.

3.4.1.5 Monitor Effectiveness of Ethical Investment in Soft Landing

As for any results-driven formal program, be prepared to restructure and redress if needed. The personal experiences I've had with even the most prestigious large placement firms that do not receive monetary compensation for placing workers has been mediocre at best. Usually they did not understand the particular subtleties of the complex IT job market, and offered little more than resumé writing workshops. These services did not display the "out of the box" creative thinking that is usually required in difficult employment markets and situations. Although I thankfully did not have to rely on these firms to identify my next job, I found the prospect rather frightening.

Payment for results, or another type of results-based accountability, would cut through a lot of the resumé workshop mentality, and is often again strangely absent in a way that would not be tolerated for the purchase of customary corporate services, as if to underscore the inevitable march toward invisibility of impacted individuals. Public reporting results of these programs as statistical percentages of success may serve to correct the casual approach to results that often inexplicably rules these placement firms.

3.4.1.6 Utilize Ethics PMO to Create and Enforce Ethical Constructs across the Entire Firm

Perhaps one of the more concrete opportunities is for a firm to review the often destructive, mindlessly tactical focus on quarterly profits without a view to the larger consequences. Recent events in the U.S. economy illustrate the fact that regulatory agencies simply cannot keep up. Clearly, firms are built upon the fiscal principle of seeking short-term profit. However a worker blindly trying to meet relatively arbitrary financial goals may do enormous damage to future generations simply because he or she has no reason to step back and ask—"is it really right to destroy the last local habitat of an endangered species or despoil a priceless natural resource" to meet this month's numbers?

All of us in the United States, as products of large schools and hospitals, have experience interfacing with governmental agencies and other large institutions. We have all been personally affected at one time or another by the arbitrary rules that turn the wheels of large institutions. The focus of the Ethics PMO is to provide a means of providing more humanity and balance, with less impersonal alignment, to what can be the very destructive rigidity of large firms.

Given the speed of "tweet-time OMG," the establishment of a broad, empowered Ethics PMO may ironically be one of the most pragmatic, self-preserving corporate investments of modern times. No firm, no matter how large, no matter how much of the market it monopolizes, can afford to become a villain in popular culture or the butt of jokes about selfishness, greed, and destruction and remain unscathed.

3.5 Case Study: Launching a New Offshore Program within the Context of an Ethics PMO

Please note that this case study is structured to maintain the privacy of the firms involved, and the identifying facts have been altered accordingly.

A large consumer goods company was struggling with profitability, suffering from both the recent economic malaise and a personal touch sales model that was not updated to reflect customer web access preferences, particularly those of the younger generation. Plagued with a sales model that was not reaching new potential customers, exacerbated by an unexceptional website, their traditional customer base represented a rapidly shrinking sales channel, with younger and younger customers drifting further away.

To ramp up Internet sales, the company decided to create a new focus on international markets where firms in other industries with similar sales models seemed to be booming.

As a traditional firm, the executive team in general did not partner effectively with IT. Technology was an "over-the-wall" exercise, viewed as a necessary cost instead of a strategic investment. At times the relationship was so challenged that destructive finger pointing occurred when the quarter was showing particularly low financial results. IT was deemed a contributing factor due to the inflexibility of the website.

Caught in the corner of needing to invest in new technology to upgrade the customer web experience, but unable to justify the investments in challenging financial times, the firm decided to offshore new technical development along with maintenance and support. The savings would generate enough to invest in new systems without imposing huge strains on the bottom line.

Bringing in yet another new CIO with IT outsourcing background, the firm also invested in another consulting effort to establish a more finely honed business strategy. The strategic consultant analyzed the strategy against peer firms in the marketplace and devised projections that looked very challenging for future growth—in particular the firm would continue to experience increasingly shrinking market share for every generation beyond the baby boomers unless significant changes were achieved.

The existing computer systems technology had not been updated for some time and was highly rigid. As a result, implementing a new business model would be challenging. Creation of a new computer environment reflecting an updated business model would be difficult as the changes could not interfere with "lights on" business as usual for the sales website. In order to effective in meeting the new potential international and web-based market, the entire value chain of marketing, sales, manufacturing, and order fulfillment would require overhaul. We now explore how the principles of ethical outsourcing management may be helpful to this firm and its current business challenges.

3.5.1 Define IT Ethics Program Management Office (Ethics PMO)

For an organization already challenged by an outmoded business model and antiquated view of information technology enablement, establishing a central, very senior point of accountability and leadership is essential to the success of any ethics program. It is easy to imagine the many challenges associated with change in this scenario. Outdated technology is challenging to update, and key to success would be achieving a reasonable balance between creating and implementing the new vision while maintaining excellent service for existing customers.

It is critical that the new CIO be empowered as a peer, and the function he or she represents is also empowered. This means having a voice in critical decision-making meetings that evaluate the feasibility of new marketing, delivery and sales functions and strategy, not simply playing the passive role of implementing a business approach that others have envisioned. This is the meaning of technology as an enabler—the visionary options are established via a close partnership with the IT function, not only at senior levels but throughout the organization. This is because IT represents, in these meetings, the art of the possible. It is no longer possible to design efficient, customer-sensitive systems without a close, creative collaboration across all organizational stakeholders. Thus, particularly in the above environment, a centralized steering committee that empowers an ethical PMO is critically important to encourage robust and frank discussions across all executive stakeholders in a way that cuts through old and outmoded alliances or rivalries. Assuming that a strategic alliance between enabling IT and other functional leaders is in process, a relationship framework for success has been established to work through the visioning and change process.

The consumer goods company in this case study was primed about ethics due to a highly publicized incident involving a close competitor and a soldier in Iraq. The competitor received a great deal of negative press from the handling of a consumer product complaint. The publicity went viral on the Internet and produced an immediate, unforeseen, and very negative impact on sales. This incident served as a very strong lesson to the entire industry and primed the senior leadership of the case study firm to view the costs of potential ethical violations very seriously.

3.5.2   Analyze Potential Impacts

Analyzing the impact on individuals and communities can serve as a guidepost to determine the level of investment that will be required. To meet the requirements of potential new customers, the firm decided to pilot some representative programs in China and launch a web-based marketing campaign. Roughly 180 IT positions among about 2,000 worldwide IT jobs would be moved offshore. These were primarily comprised of legacy IT maintenance functions that were usually performed as an afterthought by IT programmers and designers. In addition, the offshore program included consolidation of IT support and help desk functions from five sites to two, planning and implementation for a centralized IT testing capability with deployment of end-to-end testing lifecycle tools, and establishment of a significant offshore component for a new global customer relationship management (CRM) capability.

After careful analysis of the broad economy and the needs of the various departments, the firm decided on the following components for a soft landing program for laid-off workers:

First, for those within 5 years of retirement who had at least 10 years with the firm, a package was established for early retirement that met or exceeded existing retirement structures. About 40 of the 180 individuals were eligible and accepted this generous option.

Upon analysis of the 180 remaining U.S.-based workers who would no longer have jobs with the firm, the hardest hit would be the IT help desk personnel. Many of the U.S.-based programmers could shift to business analysis, project management, or other onshore roles.

The firm decided to offer individuals with programming skills and the capability to retrain a two-year process of mentorship, training, and support to fill the existing openings in these areas (roughly 35 individuals) at 80% pay plus full benefits in addition to the normal financial payout for all program participants.

Of the remaining 105 help desk workers, many were long-term, mid-career workers still very short of retirement. The external job market was dismal at the time of the program, and their limited educational backgrounds created a barrier to additional opportunities. The firm decided to offer the following choices that represented a 5% re-investment of the savings represented by the program:

- Funding for extensive retraining, not limited to the IT industry
- Financial lump sums comprising at least 30% salary, much more for long tenure workers
- Extension of existing medical care and insurance coverage for a 2-year period

3.5.3   Research Most Effective Options for Impacted Workers

Since the financial choices were complex as well as generous and represented opportunities that would not be repeated, after some research it was decided that a dedicated team of financial and career counselors would be made available to all workers to ensure that these re-entry opportunities were not squandered. These counselors offered tools such as aptitude tests. Workers were required to take a minimum of two seminars on financial management prior to receiving their lump sum payments.

The program was extremely successful. One individual was able to launch a successful local PC repair business. Many younger workers re-enrolled in training and education. Several mature workers were able to cut their living expenses by utilizing the lump sums to minimize mortgages. This allowed them to remain in the area and work at lower paying service industry roles. The generous program had the desired impact and the firm received a "community service leader" award from grateful local government officials.

As to be expected, there remained a handful of unhappy workers. One had difficulty finding a niche but the general view was that these workers would have been unhappy with any change and would have been challenged in any long-term employment situation.

The availability of a tailored set of support services via the dedicated counselors represented a small investment but it enabled most workers to individually construct workable long-term plans. This revealed a greater positive impact than anticipated when officials of a locality hard hit by firms less willing to attenuate worker impact recognized the company's efforts.

3.5.4 Create Program-Specific Pragmatic Ethical Guidelines

To continue our example, the steering committee established the following goals of the Ethics PMO for the consumer goods outsourcing program

1. Support each worker in establishing viable alternatives for long-term employment.
2. Demonstrate that support via direct contributions, primarily a combination of training programs and direct financial investment.
3. Actively support workers in the program options and choices via financial management as well as career counseling.
4. Evaluate program success at regular (1-, 3- and 5-year) intervals.
5. Publish and communicate program success to the community.

3.5.5 Factor in Program Costs

Five percent of the estimated returns on the offshore program represented a very considerable investment, with most workers receiving total benefits of roughly 120% of their annual salaries, not including an additional one-time payout. Through various financial mechanisms, the program still showed a return on investment of over 100% with a full recoup of cost in 3 1/2 years instead of 2 years.

3.5.6 Establish Community Communications

While the specific details of the program financials were not shared with the community, the program goals and overview were published in a series of interviews in the local newspaper. As the first firm to do more than simply make a terse announcement (or even worse, no announcement at all), the company reaped huge dividends in good will, reaching much further than originally anticipated.

Sales personnel reported significant increases in corporate purchases as a result of informal, word-of-mouth appreciation of the program. In one instance, the young son of a very important potential client participated in the program. He was successfully repatriated in a new job he loved.

3.5.7 Monitor Effectiveness of Ethical Investment

Follow-up on the program was reported to the firm, community and participants. One of the lessons learned from the program was to emphasize training for the new roles. Ironically many of the new onshore jobs went unfilled as the firm was funding workforce repatriation, and the firm felt that perhaps some of the former workers should have been given more opportunity to ramp up to these new roles.

3.5.8 Consider Expanding Reach to Utilize Ethics PMO

At the end of the program, successful in terms of community impact and even in unanticipated revenue generation, the firm established a formal Ethics PMO review process for all decisions impacting the community.

3.6 Summary

In this chapter we had our first look at the Ethics PMO methodology, the structure of the ideal Ethics PMO organization, and a relatively detailed look at the roles and responsibilities associated with an Ethics PMO.

The underlying ethical goal of the Ethics PMO is minimizing negative impact on workers losing their jobs due to IT Outsourcing. Even a cursory look at the profit model of a large offshore program demonstrates that it can easily fund a soft landing for impacted workers. The ROI for IT outsourcing is so high relative to other programs, that it is structured for success even with this additional expense. The soft landing costs may in actuality be only on the surface. In reality, they probably reap many revenue dividends. It is difficult to believe that the good will these corporate actions engender does not also impact sales in a positive way.

A major focus of the Ethics PMO is to bring to bear the full weight of financial accountability and project discipline to investments made on behalf of repatriating workers into the workforce. Today, such programs are routinely managed in a notoriously casual manner with a minimum of tracking, reporting, and accountability. As a major investment with formal goals and metrics, the repatriation program achievements are no longer invisible—and no longer invisible are the people the program is designed to serve.

We will look further at implementing the Ethics PMO methodology in later chapters.

Chapter 4

Alignment of Existing IT Offshore Programs

"Personal leadership is the process of keeping your vision and values before you and aligning your life to be congruent with them."

Stephen Covey

4.1 Applying Ethics PMO Methodology: Effectively Aligning Existing Offshore Programs with Ethical Principles

Organizational realignment is something of an art as well as a science. In the alignment of existing offshore programs, one great advantage comes from the understanding that accrues from undergoing the actual offshore implementation experience, even if serious flaws and challenges remain. Most of the tweaking required for optimization of existing offshore programs relates to one of three challenges:

1. Too much attention to the mechanics and logistics and not enough focus on the strategic context of the offshore program, especially as it relates to strategic staffing over the next 3 to 5 years
2. Misunderstanding of the fundamental skills and roles required for successful implementation

3. Exacerbation of existing organizational silos or other less-than-optimal structural challenges

If an offshore program is not working, how does that relate to the ethical constructs behind the program? When large firms notice a challenge, it is usually in the context of cost. Suddenly customers go elsewhere or spend less; the challenge is to analyze how and why among myriad moving parts.

Note that the establishment of an Ethics PMO is quite pragmatic. It is not unusual for firms to experience an exodus of top tier talent, for example, if offshore program communications and the underlying principles behind them are not ethically robust. This can later manifest in increased customer dissatisfaction related to changes in quality, as well as an overall increase in operational costs.

All phases of an Ethics PMO methodology (Figure 3.1) can be tailored to the needs of existing offshore programs to address the unforeseen and costly gaps in ethical redress.

4.1.1 Assess Requirements by Departments and Individuals

The post-offshore program implementation period is not too late to evaluate whether displaced workers received the support they needed, and establish a program of redress if necessary. The best neutral way to evaluate support issues is via an anonymous survey to assess how former employees view the separation process, and whether they received what they needed to establish a work life alternative.

4.1.2 Establish IT Ethics Delivery Organization (Ethics PMO)

If an IT outsourcing PMO already exists, it may be tempting to cross the Ethics PMO off as already complete. However, establishing and empowering an organizational structure focused purely on evaluating and making ethical decisions on behalf of IT offshore programs remains important.

A new Ethics PMO within the context of an existing IT offshore program can be established by borrowing from traditional IT program management processes. The first step is to generally review and tailor the Ethics PMO methodology to meet the needs of the specific program. This may need to be performed iteratively and may be best implemented as a milestone at the end of each phase in the methodology.

The assessment of the individual needs outlined above will provide the grounding to establish the goals and funding of the Ethics PMO. It will also serve as the basis for tailoring the methodology. It is best that an Ethics PMO be established independent of the IT PMO managing the offshore program. This ensures that the IT PMO will be subject to the same reviews and assessments as other aspects of the outsourcing program. The Ethics PMO update should define the goals, prerequisites, deliverables, responsibilities, success criteria, metrics, and reporting associated with each step in the methodology.

This section continues with examples of select activities that are typically parts of a tailored methodology to implement an Ethics PMO within the context of an existing offshore program.

4.1.3 Establish Scope

An effective technique that the Ethics PMO can borrow from traditional IT PMO methodologies is defining scope via a one-page scope diagram (Figure 4.1). Items listed on such diagrams are designated "in" or "out" of scope.

The figure outlines scope at a glance, with a particular focus on making a distinction between an existing traditional offshore IT PMO and the Ethics PMO. If the Ethics PMO is focused on other programs in addition to the offshore program, this can be illustrated as well. A scope diagram is best placed in the context of a full program charter that incorporates a complete project description. Note that the IT PMO is focused on program execution, while the Ethics PMO focuses on more delicate topics such as workforce management within the context of ethics. The appendix at the end of this chapter is illustrates table of contents for an ethics program charter.

4.1.4 Document Requirements

Another traditional activity borrowed from an IT PMO is the formal updating of existing requirements. Translating the information garnered from the assessment of displaced workers is always the place to start to evaluate the ethical issues and

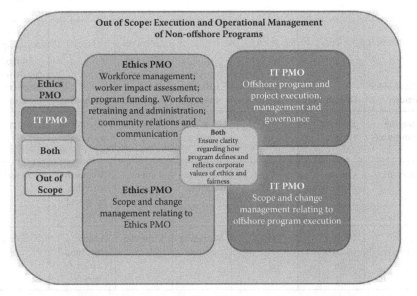

Figure 4.1 Ethics PMO scope diagram.

needs specific to a particular department or section of the worker population. After those needs are verified, they can form a basis for establishing the goals of redress, if any, to build the program.

4.1.5 Establish Process, Communications, and Reporting Standards

The sample communication plan (Figures 4.2 and 4.3) shows the audience assessment and a tailored set of communications that vary according to frequency, audience, channel (email or meeting), author, and content as reflected by the specific needs of the audience. Generally the higher the level, the more information is presented in summary form. Another requirement is alignment of strict privacy policy enforcement regarding worker information.

What is the strategy behind the goals of an Ethics PMO, and how is implementation of this strategy monitored for quality? For existing offshore programs, the messages outlining strategy and goals are still important, and it is never too late to address the unmet needs of former employees or the community to build good will.

Below are some sample communications that can be used to help clarify and support the strategy of the offshore program.

4.1.5.1 Sample External Statement

It is important that the firm implements an offshore model to remain competitive in the marketplace. The firm has established an Ethics

Stakeholder Group	Description	Importance to Effort	Change Impact	Change Effort (1 is low, 5 is high)	Concerns	Current View of Change (positive/ negative/ neutral)
Steering committee	Executive team	High	Leading change	4 out of 5	Alignment with each other	Positive
Managers	Opera- tional team	High	Change agents	4 out of 5	Alignment with the proposed change	Neutral
Project managers	Project operational team	High	Managing change	5 out of 5	Ability to shift model to include overseas	Negative

Figure 4.2   Communication plan audience assessment template.

Stakeholder Group	Communication	Message Content	Frequency	Channel	Author/ Delivery	Schedule
Steering committee	Status	One-page summary status including budget, schedule, plan, and metrics	Weekly and Monthly	Email	Ethics program manager	Friday noon (weekly); last Friday of month (monthly)
Managers	Program coordination meeting	Detailed status of program	Weekly	Direct meeting	Ethics program manager	Monday 1:00 pm
Project managers	Program coordination meeting	Detailed status of projects	Weekly	Direct meeting	Project managers	Monday 10:00 am

Figure 4.3 Communications planning.

PMO to ensure that the decisions regarding the offshore program reflect the values of the firm, including reviewing the investment designed to support former employees displaced by the offshore program. It is the intent and belief of the firm to actively support former employees in their career goals through these investments, which will total $_____ over a 3- to 5-year period and is made available to all employees according to a formula that calculates factors such as length of service and eligibility for early retirement. The firm is also investing $_____ in the community to support it during this time of business transition.

4.1.5.2 Sample Internal Statement

As market changes demand, the firm regretfully must separate some IT employees as part of deployment of an offshore model. An Ethics Program Management Office (Ethics PMO) will be providing oversight on the administration of a generous—compared to industry standards—program designed to support those employees displaced by the offshore program. The program incorporates early retirement for those who are eligible, retraining opportunities and funding, one-time separation payments, and optional, extensive, and high quality financial and career counseling and support.

The Ethics PMO will be measuring the performance of the program like any other investment, with a specific focus on maintaining positive relationships with the community and with former employees.

The effectiveness in supporting former employees will be measured and reported; and it will be important that the administration of the program reflect objectivity, fairness, and return on investment goals.

In addition to these components, the firm will be investing in the community.

It is important to the firm that we retain as many positive community and business relationships as possible while we also position ourselves for success. To this end, the Ethics PMO steering committee will consists of [list executive team members].

The Ethics PMO will ensure that the following principles are enabled through the program. We look to all firm members to actively support the Ethics PMO is ensuring the following:

- Objective criteria will be established and followed for all personnel decisions.
- The firm will maximize value of investments supporting employees in their chosen paths (early retirement, investing in their own businesses, or training for new careers). The investment will be managed professionally, with close oversight by the Ethics PMO steering committee.
- All business relationships including community relationships are important to the firm. Former employees are to be treated as program customers and included in satisfaction surveys.
- Impacted employees are to be given preference for current job openings in the firm.

Look for frequent updates and communications, including opportunities to present your perceptions and feedback as the program progresses. We will be tracking and sharing our success stories and results with you, our valued employees, and the community, our valued partner.

4.1.6 Risk Assessment and Management

A list of typical risks relating to the Ethics PMO is illustrated below (Figure 4.4). Many risks relate to ensuring clarity of team member communications on offshore outsourcing. Within most existing firms there is often no vocabulary to discuss these matters, as there have been strong taboos in discussing ethical issues and conduct outside the private offices of human resources. It is entirely likely that initial discussions may appear to end in agreement but in reality support a wide divergence of views that are not brought to light because of confusion about vocabulary. Some organizations will find it difficult to break strong cultural taboos that regard open ethical discussions as inappropriate for business focus.

Risk	Tools for Mitigation
Lack of Executive Program Agreement • Unclear vision • Inconsistent leadership • Lack of accountability • Undefined business value	• Values alignment exercises • Detailed written goals tied to metrics • Steering committee structuring • Strict escalation process • Project charter enforcement • Effective governance • Professional program and project management
Program Overly Complex • Unanticipated process gaps • Data gaps • Lack of system integration • Lack of coordination across organizational silos	• Values map to concrete realization metrics • Process standards development and deployment • Controlled professional program management throughout life cycle • Detailed communications and training planning • Engage experienced process and integrators • Formal change management • Stakeholder assessments and change agents
Scope and Timeline Control • Unclear or frequently changing scope • Missed deadlines, milestones and extended schedule	• Clear goals set by steering committee • Metrics managed at program level for each project • Definition and adopt of best practices • Early identification of challenges and pro-active risk management
Lack of Team Self Sufficiency for Change Adoption • Negative perception of change • Lack of support for change across internal team members	• Building strong core internal teams that are able to dialogue, ask questions, provide input • Balanced teams with change agents • Clear identification of business drivers for change and impact on business if change is not adopted by organization
Confusion about Roles and Responsibilities during and after Change • Lack of subject matter experts • Team members suffer change fatigue • Challenge to maintain operations while implementing change • Conflicting, unstated project priorities across team members	• RACI chart tied clearly to methodology • Reach out to peer organizations in noncompeting industries for lessons learned • Reward rapid change adopters • Realistic scheduling and task assignment reflects current and change requirements • Analyze and address stakeholder concerns via formal change management effort
Widespread, Unanticipated Process Change • Unanticipated skill gaps • Metrics that do not reflect actual program requirements or drive appropriate behavior	• Update and refine each role's skill definitions and training requirements • Map desired behaviors to job rewards • Map desired behavior to metrics • Research, apply and leverage industry best practices in managing process change
Transition of Personnel • Widespread concern, especially from top performers • Community concerns may impact view of firm	• Communicate level of commitment to supporting those impacted by program to internal and external community • Update community regularly on jobs impact and support provided by firm • Establish a clear personnel support plan, budget and timeline • Establish clearly personnel cut-over strategy and timeline

Figure 4.4 Ethics PMO risks and tools for mitigation.

To state the obvious, for most large corporations the functions of training, skills assessment, job selection, and placement are not accountable to any kind of overt ethical review via a dedicated Ethics PMO. For example, it is important that the process of evaluating options for shifting personnel go beyond the normal resumé evaluation to incorporate assessment, training, re-skilling, and other employee development tools and programs when filling roles and positions. Creating an organizational path for laid-off workers to fill open positions may be one of the areas of redress. The Ethics PMO should work with the finance organization to ensure that these exceptions are workable within the offshore program accounting principles.

4.1.7 Program Expectations and Norms

In aligning program expectations and norms for existing programs, it is useful to look closely at macro trends to evaluate where the program falls within the existing data. Although the data are somewhat limited because macro level data have been collected only for a few years, even this limited trending can provide an initial set of benchmarks.

Figure 4.5 shows the trends from the U.S. Bureau of Labor Statistics for separated workers resulting from mass layoffs since the initial data were collected in 1999. The overall impact of the percent of unemployed caused by mass layoffs and offshore outsourcing is summarized in a report of the Congressional Research Service [1] as follows:

The BLS series shows that outsourcing—particularly of work moving offshore—is uncommon in long-lasting, large-scale layoffs and accounts

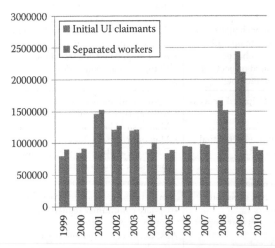

Figure 4.5 **Comparison of UI claimants and separated workers from mass layoffs. Data cover employees in all industries In the private nonfarm sector and excludes agriculture and government. (*Source:* U.S. Bureau of Labor Statistics.)**

for fairly few of the workers terminated in these actions. In 2009, for example, 61,994 workers were laid off as part of the 351 extended mass layoffs that involved movement of work within the same company or to a different company within or outside the United States. These workers accounted for 4% of all workers let go in long-lasting large-scale layoffs conducted for non-seasonal/non-vacation reasons.

Organizational change (i.e., restructuring of a company or business ownership change) was the reason underlying more than 60% of these layoffs. In 2009, employers were able to provide specific information.

According to employer-provided specific information on 317 movement-of-work actions, only one in four of the actions involving work moved outside the United States was caused by offshore outsourcing [1]. Mexico and China were reported to be the countries to which work was relocated in over one-half the events.

We will utilize the benchmark of 4% cited in the report to establish the goals for initial and redress soft landing offshore programs. In other words, the expectation is that the investments for supporting employees to repatriate in the workforce will meet at least a 96% success rate. In reality, the benchmark should be 98%— better than the norm set in the research.

Not all expectations and norms are focused upon financial equity. For example, not all divisions or departments within a large firm share the same characteristics. An offshore program may have been originally launched without reference to departmental differences in size, complexity, strategic importance to the firm, depth of required change, importance of intellectual capital, or other factors. Some major offshore program reconstruction that also impacts staffing may be required. Some divisions that hold unique capabilities may need to retrench their offshore investment to maintain a larger percentage onshore, minimizing risk for losing market share due to breaches in unique company knowledge and skills. Others may expand what was an artificially limited program. In both cases, it is important that the criteria for all decisions and individual placements be designed and implemented within an objective framework that reflects the stated values of the Ethics PMO and the offshore program.

4.1.8 Budget Management

Budget management includes the direct reporting and tracking related to the legitimate costs of IT ethics management, as well as methods by which the budget is defined, approved and managed.

A typical budget for an Ethics PMO within an offshore program includes the cost of providing separation benefits, administering the program, and evaluating the program to improve on past results. The relative cost for maintaining a large financial soft landing for separated workers may appear large. As illustrated, over time, the ROI on these programs is so great that even the relatively large one-time investment is offset by program savings within a 2- to 3-year timeframe (Figure 4.6).

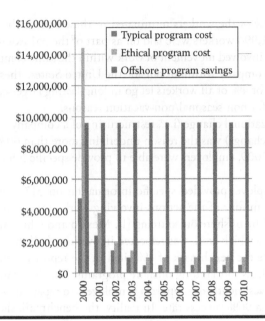

Figure 4.6 Comparison of costs of typical IT program, ethics program, and off-shore program, 2000–2010.

The example above assumes a 10% reduction in force of a 1200 person IT department (120 people) at an average loaded salary of $ 80,000. The first year cost for separation payments is 125% of program cost as compared to the more typical 50%. After year 4 (2004 in this example) the maintenance cost is 10% as compared to the more typical 5%.

Pragmatically this means that each worker can receive the equivalent of an annual salary plus benefits upon separation in the form of a combination of direct cash payout, retraining opportunities, seeding new businesses, or other arrangements. The additional 25% may be utilized for counseling, administration, or extended benefits. For year 2 (2001 in our example), the typical program cost is 25% and the extended benefits represent 40%.

4.1.9 Return on Investment (ROI) Estimation and Management

ROI estimation and management involves identifying, reporting, and managing the financial benefits of ethics management across the organization. Now that we have compared the cost of a typical versus an extended benefit program, let's turn to the potential financial benefits of the additional investment. As mentioned above, depending on the risks related to customer and community backlash, the upfront investment may be very pragmatic indeed.

The focus of the Ethics PMO, in some ways, can be likened to risk mitigation of certain kind of large institution myopia. Recently, a New York hospital was revealed to have a tape of a woman who collapsed in a waiting room and died while a seemingly unconcerned hospital worker sat next to her. A You Tube video showed a worker in Iraq shooting his gun into the product of a well known and respected technology firm to demonstrate his frustration about a charge for customer service incurred in simply getting the product to work properly. These are two examples of an internally focused culture taken to extremes, where the emphasis veers away from customers and onto procedures and policies to the point where the raison d'être of the entire organization became lost in the shuffle.

Some firms may consider themselves secure in their markets and beyond the vagaries of public opinion, in essence holding themselves not accountable to the public at large for gross ethical violations. How realistic is that view? Are large firms so large that they become immune to market forces? We can again turn to historical data for answers.

The 30 or so companies that constitute the "blue chip" segment of the Dow— the largest of the large—have changed relatively frequently over the years: "There were 34 changes in Dow components in the first five years. Many were dropped and then added back in. It was a VERY fluid index. . . . The past two decades hardly qualify for buy and hold" [2].

While it is clearly an overstatement to state that the firms disappearing from the top 30 did so due to ethical violations, it is also clear that even the biggest firms of one age may struggle to maintain a high level of business relevance from one decade to the next. It is the very myopia of large institutions that in and of itself contributes to their obsolescence, and historically at least—size is no guarantee of longevity.

4.1.10 Quality Assurance

Quality assurance provides measured oversight in meeting Ethics PMO goals. In the context of a newly launched Ethics PMO, quality assurance requires that the following components work together and in concert:

- Clear goals for the Ethics PMO are established and regularly reviewed by firm leadership
- Goals are aligned with communications across all levels of the organization
- A full financial commitment to enable the goals of the Ethics PMO is in place so that they have meaning to the program participants and to broad stakeholders such as the community
- There is a clear document showing the mapping of the strategy behind the Ethics PMO to the program components so that all aspects of the organization work together efficiently within budget and time constraints. For example, if part of the strategy is to maximize the opportunity for displaced workers to be placed in open jobs, an expedited process for those employees to be hired into those positions is outlined and enforced.

4.1.11 Procurement Management and Vendor Selection

Procurement within this context refers to the process of establishing guidelines for hiring and management of external resources as part of the Ethics PMO. Procurement management from an Ethics PMO perspective generally means objectively evaluating the ethical principles of the prospective vendor firms providing the staff for the PMOs. As noted frequently throughout this book, ethical violations tend to surface at the most inopportune times. One firm recently negotiated with a sports team to purchase the rights to name a stadium, only to be turned down when the firm's past ethical challenges surfaced.

In business, it is an ironic reality that fraud seems to be more tolerated in the large but not in the small. Professional and personal reputations are closely guarded and held when individuals are building and maintaining professional careers. It is not uncommon for business relationships, especially in offshore deployments that tend to be more mergers than arm's length consulting engagements, to be heavily influenced by the perception of character strength, personal integrity and reputation of the specific offshore program manager.

Research into a firm's ethical conduct over its history may render many seemingly leading candidates ineligible; however, it is also important to recognize that corporate culture tends to be self-perpetuating. As all employees watch the firm closely to personally evaluate how their peers are treated during an offshore separation, so too the value of firm reputation must be closely guarded.

A recent survey reported by *USA Today* [3] found that over 50% of the buying public considered social contribution an important reason to value one purchase over another. Consistent scandals relating to large firms are creating a heightened awareness that not all businesses are created equal and current buyers beware, not simply for a product or service, but also based on quality of and valued underlying the business relationship. Figure 4.7 depicts an Ethics PMO checklist for potential business partners and vendors.

4.1.12 Process Change Management

Process change management refers to standardization of how "before" and "after" processes are developed, documented, approved, and managed. Updating outmoded business processes is the most common need for offshore programs. As the typical work relationships are upended, the early years after an offshore program is implemented represents an ideal time to review and update the quality of business process change management.

Clarity of artifacts, roles, responsibilities, metrics, oversight, and management is central to any effective PMO. While business process standardization and management as a discipline is beyond the scope of this book, some business process management components are uniquely important to an Ethics PMO. One is the importance of analyzing the impact of outmoded employee evaluation

Ethics Categories and Issues	Source of Ratings	Rating Weight	Rating	
			Rating (1–5): 1 = Low; 5 = High	Rating Total
Financial				
Overall reputation for fiscal responsibility	News sources	H		
Active contributions to community and charities	News sources	M		
Collection and debt practices	News sources	M		
Employee separation experiences	News sources	H		
Customer fairness reputation and rating	Customer satisfaction ratings	H		
Undue financial influence (e.g., strong financial ties to political party)	Public records	M		
Transparency in financial reporting (e.g., annual reports)	Annual and quarterly reporting	H		
Employee Practices				
Equity complaints by employees	Public records	H		
Feedback about employee experiences on anonymous websites	Glassdoor.com	M		
Workforce diversity (gender and race)	Public records	H		
Executive team diversity (gender and race)	Company public records	H		
Average salary and benefit package as compared with competition	Glassdoor.com; news sources; public records	H		
Salary and benefit package as compared with competition	Glassdoor.com; news sources; public records	H		
Equity of financial compensation for similar jobs and experience across gender and race	Glassdoor.com; news sources; public records	H		

Figure 4.7   Ethics PMO vendor rating scorecard.

Ethics Category	Typical Questions/Source of Ratings	Weight	Rating (1–5): 1 is Low to 5 is High	Total
			Rating	
Business Practices				
Environmental practices and track record	Agency and public ratings	H		
Ethical scores of affiliated firms	Public records	M		
On-time payment record	Public records	M		
Industry leadership related to ethical practices	Industry groups	H		
Pricing practices for economically disadvantaged customers	Public records	H		
High profile incidents ; negative press	News sources	H		
Post-buying experiences of customers (e.g., technical support)	Customer satisfaction ratings	H		
Overall quality of products and services	Customer satisfaction ratings	H		
Level of active participation in industry regulation	Industry groups	H		
Governmental lobbying practices	Industry groups	H		
Humane animal practices (if relevant)	Oversight groups	H		
Health and safety record	Oversight groups	H		
Total				

Figure 4.7 (continued) Ethics PMO vendor rating scorecard.

Skill	Performance Measure
Original	
Document high level business requirements	Customer feedback and validation
Development of pilot or model systems	Accuracy of models
Requirements development	Accuracy and thoroughness of requirements
Functional specification development programming	Accuracy and thoroughness of specifications
Alignment of code to standards	Speed, efficiency, and robustness of code
User acceptance testing	End user feedback
Updated	
Facilitating, communicating, and overseeing development of high level business requirements	Customer feedback and validation
Facilitating, communicating, and overseeing development of pilot systems	Mentorship skills and clarity of communications
Facilitating, communicating, and overseeing development of requirements	Mentorship skills and supervisory skills
Overseeing development of functional specifications	Technical supervision skills
Overseeing programming	Technical supervision skills
Understanding and supporting programming standards	Global team membership and coaching
Setting expectations	Ability to build and maintain relationships overseas
User acceptance testing	Supporting team process to achieve excellent testing results

Figure 4.8 Measures of original and updated employee performance.

criteria (Figure 4.8). Offshore IT roles and skills shift significantly, and revamping employee performance metrics is often overlooked. These are examples of the kinds of business process shifts that need to occur to make offshore programs successful, not only in the behavior drivers such as the employee evaluation process, but also in employee training and skills development.

4.1.13 Metrics Management

Metrics management within the context of an Ethics PMO refers to establishing standards to evaluate program success, including deliverables acceptance and review. The Ethics PMO will be tracking successful execution of the firm's investment in creating a soft landing for impacted employees and the community, including the efficacy of the program in supporting former employee repatriation into the workforce.

It is important for each metric to be incorporated into a well constructed communication plan that it is appropriate for the audience, and timed in such a way that the audience can take action if the metric reveals that the program is not working as planned. For example, if the goal is to repatriate 55 of 100 impacted workers into the workforce within 6 months, and the actual result is 35, it will be important to delve into the reasons that the goal was not achieved. It may be that the goal of 55 was reasonable at the time but that unexpected economic factors at play ultimately rendered it unrealistic; perhaps the individuals had personal reasons to be struggling to build an alternative path. Often, it is not the one most qualified but the one most skilled at job hunting that is rewarded with a new opportunity. Long-term, loyal employees long out of practice may find the new, highly Internet-focused process of job hunting to be both daunting and difficult, even with excellent professional support.

Job loss invariably involves a loss of identity; the ability to objectively step back, look at current opportunities, and create a path forward cannot always follow a strict timetable. It is important that everyone participating in a program move through these stages of loss and acceptance as quickly as possible so as to take maximum advantage of the time-limited support options.

If personal and/or market conditions do not enable an immediate fit, it is important that pragmatic short-term solutions be established. This may include reduction in living costs (moving, finding roommates), taking short-term and/or lower-pay temporary work, or other measures to establish some stability while also creating a long-term plan more aligned with the true potential of the displaced employee.

Not all former workers are able to handle payouts responsibly or plan effectively for the long-term when the immediate future appears secured through separation pay. Counseling programs should include written statements in which former employees acknowledge that lack of long-term financial and career planning or failing to pursue career development opportunities or recommendations will have deleterious impact.

Of course these programs do not offer guarantees. It is certainly reasonable to anticipate, however, that if such programs are well funded and designed, most if not all former employees, will find themselves with new work lives that provide long-term security and satisfaction. Applying the checklist and framework established in Chapter 3, some of the focused activities of the Ethics PMO are described below.

Evaluate the actual versus projected impact — While not every aspect of the investment will yield unquestionable benefits, it is unusual for any kind of employee investment program to receive the same focus, intensity, level of accountability, and reporting that similar business-focused investment programs accrue. The sheer extent of this investment requires that its focus be as professional and results-driven as any business investment.

Evaluate the most effective aspect of the existing program — An often overlooked aspect of communication for existing offshore programs is evaluating how the cash flow resulting from the offshore program is to be utilized to establish the firm in a stronger market position. Communication of these strategic results is often overlooked in the focus of either launching or improving the extensive process changes often required by offshore programs. Reporting on the success of the offshore program vision, as well as any updates to the strategy, is important to redirect the focus to where it belongs—on the success of the business.

Create program-specific pragmatic ethical guidelines — The period after launch of an offshore program represents the best time to evaluate the need to expand the purview of the Ethics PMO across other functions and departments. The larger the firm, often the more myopia, and the greater the need to have a voice of sanity and reason look across the inwardly focused measures of success to ensure they are not losing touch with reality.

Factor in program costs — Let's look at another example of the "down side" of the loss of reputation. Considering the investment required to support a positive reputation, it may be instructive to look at the cost of a bad one. Figure 4.9 shows an analysis of stock impacts on the top 10 large companies with the worst reputations between June 2010 and June 2011 by the Flame Index. This website publishes via a proprietary algorithm the total number of negative large company reviews indexed 24 hours a day from over 12,000 news sources. While the cumulative drop of stock price over a 1-year period for the top ten large firms was only 3%, the 99% loss for firm 3 is quite dramatic.

Maximize and enhance community communications — Ideally, the ethics program will serve to minimize potential damage, and perhaps even improve community communication, ties and relationships. Ultimately, it can provide a better understanding of how and where the firm can most effectively support the community and obtain positive, measurable results from its contributions and investments.

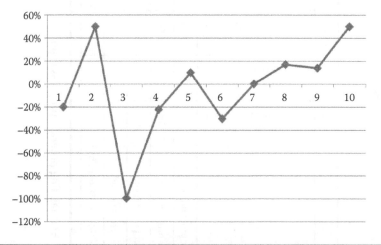

Figure 4.9 Graph of one-year impact of negative publicity on stock prices of top ten large companies with most negative press, June 2010 through June 2011. (Based upon data first posted at: http://www.huffingtonpost.com/2011/06/14/american-companies-burned-by-media_n_876860.html#s291863&title=1_BP)

Metric	Program Results—Details											
	New Job same firm (training)/Planned	New Job same firm (training)/Actual	Same or new job with different firm/Planned	Same or new job with different firm/Planned	Early Retirement/Planned	Early Retirement/Actual	New Career Training/School Planned	New Career Training/School Actual	New Business/Planned	New Business/Actual	Participating—No Results/Planned	Participating—No Results/Actual
6 months after program end	0%	0%	15%	5%	20%	20%	15%	18%	16%	20%	34%	37%
9 months after program end	5%	3%	20%	10%	20%	20%	18%	21%	18%	23%	24%	23%
12 months after program end	10%	5%	25%	10%	20%	20%	20%	22%	20%	25%	15%	18%
18 months after program end	10%	5%	30%	15%	20%	20%	25%	27%	22%	25%	3%	14%
% Difference (+/−) after 18 months	−5%		−15%		0%		2%		3%		11%	

Figure 4.10 Soft landing program progress report.

Monitor effectiveness of ethical investment — Ultimately it would be helpful to be able to publish something like Figure 4.10, to report program results based upon the metrics above. This sample soft landing program underperformed by 5% in providing new jobs within the firm, and underestimated the strength of the market in supporting others finding new jobs by 15%. Early retirement met the projection. Two percent more program participants chose to develop new skills for new careers and a large number (25%) decided to invest their program dollars in building new businesses. Those who participated in the program but did not pursue new jobs, training programs, or building businesses (11%) exceeded the projection by 8%. For a program involving 120 people, 12 were still unemployed after 18 months of program participation.

It is important to consider during program planning how to handle the possibility that a relatively large number of individuals may not be successfully repatriated into the workforce. The firm should consider offering further help in the form of extended training and additional support.

Expand Ethics PMO beyond outsourcing to create and enforce ethical constructs across firm — One can make a case that the ultimate ethical management of IT outsourcing is to utilize it as a basis for building a global strategic staffing strategy. Ultimately, the goal is to preserve both U.S. and internationally-based positions via robust growth and market leadership. In other words, the Ethics PMO has been so effective in strengthening the core business that reductions in force are no longer needed across the rapidly growing, healthy global enterprise.

The next section explores in detail the meaning, benefits, and value of a robust strategic sourcing capability.

4.2 Global Strategic Sourcing: Definition and Benefits

Strategic sourcing is an important tool to establish the strength of a firm by maximizing employee skill alignment across the globe. As different countries invest in education of their workforces, they present different opportunities for adding new employee skills across locations, time zones, languages, and cultures. It is important to track and participate in these trends. For example, in financial services sourcing, Canada has built a powerful near shore base of industry-specific knowledge, enabling a kind of three-tier set of services that supports greater alignment to U.S. time zones and a financial services-specific IT culture. Instead of utilizing business analysts in the U.S coach, oversee, and interpret customer needs to programmers in India, for example, these responsibilities are shared between the U.S. and Canada, thus decreasing pressures during the early and late hours worked by U.S.-based personnel. While the Canadian resources are more expensive than those in India, historically they cost less than U.S.-based resources. They also create a kind of middle buffer that has proven effective for website design, business analysis, training, and other functions that require heavy industry-specific knowledge and expertise along with time zone overlap.

As countries compete across the globe, the better educated, less expensive workforce creates the highest draw. Factors influencing relative standing across countries shift frequently, and some large firms attempt to have a finger in every geographic pie to be positioned early in a beneficial labor market. In India, the recent glut of firms competing for offshore resources has shifted the cost paradigm, not so much of programmers and general workers, but for team leaders. This has led to higher turnover rates due to scarcity of leadership resources, which in turn translates into higher costs for customers of offshore firms, in the form of the need for more frequent retraining.

As demand for workers from countries like India grows, unanticipated cultural and other types of impact may ensue. For example, a kind of self-referential megalopolis may develop that may cause Indian workers to lose touch with their U.S.-based customers. I note an increase in the use of United Kingdom styles of communication, spelling, and acronyms because most India workers are schooled in U.K. English. It is important that the culture of the U.S. customer be retained as the primary focus in order to best serve the business relationship. Some firms utilize such large numbers of offshore staff over so many organizational layers that they struggle to maintain customer awareness.

Several questions relate to strategic sourcing:

- Skill planning: What skills do we need now, 3 to 5 five years from now, and for the very long-term?
- Skill sourcing: What skills and jobs do we want to retain in- vs. outsourced? What factors are we looking for (price, breadth and depth of workforce, time zone compatibility, industry as well as technical knowledge, etc.) to support these decisions?
- Geographic placement: What are our long-term skills needs? What factors would create an ideal work force to fill those needs? Which countries can provide them? Do we have the presence we need in promising new countries to establish a base so that we can ramp up quickly if needed?
- Strategic or competitive significance: What level of importance to our overall business strategy does staffing represent?
- Global staff development: What kinds of training and development programs are required to maximize investments in staffing resources around the world? What is the best way to identify and retain top talent?
- Resource management: What is the current status of vendor process management related to commoditized versus strategic resources, including vendor selection, negotiation, management and reporting, and pricing? Are these optimized for the short and long term?

4.2.1 Skill Planning

Given the financial constraints that many firms have faced in recent years, the de facto go-to position has been extremely conservative, with the perception of staffing as an expense to be minimized, with exceptions in key areas. Like any strategy, this can backfire, and firms face the risk of losing business due to lack of ability to ramp up to meet demand.

The IT services industry, for example, is running hot for low-cost providers after a long period of relative dormancy. This in turn has resulted in large shifts in size and market standing across offshore providers. The lack of investment in deployment-ready IT resources significantly hampered the growth and relative leadership positions of competing firms.

Extrapolating a skills map from a business strategy is as much art as science, and staffing based on a poor business strategy can easily backfire. The understanding of the requirements of particular business cultures—companies and even divisions can differ dramatically in their so-called softer, more communication-oriented requirements—layers on additional complexities. It is not unusual, ironically, for firms well down the road in IT outsourcing to find that the emphasis on face-to-face, co-located, internal customer meetings to have increased markedly in some select high visibility roles. Some kinds of new concepts, ideas, projects, and organizational development simply need to be shepherded via the personal touch, and cannot be achieved via memos or video meetings.

Figure 4.11 shows the mapping of a business strategy to IT roles and skills over time. Note that only one focuses primarily on cost cutting. The others concern

Business Strategy Timeframe	Competitive Capability	New or Expanded IT Skill Requirements
1 to 2 Years	Launch new set of products with more complex capabilities	Unique detailed product- specific IT design, test, and product development skills
	Launch new set of products with lower price point	Lower cost of IT production; expand outsourcing
	Expand existing customer loyalty by purchasing businesses that align with our products and offer broader package solutions	Integration of IT business systems such as accounting, customer relationship management, and sales and marketing
3 to 5 Years	Enable greater cross-sell by building clear upgrades from low- to higher-end products	Unique detailed IT product- specific design, test, and product development skills
	Emphasize growth in new markets overseas, particularly China and Australia	Country-specific IT integration, language and capability development skills
	Differentiate products by establishing and marketing independent verification of quality	IT Quality leadership, analysis, and reporting
Long Term	Add to capabilities; in addition to being a product and service provider, we want to sell data about our products to users of those products	Expertise in strategic IT data collection, management, and marketing
	Enable product, services, and data diversification unique to geography and location	Expansion of unique detailed IT product- specific design, test, and product development skills

Figure 4.11 Mapping of business strategy to short- and long-term skill requirements.

expansion of relatively specialized skills for achieving new capabilities or market locations.

4.2.2 Skill Sourcing

The next step is to identify where and how the staffing footprint for the firm could and should be established. There is a trade-off. Too much geographic diversity can weaken the focus of the firm. Too little geographic diversity may diminish the opportunity to expand quickly in key strength areas. The decisions quickly become complex but they can also offer equally sophisticated solutions such as the ability to provide an around-the-world development staff that never sleeps, or a complex safety net of critical data that moves around global data centers, creating robust fail-safe security for disaster recovery.

Figure 4.12 expands on the strategic staffing baseline by providing an example of these factors for one strategy. Note that the factors (e.g., emphasis on specialist skills) may not change, but the optimal geography to meet those criterion changes over time. The decision then involves the trade-off between establishing a presence for fast ramp up and becoming stretched too thin, creating an environment where production becomes strained or overhead costs are too high.

4.2.3 Geographic Placement

Now that the business strategy has been directly linked to IT skill needs by time-frame and the factors relevant to each country, it is time to evaluate the options. Often the ability to expand in a market from a sales perspective drives a decision to establish an IT services presence, as does the existence of an offshore facility provided by the offshore vendor of choice.

While it is difficult to predict many decision points such security requirements or availability of particular workforce skills over time, two factors to watch closely are (1) the investment in and quality of technical education of the geography and (2) the relative global standing of the countries' technical and business education. The smarter countries provide large incentives for new business establishment and significant investments in technical education for their working populations. Of course, many of these factors already factored into the vendor analysis. In other words, choosing a vendor means that the representative countries' educational structure is often already in place.

4.2.4 Strategic or Competitive Significance of Skills

The value of IT staffing is often glossed over in the establishment of offshore programs. Is all IT staffing best subject to a commodity model of procurement within an offshore implementation? Unfortunately in my experience, given the complexities of creating, mapping, communicating, and socializing a competitive sourcing

Business Strategy Timeframe	Competitive Capability	New or Expanded IT Skill Requirements	Notes	Location Decision Factor Importance—High (H), Medium (M), Low (L)						
				Price	Security	Depth of Workforce Skills	Time Zone	Industry Specialized Knowledge	Tax Advantages	
1–2 Years	Launch new set of products with more complex capabilities	Unique detailed product-specific IT design, test and product development skills	* Evaluate near shore design centers that specialize in our products (e.g., Brazil)	M	H	H	M	H	M	
	Launch new set of products with lower price point	Lower cost of IT production—expand outsourcing	* Expand current offshore program in India	H	M	L	L	L	M	
	Expand existing customer loyalty by purchasing businesses that align with our products and offering broader package solutions	Integration of IT business systems such as accounting, customer relationship management, and sales and marketing	* Evaluate business partners located in EMEA, particularly UK	M	M	H	L	L	H	

Figure 4.12 Location decision factors for IT skill sourcing.

strategy across large offshore providers, many of these questions are never asked. It is as if just jumping on the offshore highway is difficult enough, so that the direction of the highway is never addressed.

Existing offshore programs have already handled many of the "nuts and bolts" of implementation. Two to three years down the road, they may have to further refine how they have addressed these concerns and they should do so in order to build a strong foundation of growth and strength in IT capability. Reduction of staffing expense does not replace a growth strategy or even represent a viable, realistic long-term expense mitigation strategy. Figure 4.13 shows a simplistic mapping of the changing strategic or competitive value of various IT skills and roles over time, reflecting changes in business strategy. For example, over the next 1 to 2 years, this firm will focus on three strategies: (1) expansion of capabilities of high-end products, (2) launch of low-end products, and (3) judicious purchasing of companies with existing complementary products.

For the first strategy, IT research, development, and testing are of paramount competitive importance. The second strategy requires an offshore capability utilizing low-cost resources where possible. For the third strategy, system integration across multiple redundancies (global program leadership) becomes vital. Note, however, that a longer term (3 to 5 years) strategy for this same example firm focuses on and promotes product quality. This moves quality assurance into the strategic spotlight up from commoditized IT skill during the first 1 to 2 years. It is important to ensure that the IT quality management capability is preserved and supported to realize this strategic goal.

4.2.5 Global Staff Development

Clearly, the criticality of the IT function shifts with the industry, products, and strategy of a particular firm. Global staff development is challenging for very large firms because of the sheer complexity. There is little that can replace an extensive training program that takes nothing for granted, and teaches not only common skills and disciplines, but also the strategy and value of the firm and the stated value equation for customers.

As global counterparts make daily decisions on the deployment of resources for products and projects, it is important that they all understand the relative strategic importance of their efforts so that they can work well together and also make the right choices for their specific deployments. We will look more closely at this component in the case studies in the following chapters.

4.2.6 Resource Management

As geographic reach becomes more complex, vendor management becomes more challenging. In our next case study, we will look at these challenges and opportunities in detail.

Business Strategy and Timeframe	Competitive Capability	New or Expanded IT Skill Requirements	Strategic (S) vs. Commoditized (CO) Skills/Roles (Roles designated as both depend upon particular project or program)											
			Technical Research	Requirements Analysis	Technical Design	User Acceptance Testing	Global Program Management	Data Management (Availability/Quality)	End-to-End Product Testing	Web Design	Coding	Code Verification	Quality Gate Management	Documentation, Maintenance and Support
1–2 Years	Launch new set of products with more complex capabilities	Unique detailed product-specific IT design, test and product development skills	S	S	S	S	S	S	S	Both	CO	CO	CO	CO
	Launch new set of products with lower price point	Lower cost of IT production—expand outsourcing	Both	Both	Both	Both	Both	Both	Both	Both	CO	CO	CO	CO
	Expand existing customer loyalty by purchasing businesses that align with our products and offering broader package solutions	Integration of IT business systems such as accounting, customer relationship management, and sales and marketing	S	S	S	S	S	S	S	S	CO	CO	CO	S

Figure 4.13 Changes in strategic values of IT roles over time based on changes in business strategy.

Business Strategy and Timeframe	Competitive Capability	New or Expanded IT Skill Requirements	Strategic (S) vs. Commoditized (CO) Skills/Roles (Roles designated as both depend upon particular project or program)											
			Technical Research	Requirements Analysis	Technical Design	User Acceptance Testing	Global Program Management	Data Management (Availability/Quality)	End-to-End Product Testing	Web Design	Coding	Code Verification	Quality Gate Management	Documentation, Maintenance and Support
3–5 Years	Enable greater product cross-sell by building clear upgrades from low-end to higher-end products	Unique detailed IT product-specific design, test and product development skills	S	S	S	S	S	S	S	S	CO	CO	CO	CO
	Emphasize growth in new markets overseas, particularly China and Australia	Country-specific IT integration, language and capability development skills	S	S	S	S	S	S	CO	Both	CO	CO	CO	CO
	Differentiate products by establishing and marketing independent verification of quality	IT Quality leadership, analysis and reporting	Both	Both	Both	Both	Both	Both	S	Both	CO	CO	S	S

Figure 4.13 (continued) Changes in strategic values of IT roles over time based on changes in business strategy.

Business Strategy and Timeframe	Competitive Capability	New or Expanded IT Skill Requirements	Strategic (S) vs. Commoditized (CO) Skills/Roles (Roles designated as both depend upon particular project or program)											
			Technical Research	Requirements Analysis	Technical Design	User Acceptance Testing	Global Program Management	Data Management (Availability/Quality)	End-to-End Product Testing	Web Design	Coding	Code Verification	Quality Gate Management	Documentation, Maintenance and Support
Long Term	Add to capabilities—in addition to being a product and services provider, also want to sell data about our products to user of those products	Expertise in strategic IT data collection, management and marketing	S	S	S	S	S	S	CO	Both	CO	CO	CO	CO
	Enable product, services and data diversification unique to geography and location	Expansion of unique detailed IT product-specific design, test and product development skills	S	S	S	S	S	S	S	Both	CO	CO	CO	CO

Figure 4.13 (continued)   Changes in strategic values of IT roles over time based on changes in business strategy.

4.3 Summary

The Ethics PMO methodology enables firms with investments in existing offshore programs to benefit from the discipline of ethics, and potentially redress earlier decisions that may have impacted both former employees and the firm negatively.

References

[1] Linda Levine, Unemployment through Layoffs and Offshore Outsourcing. Congressional Research Service 6, Cornell University ILR School, 2009.
[2] Feddern Financial Consulting Group, eNewsletter, April 20, 2009.
[3] American Companies Burned Worst by the Media: 24/7 Wall Street. First posted June 15, 2011. http://www.huffingtonpost.com/2011/06/14/american-companies-burned-by-media_n_876860.html#s291863&title=1_BP)

Appendix: Sample Ethics Program Charter Table of Contents

- Document Overview and Audience
- Ethics PMO Objectives
  - Why Ethics as related to IT Outsourcing?
  - Why Change Management?
  - Change Management: "Before" and "After"
- Project Components
  - Scope: Ethics PMO versus IT PMO
  - Methodology
- Project Approach and Phases
  - Timeline
  - Milestones and Deliverables
  - Roles and Responsibilities
- Project Management Process
  - Scope Management
  - Communication Management
  - Risk Management
- Project Organization
  - Team Members
  - Deliverables Roles
- Project Assumptions
- Project Schedule

Chapter 5

The Ethics of the Personal: Avoidable Ethical Compromise

"Deprived of meaningful work, both women and men go stark raving mad."

Fyodor Dostoevsky

Walking into the typical large information technology department of a Fortune 200 firm today, the cultural landscape is vastly different from my initial impressions. In the early 1980s when I started my career in information technology with a large U.S.-based firm, the anomaly was the handful of women among the legions of men. It was not atypical to find fewer than 5% women, mostly in junior or less prestigious roles.

Fast forward to the 1990s and the memorable launches of large offshore projects. I recall watching a handful of women in colorful saris get off an elevator in downtown Manhattan, a punch of color in a sea of gray and black business suits.

Although the saris are gone, it is now common to find a larger number of both onshore and offshore personnel to be from India and other developing countries. In someway, offshore outsourcing has achieved, through economic necessity, the broadest cross-cultural melding in history. While clearly the business culture of the United States, the seat of the "hiring" firms, most often prevails, the cultural cross-pollination is dramatic and noticeable, from the promulgation of Indian grocery stores in large U.S. cities to the ever-increasing numbers of U.S. IT personnel relocating to India to further their careers.

5.1 Ethics of the Personal in the Cross-Cultural Melting Pot

The shifting of the workforce to incorporate legions of individuals around the world—primarily from India—into the United States has not been achieved without pain, and nowhere has this pain been greater than in the realm of the personal. Change is usually uncomfortable, but incorporating a multitude of individuals who speak another language into daily work life certainly is not the business process reengineering (a catch-all phrase for doing business differently) of yesteryear. A generation ago, the thought that the large, close-knit families of middle-class India would routinely be separated by a continent from their highly prized children and grandchildren was unthinkable, as was the prosperity it engenders. Prior to the advent of outsourcing, the best a young up-and-coming worker from India could hope for, other than working for the family business, was a job pushing papers in the labyrinthine Indian government.

The sense of being invaded, of invisible borders being crossed and with that a sense of not only a confusing, vast sea change, but also an era passing, is difficult to avoid. As the values of the homes we live in suddenly become rocky, the economic foundations of the American family may be crumbling. This sense of economic uncertainty has not left anyone untouched. At a recent lunch with my peers, two men in their professional prime who work successfully for one of the fastest growing, largest IT firms, the subject turned to the impact of personal economic uncertainty. One had lost a high paying job out of the blue as a result of 9-11, and the resulting 12 months of unemployment not only devastated his savings, retirement, and family life, but also left a permanent sense of instability and vulnerability that had been completely foreign to his prior work life. The second was caught in the housing crisis, buying a second home before the first one sold. Supporting both homes drained his resources. Both men were worried about the impact of their credit ratings on upcoming travel. Would the corporate credit card cover the long trip to India? Would their past credit catch up with them?

These conversations would have been unheard of in the 1980s, and especially the late 1990's during the dot-com boom, when this same group of professionals would have competed to demonstrate how quickly they could build a private wine cellar or similar indulgence. There is a new austerity and sense of unassailable change that informs even the so-called survivors.

In a scenario of too-rapid, uncomfortable change and the consequent fear that may result, it is tempting apply black and white thinking or blame—and many individuals do so. The lines of loyalty may be drawn according to color, cultural affiliation, or even conceptual support of the offshore model.

Ethical considerations aside, the winds of change tend to blow many ways, and those who hold to a particular orthodoxy of any kind tend to be most vulnerable when the winds shift. The inexorable people movement due to adoption of inexpensive labor clearly is here to stay, and the pragmatic adapt. Who is to say that an individual in India is less deserving of $29 per hour for the same work for which a U.S. employee receives $55 to $80 hourly? As group membership shifts and forms, a broader definition of those who belong ("us") is naturally extended. In some ways, outsourcing can be viewed as a kind of love affair between the United States and India, celebrated even in movies. Why, Americans have even voted the coveted Oscar for Best Picture to India!

5.2 Applying the Ethics of the Personal within the New Austerity

This new austerity demands a shift in the level of sensitivity and sense of fair play. Blanket commitment to cost savings without taking into account the human impact is not sustainable over the long term. It is, perhaps, as historically short lived as the tulip market craze in 16th century Holland. At its height, historians tell us, a large estate was traded for a handful of tulip bulbs (yes, a long history of market crazes precedes our recent booms and busts). Just as a corporation cannot sustain wild growth based on soft or even nonexistent revenue and profitability, this same culture cannot sustain living under the dark cloud of drastically reduced employee loyalty and trust. Unsurprisingly, over the long term, the corporate identity becomes one in which employee loyalty to the firm is held as lightly as firm loyalty to workers. This impacts the firms' ability to attract and retain top performers, leading to a culture that does not effectively compete at operational levels and even executive levels.

A self-perpetuating culture in which it is openly acknowledged that a the firm is driven by financials at the expense of loyalty or even the intangible concept of concern about employees runs the risk of becoming the company that everyone loves to hate. The damage can be lasting and vast. As we noted earlier, many United States banks have lost their hard won reputations as institutions of security, careful accounting, accountability, safety, and fidelity. The recent shifts in the public perception of banks may take years (if ever) to undo. When it gets to the point where popular websites cry "boycott" based upon unethical or poor business practices, the damage is done, and it is too late. Continuing our look at United States banks, have they incurred damage? They don't seem to be losing too many customers, and the profitability is maintained—at least to the point where they remain afloat. So what if a large number of U.S. citizens carry deep resentment and distrust? Where else will they keep their money—in the mattress?

Part of the problem is that it is difficult to measure these losses of customer fidelity. If a bank raises customer fees, declares losses, requires government bailout, and then rewards executives with massive bonuses in the context of a shrinking economy within a short time, what is the cost? Is it old fashioned to believe that one unhappy customer is one too many, or is there simply a group of individuals who are so economically above or below the radar screen that it just doesn't matter?

The principles of ethics suggest simply that what goes around comes around. One material example is our own President Obama, one of the many children whose families were denied insurance coverage, now all grown up and focusing his power upon that national debate. Who can deny him the pain of losing his mother to the denial of benefits dealt by the kind of faceless insurance bureaucracy many fear and loathe?

The bottom line is that when masses are treated unfairly and humanity is missing from a culture that consistently favors financial priorities, eventually the "wrong person"—one who comes into a position of real power—is wronged. Then the embarrassing details inevitably come to light, and the damage is done. Like the individual who is caught cheating in a hotel room or the accountant who takes a little here and there for his own use, the likelihood is that all will be revealed. Once an individual is exposed as a cheater or thief or a corporation is shown to be a "heartless" entity, business may appear to continue as usual but these characterizations will never be forgotten. The cost can ultimately be dissolution of the firm itself, as in the poster child of Enron.

Part of the challenge, of course, is that it is difficult to create an actionable set of ethical guidelines, given the complexities of modern business model. Firms are primarily financial entities, bound by laws and commitments to return on shareholder investment and alignment with industry "regulations," but are not necessarily bound by ethics. Yet these same firms are made of individuals who can create a powerfully positive or negative individual or collective environment. This environment, in turn, can serve to either further or limit business opportunity based upon the elusive quality of character.

There is an opportunity, however, to define a high level set of ethical guidelines that reflects the reality of the new austerity and the danger of deep collateral damage to a firm's reputation. An initial set of these guidelines is outlined in the following case study, where we explore the impact of the promulgation of these principles.

1. Communications reflect the level of integrity that meets the level of austerity.
2. Overt values are actively supported, not passively drawn.
3. Prized values are maintained (or not maintained) bilaterally.
4. The needs and consequent responsibilities of the individual are acknowledged within the whole.

5. Raw abuse of power—defined as the suspension of the normal rules of business and ethics within that business—is perceived as damaging to the operations and reputation of the organization.

Let's look at these principles one by one and review them within the context of a Fortune 100 firm.

5.2.1 Communications Reflect the Level of Integrity that Meets the Level of Austerity

The proverbial austerity test of being dropped in New York City's Times Square with just a quarter to spend, in former times utilized as a kind of character building exercise, is today perhaps all too real for some. Times Square is not the center of danger and crime it used to be, but the concept remains valid. Situations of financial extremes—when the relative difference of a small amount of money has huge implications—have become common. In today's new austerity, the ethics of personal conduct must reflect that reality.

One of the characteristics of the new austerity is the wide impact of financial challenges across individuals for whom the idea of struggling is completely new. Friendship loyalty may now be measured on a completely different scale—similar to other personal cataclysms—such as those tested by such major personal challenges such as divorce or grave illness. The effects on friendships that stand the test, for example, of even short-term unemployment, are often hard to predict and somewhat surprising, as those who have experienced personal cataclysm know. For the so-called lucky ones, determining where and how much to give to the newly disenfranchised can be painful for all parties.

In a business context, this ethical principle means that all communications and actions are crafted with the care that constrained economic circumstances demand. The impact of a bad job review, or in fact any decision to cut costs in a way that impacts workers financially, may have a cascading impact on an individual worker's long-term career that is dramatic and lasting. While the unscrupulous may not allow these considerations to factor into these types of decisions, it is important in a discussion of ethics to recognize these factors and to hold ourselves to a higher standard of objectivity and personal honesty.

5.2.2 Overt Values Are Actively Supported, Not Passively Drawn

A negative job performance review may be based upon internal politics rather than job performance. Over the long term, it may result in a loss of employment that impacts the career of a worker and also his or her family over the long term. These are material issues in the realm of the ethics of the personal.

Speaking personally over a 25-year career, the firms that overtly address the issues of fairness and economic impact of career management are few and far between. These concerns are more generally expressed in undercurrents. The more the undercurrent differs from the reality, often the worse the impact on the firm in terms of retention of top performers, who usually have multiple employment options and tend to skitter at the first sign of workforce reductions.

One company that demonstrated awareness of the ethical implications of career management on a large scale was Digital Equipment Corporation (DEC), founded by Kenneth Olsen (more familiarly, KO). I was fortunate to work for KO's DEC during the heady 1980s, when the 128 highway circling Boston was proudly labeled "America's High Tech Highway," and MIT and other universities around Boston fed such technology giants as Data General, Wang Computers, Raytheon, Lotus Notes Corporation, and many others.

A unique egalitarianism sensibility imbued the corporate culture at DEC. During its heyday, employment was considered a contract to the employee, and one of the memories I have is of the upheaval when a worker was dismissed for an ethical breach of tapping into a co-worker's email without authorization. In good economic times, such firings were very rare.

One way that the corporate culture was established at DEC was circulation of the sayings of KO. Stories circulated (probably deliberately) that served as guidelines for worker decisions. One well known fact, for example, was that KO was one of the few Fortune 100 presidents who did not have a reserved parking space. KO walked the 10 minutes from the back of the large parking lot to the main building along with the rest of the workers.

When a computer line failed to sell, KO was said to have remarked, "Why should I fire a factory worker when some VP of marketing messed up?" KO set the tone from the top, creating a fierce loyalty that exists even today in DEC-related websites discussions and long-term relationships. Although I never had the privilege of meeting him, KO was the single most beloved leader of any firm I ever encountered. My tenure there was one of the only times I felt that personal ethics as related to the financial impact of career management decisions was a sanctioned topic of conversation within a large firm.

If I were to interpret my personal experience at DEC, looking back now over a long career consulting with dozens of the largest global firms, I would say, "A fairly treated, happy employee treats the company fairly, and is empowered to do best by the customer within his or her professional purview." Quite honestly, I could recognize, even at my relatively tender age, that not all DEC employees lived up to that promise—but many did, and in a way that was outstandingly positive, creative and often, proud. I remember a certain pride of contribution that I don't see often—a sense of believing a vision, and contributing to that vision that was heady and ultimately, very productive.

DEC was ultimately sold from inside the company part by part and piece by piece, and many "DECies" went their way into the world, in what was a shattering and very quick fall from grace. At its peak, DEC had over 200,000 employees. In the early 1990s, major assets such as the RDB database product line were sold to competitors and the exodus began. DEC remains a model for many of us, and it demonstrates how well an employee-centered corporate culture can create incredible creativity, growth and profit. That DEC technology went on to benefit other firm's growth and profitability does not minimize its achievements. In the case studies cited in this book, DEC will be featured as a unique firm created by a set of unique individuals.

In sum, the ethics of the personal in which communications reflect the level of precision and integrity demanded by today's austerity means that we hold ourselves to a higher standard of precision and honesty. We understand that the constraints of the economy mean that the typical power of a manager may be expanded, and the consequent commitment to clarity and fairness is also heightened.

As explored elsewhere in this volume, note that the demographics inevitably point to the proverbial shoe to be placed dramatically on the other foot for employers. Baby boomers are aging out rapidly over the next decade, and the Internet creates a level of personal accountability and exposure that surprises us constantly with dramatically higher bars and levels of disclosure. In short, the ethics of the personal in which we carefully consider and reconsider-the financial impacts of our actions (as KO so dramatically embodied) is good business.

5.2.3 Prized Values Are Maintained (or Not Maintained) Bilaterally

Pro forma expectations of workers include loyalty and enthusiasm starting from interview, but firms often do not return that expectation and seem to go out of their way to demonstrate (despite individuals who may buck the trend, sometimes to their own peril) the opposite as a tough "willingness to go the distance" for shareholder value. Many of my earlier written contributions on this topic [1] outline the view that the savings from offshore outsourcing more than allow for generous financial compensation to loyal displaced workers. In many business cultures, this is a quaint, naïve notion. But those corporate cultures that most often demand loyalty from workers are perhaps the first to fail to return that loyalty when the winds shift. This is perceived as pragmatic recognition of reality.

The cost of this so-called pragmatism may indeed be high. While few studies have been performed—it is almost as if the topic is radioactive—no one who has been part of an extensive layoff can minimize the impact to the ensuing organizational culture, often for years to come.

In some circumstances, management teams have the luxury of establishing alternative positions to minimize layoffs, or supporting training programs or other means of cushioning the blow. Such steps do indeed help employees withstand the shock and more importantly preserve the fragile trust that once broken often never returns. The handful of workers that comprise the best and brightest are always in demand, and often leave for the competition en masse. Perhaps even more destruction is wrought by the so-called survivors.

I worked with one of the world's largest firms, a Fortune 10, shortly after it implemented its first major layoff in history. I was among the first large wave of hires representing the new skills the firm wanted to develop and many loyal, middle-aged workers were taken very much by surprise. The culture of the firm was extraordinarily dysfunctional. It was not uncommon for middle management decisions (e.g., members of an account team for a large, profitable client) to publically align only with the individual career of the manager. I often heard statements that could be summarized as "it's best for me—that's what goes—I don't care what is best for the company, the client or the business."

I personally got burned when an individual I hired was about to lose her job. She lied to my management team a year later about some negative feedback she supposedly received from a customer. My managers never talked to me about the feedback or gave me an opportunity to refute it until it appeared in my review. These kinds of games make it difficult to focus on the work. The welfare of the business is clearly secondary in these kinds of cultures.

Indeed, 74% of retained employees reported negative effects on their job quality and performance after layoffs; 69% said the layoffs negatively impacted the quality of the product and/or services and 87% were less like to recommend their company to potential workers. On average, a 10% reduction in workers resulted in only a 1.5% reduction in costs. [2] A study based upon 2.5 million surveys over a 10-year period found that firms in which employee morale is high outperform their competitors. The same study compared morale and share prices for 20 companies employing almost 1 million people. Share prices for companies with high morale increased an average of 16% as compared to their industry average of 6%. Low morale company share values increased only 3%. [3] Finally, the stress induced by layoffs is long term. A stress study among managers found that they reported heightened stress symptoms as long as 3 years after layoffs [2].

These findings, which seem to validate every individual's personal experience and intuition that has ever been on the receiving end of a bored, hostile customer representative, are still debated by some. A study of clerical employees in a federal agency found that "enriched environment" employees were happier but that it did not enhance their productivity [4]. One must wonder how increased productivity would be measured in a clerical role in a federal agency—faster words per minute typing or filing more rapidly and accurately? Researching a group at one extreme end of the organizational hierarchy in pay and probably job satisfaction leads to questions about the applicability of the study for drawing conclusions about all levels of employees. It is the equivalent of researching increases of creativity by focusing on a control group of janitorial staff or a group of peer Fortune 100 CEO's [5]. This kind of lack of common sense in these studies lead to broad conclusions in many academic journals that there is no documented relationship between job performance and employee satisfaction. [6] Anyone who has ever earned a dollar working for someone else knows better.

The bottom line is that, visionary leaders such as Ken Olsen understand that employees mirror to the customer what the company in turn reflects to the employee—an immediate kind of "what goes around, comes around." As consumers, we know the difference between passive compliance and enthusiastic excellence in products and services. Creation of a corporate culture in which loyalty, excellence, and deep commitment to quality are nourished is a delicate process that includes the challenging components of team building and visionary leadership. To expect loyalty, excellence and commitment not to go by the wayside without a mutual commitment to values and team welfare is unrealistic.

5.2.4 The Needs and Consequent Responsibilities of the Individual Are Acknowledged within the Whole

There is a limit to group think. The price we pay for absolute obedience to a vociferous leader, no matter how charismatic, represents a failure to think outside the current narrow view. As an example, today's marketing leadership requires a fluency with social networking and alternative media that wasn't even on the horizon 10 years ago. Tomorrow's winning business strategy and framework are just as elusive and hard to predict.

The corporate maverick, the visionary who quite doesn't see the world the same way and thus brings fresh thinking and vision, remains essential. The larger the firm, the more difficult it may be to find a place for these key individuals. It is a paradoxical truism of many large U.S.-based firms that individual performance accountability becomes more difficult to track as the firms grow larger. Often within large matrix organizations different disciplines develop competitive relationships. It is not uncommon for very large departments to act as firms in and of themselves due to their sheer size as well as a corporate structure that does not share common managerial oversight until many layers of management above the operational management layer. This means that while different groups are pragmatically required to work together within that management matrix, they do not share the same views, values, priorities, and measures of job performance. Credit for a job well done is based on strength of personality rather than objective contribution. Within the stress of these kinds of internal jockeying work cultures it is the maverick voice that may fall silent.

An overt focus on a corporate value that prizes objective analysis and evaluation—set by the leadership team—may go a long way to establish room for these original contributors. We have all felt the impact of the closed system on creativity—and the opposite—the breath of fresh air that encouraged our personal best. It is no different for the corporation. Piero Formica [7] states:

Different communities of knowledge practice coalesce in a knowledge pool. Knowledge pools relate to collective networked intelligence of knowledge workers forging relationships to prove the power of their business ideas and stretch out their capabilities. Different knowledge pools form a knowledge cluster.

The value of the individual—the encouragement of the new even as it may obliterate the tried and true—requires a delicate balance. It is clear no organization can survive for long without that elusive factor. From an ethical perspective, the firm must support the lone voice, even if it means an unknown in the balance of power as business processes shift and merge to incorporate the new vision.

5.2.5 Raw Abuse of Power Is Perceived as Damaging to an Organization

Raw abuse of power is defined as the suspension of the normal rules of business and ethics that serve as a kind of the ethical equivalent of the Generally Accepted Accounting Principles (GAAPs). While these abuses have been around since the first company was established, it is sad fact in modern corporate life that we are now in a period in which new discoveries of these violations is a daily event. The days when business per se conveyed a sense of ethics and community contribution are fast waning. A business model predicated on the cheat—no matter how complex the cheat or difficult to discover in that particular industry—will ultimately be found out and hurt the business as an entity. I recently viewed a TV commercial placed by a large institution with a highly compromised public image, portraying the way the firm is helping individuals and businesses. No commercial can address concerns about a firm that is synonymous with cheating and unfair business practices. Without honesty as a foundation, none of the corporate ethical guidelines retain any meaning. My personal reaction to that commercial, was, to use a recent popular parlance, *"Oh, Really ?!?"*

Here it is important to recognize the impact of the leader. The ethically failed corporate culture inevitably possesses a leader with a high level of personal charisma. This leader may convince the normally ethical individuals around him or her that the redefinition of the rules is simply a new form of creativity and not a true ethical breach. A way to evaluate whether this is true is not simply to understand the legality of these actions—although this is clearly one applicable benchmark. The key is to focus upon the impact on the powerless and voiceless—those somehow disenfranchised by the firms activities. The charismatic tend to prey upon the powerless, and the underlying threat that brings a negative kind of excitement is that it is acceptable, for a short time at least, to vent negative consequences upon them. Increased complexity and the tendency for large firms to grow even larger in impact and political influence as well as revenue, has led to avoidance and general befuddlement of any kind of regulation. One can't help but wonder what the answers to the following questions are for those in a position to influence wealth on a global scale:

- Are you creating the kind of world that you want your children to inherit? The creation of a mass of poverty for the exercise of ego-driven amassed wealth even if accompanied by the requisite high profile individual "philanthropy" creates a prison for your grandchildren, no matter how much wealth they may inherit.
- Does your corporation contribute to a scenario of a wealthy few surrounded by masses of poverty? If it does, you are condemning your descendants to isolated, fear-riddled lives in camps of luxury.

In an interesting historical snapshot that produced a broad impact on popular U.S., culture, President Truman personally brought the heads of the Hollywood film studios to visit the concentration camps in Germany immediately after World War II. Most of the films they took of the camps there were never shown, deemed as too gory, but for these men- mostly Jewish in origin—it must have been a truly awful and awe-filled experience. Truman also had mostly military men underwrite the new constitutions of Europe, which were carefully structured so that there would never be a mass of hungry and poor as was created in Germany after World War I. These hardened men wrote in these constitutions the extensive benefits to unwed mothers, the unemployed, and other economically vulnerable groups they now enjoy. Underlying these actions was the understanding, born of hard-won experience and lives lost, that large groups of desperate individuals may lead to the unthinkable—fascism—to the detriment of all.

5.3 Applying Personal Code of Ethics in Daily Business Life

It is challenging to create objective measures of a personal code of ethics, yet to put these principles without objective measurement guidelines seems an empty exercise. The following questions can be utilized on a personal or group level to evaluate whether an individual's actions are indeed aligned with their stated ethical values, and whether the firm environment supports this integrity. This tool is targeted towards individuals working in business environments.

Each topic is followed by a relevant question and a series of statements and examples designed to help individuals understand their ethical alignment in specific areas.

Instructions: Each ethical topic, such as communications integrity, is prefaced by a question, and followed by a series of statements or examples that are designed to help you understand your ethical alignment in that area. Working privately and for your own benefit, identify the extent to which each statement is true on a scale of 1 (low) to 5 (high). Scores below 4 indicate need for improvement. Be as honest and objective as possible. The results are only for you.

5.3.1 Communications Integrity

Do my personal communications reflect a level of integrity that matches the current level of austerity?
Does my firm culture expect and support that integrity?

A. **The recipients of decisions do not express surprise at outcomes.** Those to whom you provide formal feedback, or otherwise impact via your decisions, do not express surprise indirectly (via tone of voice) or directly when these views are communicated.

B. **Those who receive evaluations or decisions have opportunities for dialogue.** For example, finalists competing for a job have opportunities to expand on their answers to open questions about their qualifications or fit.

C. **Value-laden words are utilized appropriately, with an understanding of their impact.** For example, not all work subject to verbal review earns the feedback of "excellent" even during informal discussions.

D. **Decisions are made within a consistent timeframe and communication structure that supports the recipient.** For example, the timeframe for job decision making is clearly established at the beginning of the interview process. Timing of opportunities is recognized as an important factor in helping potential workers meet their employment needs.

E. **Consistency and fairness of decision making are validated by an external source even if the source is informal.** In effect, performance reviews, opportunities, and job offers are supported by objective evaluation criteria or validation by an outside party to validate the integrity of the decisions.

F. **Evaluation criteria are communicated to individuals in a timeframe that enables them to understand the information and how it impacts them.** For example, decision making criteria for promotions are published; frequent updates are provided to candidates to help them reach their goals.

G. **Evaluation criteria are applied within a robust structure of positive, published values to minimize favoritism or deference to internal politics.** For example, personal friendships, family relationships, and other factors not related to performance are understood to be outside the realm of appropriate decisions. Corporate value statements are not empty documents and are vigorously applied and discussed within the context of business practice and leadership.

H. **Formal training in decision making and ethics is required of decision-makers.** Ideally, this training is not limited to discrimination issues and covers a broad framework of appropriate and ethical decision making.

(Unfortunately, this item is the only one I see regularly enforced across most of the large companies I've worked with over the years).

I. **Decision makers to great lengths to focus on job performance and/or qualifications and minimize extraneous "noise."** For example, I recently shared an airplane row with a company owner who described his consternation when an otherwise highly qualified engineer appeared at a job interview in wrinkled khakis. This engineer was the victim of a large layoff and had several children. The company owner's wife said, "Give him a try. Just buy him a suit." The owner did so and the engineer is now one of the top performers in the firm.

J. **Feedback from those who receive the outcomes of your decisions verifies the fairness of both the feedback process and the decisions that result.** Formal and informal feedback verifies that the process is objective, perceived as fair and ideally, motivating for performance improvement.

5.3.2 Active Support of Values

Are overt values are actively supported, not passively drawn?

A. **Values are written and frequently reinforced by the leadership team in writing and by their behavior.** For example, sales personnel have realistic goals reflecting the economy and market position of their firm, and are not under undue pressure that will lead them to misrepresent products to win sales.

B. **Training includes all levels of the organization. This training is case-study based, or uses other means to convince participants to actually apply the values in question, not just passively understand them.** Ideally, real life examples of business decisions are incorporated into ethics training.

C. **Employees are measured on how well they align with corporate values as part of their formal performance goals.** Examples of excellence in performance in this area are notated and rewarded.

D. **Community programs that embody the values of the organization are well publicized and participation is encouraged but not required.** Reaching out to the disenfranchised in the greater community is a great way to give back and sends an important message.

E. **Corporate values are not separated from financial performance measures.** A sense of fair play in terms of opportunity and recognition infuses business processes. For example, the organizational culture does not single out one level of management for punishment for failed experiments or missed goals.

F. **Difficult communications are drawn within the framework of corporate values.** If the current financial environment leads senior management to cut jobs, the financial sacrifice is distributed across all levels, and the impact on long-term, loyal employees is significantly lessened by compensation, training, or other cushions.

G. **Difficult communications are structured within a market strategy that positions the firm for competitive strength and minimizes the future need to repeat job reduction measures.** If the current financial environment leads senior management to cut jobs, the workforce restructuring takes place as a last resource and is conducted via a long-term strategy that clearly identifies how the savings will enable a greater competitive position over the long term so that additional job cuts are minimized by a solid foundation for future growth.

H. **Individuals are supported for success within the framework of their responsibilities.** Employees are valued and their contributions are intended to be preserved. This may be a subtle issue, but ethical fairness extends to giving individuals who are new the benefit of the doubt and support within the new environment, not a series of obstacles to field.

I. **Successful performance is structured as reasonable and within reach.** Deadlines are not arbitrarily changed. The framework for success may shift rapidly due to market forces but not as a result of a whim.

J. **Group success plays a factor in individual performance.** One indication of success of individuals is their ability to move appropriately within the group they represent—as enthusiastic learners or as mentors and guides to new members.

5.3.3 Equality

Are prized values maintained (or not maintained) bilaterally?

A. **Openness in communication of market strategy, financial standing, and market standing is a responsibility of the firm to all employees.** Today's employees must often submit to credit checks. Open communications about such topics is a reciprocal corporate value. Part of the legacy of ethically challenged firms is a tendency to misrepresent financial results. The lack of transparency or inconsistencies in this can serve as an early warning sign.

B. **Preservation of jobs, representing loyalty to the employee, is a value discarded only under market duress.** Loyalty by employees to a firm is earned by the firm's loyalty to employees. What is your view of the loyalty you have earned in your job. Is that loyalty communicated and recognized by both your manager and the firm as a whole? If it is recognized, how do you experience that recognition?

C. **The firm has a view that establishes its vision as a societal contributor and a provider of goods and services.** Do you participate in corporate sponsored giving programs?

D. **The ever-rippling economic impact on family economic life is recognized.** Family economic life is an expending ecosystem. The impact of economic hardship clearly cascades across nuclear families and throughout community, city, and even the state, like a stone on a pond, with widening ripples of economic impact. Within the complex web of corporate interactions, do your decisions reflect the full weight of that reality even by small gestures such as car pooling with a peer who is supporting two children in college and elderly parents?

E. **The devastating effects of economics in the large are recognized in the economics of personal.** The many recent mergers and acquisitions left voids in some large cities as formerly active corporations that supported sports, the arts, and education were dissolved into a corporate entity half a world away. It is important that those large decisions be also made in the context of the impact on the personal. Examples are the little league team that no longer has a sponsor and cannot continue, or the schools and neighborhoods hit hard by mass layoffs that decimate housing values and retirement portfolios. Do you encourage and participate in community-related events and maintain those connections within the context of your corporate role?

F. **Corporate favor goes both ways.** Can and would you represent the interests of the broader community when the opportunity arose for defending those principles?

G. **The promulgation of a basic humanity when individuals are confronted with severe personal circumstances.** In extraordinary times when overtime for salaried workers is considered within the corporate culture to be part of the job, so too should the normal rules of business be bent in the event of a sick child or other personal catastrophe. This generally means some flexibility in work hours. Within the purview of your job, do you support those who are undergoing extraordinary stress and circumstances?

H. **A commitment to fairness and equality is maintained even in the face of personal emotional triggers.** Even the best of us are human—some individuals just rub us the wrong way. The extent to which these personal peeves can be indulged within a large firm is often a matter of tone. The policy at a corporate level can be quite general, leaving the actual experience to vary widely from manager to manager and employee to employee. In modern corporate America, this seems to be what is expected—the manager has the authority to not only evaluate performance, but establish favored relationships and pockets of influence. Within the realm of personal ethics, with the kind of power that bestows, it is important to embody a spirit of fairness and basic human empathy.

I. **It is important to make a distinction between gossip and feedback.** Gossip is full of emotionally laden words and represents unfounded speculation. On the other hand, feedback is based upon fact and leaves open the joint exploration of misinterpretation of intent. It is the level of intent that is often the determinant of fairness across the power spectrum. Even the most seemingly innocent remark can carry an extraordinarily loaded meaning. Learning to listen with an inner ear that registers emotional impact, and addressing the impact in kind, is a special and very important skill to cultivate and help others develop. Refraining from unfounded conclusions is a critical aspect of all human relations.

J. **Recognition that there is no such thing as a small breach of ethics.** In the ethics of the personal, there is little distinction between the business man that takes the umbrella left behind on the plane and the corporate swindler. Filling and informing your personal psyche with the belief and permission to take what belongs to others is personally poisonous. Ultimately these individuals find themselves surrounded by like others, and there is no place to turn for an honest respite that is not marked by the inevitable self-loathing.

5.3.4 Abuses of Power

Are raw abuses of power—suspensions of the normal rules of business and ethics—perceived as damaging to an operation and ultimately its reputation?

A. **A misguided belief that there are rules that "don't apply to me."** The sense of being special is a hallmark of the entrepreneur; a kind of gumption, get up and go that is part of our national pride of character. It is important that this positive hustling energy and creativity be prized but utilized appropriately. Are the rules that don't apply creatively dampening or in place to protect others?

B. **Support of the indulgence of ego.** Do you have to be the (richest, most powerful, most attractive) person in a room? If so, to what end are you using this influence? Where exactly is it taking you?

C. **Reputation of using power on behalf of others as well as yourself.** Within your purview of decision making authority, are you known for creating opportunities for others as well as yourself? Are those others independent thinkers or simply extensions of your views for building your own influence?

D. **Distribution of corporate perks.** Even if the only corporate perk you distribute is a smile, is it genuine and bestowed evenly? How do you interact with those less powerful than you in the corporate hierarchy?

E. **Mentorship and encouragement.** Almost every corporate role is shadowed by someone learning the role. Do you encourage that growth? If not, why not? If so, how?

5.4 Leader's Role in the Micro Realm of the Personal

Recognition of the impact of the leader in setting the ethical tone for corporate life is an important realization for any individual. Managers tend to hire those who reflect their values. The tone is set at the top and filters down from there. I've often been amazed at the palpable change in atmosphere after a change in executive leadership. Underlying the adjustments in personnel, business processes, and focus that normally accompany a change in leadership is also a shift in the underlying expression of values. If the overt values conflict with the unstated values, the unstated values win (think Enron). Some additional components of successful navigation of murky ethical waters include:

- Know your own non-negotiable ethical line. A basic principle in business dealings is to know and protect your own non-negotiable line beyond which you will not compromise. Know your line and be comfortable looking your face in the mirror. We look more deeply at this in later chapters.
- The greater the informational power over another, the greater the responsibility for situational objectivity and fair play. As businesses get more complex, regulatory bodies struggle to keep up with productivity and technology improvements. This creates an opening for the unscrupulous. There is a concept of earning an honest dollar, as old-fashioned as that may seem. Often it takes one lone individual to stop the short-sighted focus of the dollar at any cost. The recipients of professional silent resentment based upon unfair advantage often find that difficult to mitigate later when the advantage is gone.
- Those who depend upon a certain unfair advantage as the source of power—say a special relationship with a powerful person who in turn bestows power based upon shared negative values—often find that these disappear quickly. Also compromised is the opportunity of developing more authentic sources of empowerment (such as demonstration of excellent skills and performance).
- In speaking truth to power, actions rather than words may be most impactful. I spoke to a co-worker in a large Fortune 100 company who was clearly extremely competent, respected and acknowledged as effective in her role. During an earlier project, she was unfairly blamed by many levels of management for a failure. No one in the management chain above her had the integrity to look into what led to her unfair treatment as a situational scapegoat. I asked her why she didn't leave the firm at that time, and she said that she would not give anyone the satisfaction of leaving under a cloud. She later became one of the most respected contributors in the firm and by the sheer force of demonstrating her capabilities, had the last word. This resolution was not necessarily fair but it was satisfying.
- Opportunity—or the lack thereof—to develop skills valuable in the general marketplace may be the most powerful incentive or disincentive in this age

of rapid shifts in employment. Ethical practices related to opportunities for growth are important measures of fair play in this sphere.

■ Corporations in which the norm is to deflect the competency of others, even as a "joke," ultimately hurt the business. There are of course those business cultures in which the de facto means of gaining prestige is to use negativity—gossip, lies, innuendo—to establish professional standing over peers. Most of us growing up in the United States have experienced the emotional consequences of negative branding—in schools, universities, clubs, perhaps even the military. Often the internal noise is so overwhelming—workers must spend so much time in defensive mode—that customer and / or market facing concerns take second place. Even in the largest firms this can mean a very serious negative impact to the business.

■ In sum, few realms are so resonant with ethical overtones than the realm of the personal. Within the large corporation, much of the focus on ethics relates to the boss–worker relationship. The questions above can help to evaluate an individual's alignment with personal ethics, as well as the level of support from the firm's culture. The experience of freedom for many U.S. citizens is curtailed by the experience of absolute authority in their daily work life, where the dependency of the family welfare upon the foibles of this one relationship can lead to outrageous abuses. This is where the clear definition of ethical decision making becomes so important, supporting the accurate perception of personal and firm consequences if these guidelines are flouted. Leadership at the top sets the tone here.

References

[1] Tandy Gold, Key Lessons in Offshore Outsourcing: Toward an Offshore Maturity Model, IEEE CS ReadyNotes, 2010. http://www.amazon.com/Lessons-Offshore-Outsourcing-ReadyNotes-ebook/dp/B004YQD5YO#reader_B004YQD5YO

[2] Ray B. Williams, Layoffs and the Stress Response. How to Fulfill Your Potential: Blog Wired for Success, *Psychology Today,* September 7, 2009. http://www.psychologytoday.com/blog/wired-success/200909/layoffs-and-the-stress-response

[3] David Sirota, Louis A. Mischkind, and Michael Irwin, *The Enthusiastic Employee: How Companies Profit By Giving Workers What They Want Based upon Years of Research with Millions of Employees,* Philadelphia: Wharton School Publishing, 2005. http://knowledge.wharton.upenn.edu/article.cfm?articleid=1188

[4] Giving Employees What They Want: The Returns Are Huge, Knowledge@Wharton, May 4, 2005. http://knowledge.wharton.upenn.edu/article.cfm?articleid=1188

[5] Christopher Orpen, The Effects of Job Enrichment on Employee Satisfaction, Motivation, Involvement, and Performance: A Field Experiment. University of the Witwatersrand, Johannesburg, South Africa, 2001. http://hum.sagepub.com/content/32/3/189.short

[6] Rachel W. Y. Yee, Andy C. L. Yeung, and T. C. Edwin Cheng, The Impact of Employee Satisfaction on Quality and Profitability in High-Contact Service Industries, *Journal of Operations Management*, 27 (5), 651–666. http://www.mendeley.com/research/impact-employee-satisfaction-quality-profitability-highcontact-service-industries/

[7] Piero Formica, *Industry and Knowledge Clusters: Principles, Practices, Policy*, Tartu, Finland: Tartu University Press, 2003.

[8] Reesa Abrams, A Study in Corporate Cultures. Digital Equipment Corporation: The Myth. A Cultural Operating Manual, Boston: Digital Equipment Corporation, 1984. Updated 1988. http://decconnection.org/ReesaAbrams-DIGITAL.pdf

[9] Curt Nickisch, Computer pioneer Ken Olsen remembered, WBUR, February 8, 2011.

Appendix: Digital Equipment Corporation: Creating an Environment for Ethics of the Personal

In November 1981, a memo titled "Talking Values" was compiled from published speeches and interviews of early architects of Digital Equipment Corporation (DEC) [8]. It gives a clear description of characteristics valued in Digital employees. This section contains excerpts from the memo and other sources.

> A DEC type is someone who is innovative, somebody who is enthusiastic, someone who is willing to work here, somebody who isn't hung up on structure, somebody who has absolutely no concern with educational background.
>
> We demand an awful lot of our people and they demand an awful lot of themselves.
>
> A core of the environment is individual commitment to whatever you are doing and a lot of integrity to achieve a very high level of expectations for yourself.
>
> We are all learning, we are all going to make mistakes and the only important thing is to know you made a mistake, know what you did wrong so you can go on.
>
> He who plans executes. You propose a plan and when you fail, you know you fail; but at least it was your plan and you don't fail against somebody else's plan.
>
> You should always be selling your plans and programs as opposed to saying: "Do it!" People should always be allowed to ask why.
>
> We want people to feel free to go and openly challenge a decision without feeling that they will be fired.
>
> Hassle is the price of an organizational structure as we have it. For those people who don't like it, it's very frustrating. It depends where you want your frustration: up front where you get people to agree with you, so that you have support, or later because you've got so many people upset with you.
>
> If you wrap those three or four things together (openness, honesty, success, fairness) you can sum it up in one word and it is caring. Caring about your job. Caring about the people that work for you. Caring about yourself.

The following list taken from DEC's *Cultural Operations Manual* indicates that you can succeed if you:

Take responsibility for yourself
Meet personal goals within organization goals
Pick tasks that meet long-range personal goals
Know who you are
Take care of your personal life
Grow continually, personally, and technically
Make sure you produce; find a way
Make sure your personal product is "the right thing"
Keep your energy positive
Be your own hero

Curt Nickisch noted recently at WBUR.org: "Ken Olsen . . . was certainly a titan in the computer industry. But he was also a personal titan to the employees. They knew Olsen for his humility and the culture of fun and excitement he created." How many current Fortune 500 executives will be remembered fondly by their former employees? *MIT Sloan Management Review,* February 17, 2011.

When I worked for DEC, I noted several practices that were very distinct from practices in other organizations.

The first was emphasis on personal responsibility. As outlined above, all workers were encouraged to fill their roles in terms of personal contributions, not only in terms provided by management but via their own definitions and contributions. To that end, DEC contributed an inordinate amount of investment in employees. I remember taking part in an extensive 10-day employee orientation that outlined the history of the company, the business strategy and future direction. In hindsight, the program was a very cost-effective investment. Employees were able to understand the structure from the beginning. DEC was a model of effective on-boarding.

DEC training was astoundingly effective and innovative. I completed a course on using the unconscious to boost effectiveness at least 10 years before the concept entered popular culture. Another powerful course, extraordinarily prescient given the current business environment, taught us how to examine company annual reports to read between the financial lines to determine their consistency, transparency, and essential honesty.

Not all those in management roles and other power positions lived up to the DEC ideals, but many did. The radical difference at DEC was the open acknowledgment and discussion of the rights of employees to feel secure in their employment. In later years, the company performance did not allow employees to feel secure. After KO resigned, the culture shifted rapidly. But for most of the roughly 8 years I worked there, part of the culture of keeping everyone engaged and loyal was the cultural belief that employees could also expect loyalty from the firm— not separate from producing results—but as a foundational element of a mutually beneficial understanding. The best comparison I can use to describe the atmosphere on the best days at DEC is the Starship Enterprise. Not for the unhardy, but for those willing to craft their own courses, an immensely gratifying experience.

DEC was not immune to corporate gamesmanship, of course. Yet being part of a company with a strong, public, foundational value of valuing employees has left a permanent sense of the kind of unprecedented creativity can be unleashed in an atmosphere of job security. DEC was responsible for overtly creating jobs in communities that had fallen under hard times and deliberately located state of the art manufacturing facilities in those areas. It was one of the earliest companies to establish an major technical presence in Europe, particularly in Ireland, and many companies followed in its footsteps.

From a business perspective, the unprecedented free fall of the cost of computing power between in the early 1990s caused by the advent of the personal computer made it difficult for many computer firms to weather the storm. Data General, Wang Computer, and DEC were among the giants that fell and the proud sign calling Route 128 "America's High Tech Highway" was quietly removed.

What I remember most was the sense that what happened to the least of us, happened to the best of us, and vice versa. There was an open dialogue about financial safety, and in the annual talks that KO gave to the troops, he usually started out by stating—"Yes, once again, we are all in good shape and we can live safe in the economic umbrella we have all worked so hard to provide each other, for yet another year." From the annual picnic in the fairgrounds in New Hampshire, to the annual distribution of turkeys on Thanksgiving, I recall with great fondness being part of that environment. I like to think that the many former DEC employees now sprinkled throughout the other firms have brought a little of the DEC humility, quality, hard work, and personal entrepreneurship to their new corporate environment.

Chapter 6

Minimizing Negative Impact

"You may never know what results come of your action, but if you do nothing there will be no result."

Mahatma Gandhi

6.1 Basic Building Blocks of Corporate Offshore Programs: A Brief Review

Before we review ethics at the molar level, let's briefly review the basics of the offshore model. The foundation of offshore outsourcing is labor arbitrage—the simple shift of work to those who live in a country with first world skills and education at third world costs and salaries. Let's take a look at the ethics of labor arbitrage at the molar or corporate level.

The offshore cost and value model has shifted surprisingly little over time. The general cost of an IT worker in the U.S. remains somewhere around $50 to $85 per hour including benefits. The same skills can be purchased overseas for roughly $20 to $25 per hour. Assuming a conservative $25 per hour difference or about $46,000 savings per worker over an 11-month year, the result for 100 workers equates to over $4.5 million annual savings. Even with ramp-up costs, that cost saving is very significant, especially over the long term.

The cost to achieve that tempting savings can be unacceptably high, however, if customers notice a downgrade in their experiences. The true underlying cost of offshoring is the business process reengineering a large U.S. firm must undergo to enable it effectively—a hard path that many simply cannot navigate effectively. The challenge of the path is that the underlying business processes involved in performing daily work must undergo an enormous transformation, shifting from informal to formal.

For example, today's process for moving a newly implemented IT software application from completion to testing may occur when two team members who work together mention to each other that the shift is ready to take place. This mutual decision may be communicated over a coffee break in the cafeteria or in the more formal environment of a group team meeting in a conference room. The conversation may launch a more formal gate review process, but the key communication—the true grease for the wheel—is based on long-term, geographically co-located professional relationships. These communications represent a type of shorthand that appears informal but is instrumental in speeding up the process via critical references to shared experiences based upon many similar efforts across past projects, often involving the same individuals in the identical roles.

The same offshore process updated for outsourcing by necessity involves layers of hierarchy, and is designed so that the myriad of team members are interchangeable. Each step now requires much more formal definition, beginning with a detailed service level agreement (SLA) that outline criteria for notification, acceptance, performance measurement, and reporting. This process definition overhead becomes necessity when task ownership is shifted elsewhere. Simply uncovering various process activities that fall under the formal radar is often an iterative discovery process, For example, the assistant that overnights design specifications is unlikely to show up on a formal process chart, and it may take weeks to identify delays associated with overlooking this process step.

The culture of work in India is very hierarchical. It is not unusual for direct communication with multiple offshore workers to be brokered only through their team leader. This approach is somewhat antithetical to the U.S. work culture where we are used to dealing directly with the individuals responsible for their work. Overcoming some of these barriers—for example, insisting that the worker actually performing the work is directly involved in team meetings—may be well-meaning. However, while junior workers may demonstrate excellent technical skills, their English communication skills may be challenged and their attendance at a meeting may not be effective. Adjustments are required for all team members.

Not every large corporate entity does well with this adjustment of culture or the requisite clean up of information and process. In addition to the challenging shifts from informal to formal processes, these changes create shifts in power within the firm. The shift of responsibility across team members ideally incorporates a well structured vendor management office that centrally manages and implements offshore program governance. Clearly, the paths of influence change as well.

Offshore program governance encompasses initial negotiations, program implementation, performance review, metrics reporting, and change management of global offshore services as they relate to delivery of IT. These activities include every aspect of the methodology, from the initial needs analysis to vendor qualification and hiring, knowledge transfer, and business process re-engineering. An effective program management office, or PMO, can be invaluable in streamlining offshore program implementation. Empowering an Offshore PMO, as distinct from the Ethics PMO addressed elsewhere in this volume, necessitates political realignment across the IT department as the focus for execution shifts to a global model. Later in this case study, we will illustrate how both the Offshore PMO and the Ethics PMO can enhance value and returns related to offshore outsourcing, even though they differ in role and focus.

6.2 Applying Basic Building Blocks of Corporate Ethical Principles to IT Offshore Outsourcing: A Deeper Look

Not all IT roles can be effectively moved overseas. The more strategic or customer-facing a role is, the greater the likelihood it must remain onshore or within the U.S. In the classic IT staffing pyramid, the largest number of workers that form the base of the triangle represent the programmers or IT application software developers. The next layer is comprised of more IT specialized skills such as technology architects, network or security specialists. The final, top point of the pyramid—the fewest in actual numbers—belongs to those holding IT strategy, design or delivery roles that require internal customer interface.

Cultural misunderstandings are possible at every staffing level of this pyramid of course, but the more strategic the role, the greater the potential for damage from cultural snafus. Interviewing those who have spent years bridging the cultural gaps between the U.S. and India, it is interesting that many of these are extremely subtle. In my last project, for example, the project T-shirts I distributed to the U.S. team members were perceived as a humorous, casual corporate gift and keepsake. The team members from India perceived the shirt as an insult, akin to asking them to wear a uniform associated with a menial task.

The most troublesome challenge is in communications across closely collaborating teams. It is considered rude to say no within the Indian culture, so that the response is silence—often disastrously interpreted as consent in the U.S. business culture.

Given the complexities of moving from informality to formality in large numbers of business processes across multiple countries, time zones, languages and departments, these kinds of underlying communications difficulties create a level of complexity that sometimes simply cannot be overcome. I held several roles in which my function was to determine why one department or group worked so well with the offshore model, while others failed miserably. Invariably the successes were due to a group of individuals who recognized the need to address these concerns and did so. This was often accomplished at the personal cost of coming in early and leaving late so that daily phone conversations between the U.S. and India personnel validated progress of the work in detail. It is interesting that even now most of the focus in implementing offshore programs is placed on the technology or technical knowledge transfer when it is the intercultural, intercountry process reengineering and communications issues that are usually behind the whopping failures (the famous global projects that take five years instead of the planned two).

Given the landscape above, we can start building a picture of the ethical challenges of offshore outsourcing, and to build an ethical model. The gist of the ethical conundrum is when loyal long-term workers are either unable or unwilling to move to new roles under the offshore model. At a macro level, it is not clear that outsourcing is devastating to the economy as a whole, as we explored in an earlier chapter. Experts are divided, and the U.S. has remained one of the strongest world economies through wave after wave of outsourcing in multiple industries for over 50 years. At a micro level, as we will explore, the ethical picture splits narrowly within an individual's personal code.

For the molar level, most ethical models assume a worker freedom of choice via a robust job market that offers plenty of career management options. Today these choices simply may not manifest in a cyclical economy. In other words, there is a good chance that workers, including IT professionals, must bend to a personally untenable work situation because there are limited external options for similarly compensated work. At a macro level, the ethical challenge is dealing with groups of workers as a whole in a way that reflects their past worth to the firm. In certain industries such as financial services, it is not uncommon to find that IT workers with families steered clear of higher risk, higher paying jobs in other industries. Perceived at the time as a tradeoff—more security, less pay—IT workers chose the former in which to raise their families, forgoing greater short-term income. Often recruiters would emphasize the relative stability of the IT workforce in these industries as compared to roles in similarly high risk/high reward firms.

Losing a position due to offshore outsourcing is particularly unfair to those employees assured of a long-term role, encouraged to develop or remain in that role, and of a mature enough age not to have many alternatives or able to start over. This core group often supports college-age children with tuition and other needs, handles the costs of helping aging parents, and represents the economic backbone of communities. Their economic disenfranchisement can have consequences for families across multiple generations.

The other side of the aptly named coin must also be presented here. It is unlikely that a corporate entity can survive in the market over the long term without implementing offshore outsourcing at equal or greater levels vis-à-vis their competition. The returns are very large and represent an enormous opportunity for reinvestment in firm assets or price cuts to gain market share, along with rewards to stockholders.

Firms that chose not to follow the trend to computerization and other technology advances disappeared long ago. Just as today there are no travel firms that are not computerized—the travel firms that chose not to follow that "trend" have long ago disappeared—it is likely that large firms that don't implement offshore outsourcing will not be able to remain afloat. This is not just because of the savings relative to labor arbitrage but also due to the enforced business process clean-up and formalization that the offshore model necessitates. Offshore outsourcing represents a kind of process efficiency trial by fire. Large firms that can make the offshore model work and enable it as a natural part of their business environment truly emerge lean and mean, and better able to quickly and effectively respond to the roller coaster marketplace.

One strong recommendation to this conundrum—a corporation that suddenly finds itself with a large group of redundant workers—is to provide them a soft economic landing. The offshore model is sufficiently profitable to ensure that these payouts do not put a real dent in the offshore program returns. There is plenty of offshore generated savings to go around, and in particular to fund a substantial and meaningful financial recompense or alternative careers and opportunities. The addition of a soft landing program component would necessitate a shift in the unfortunate and pervasive U.S. business culture of excessive financial rewards for the very few at the top and token payouts for loyal workers in the middle. This cultural norm is strange even to other countries in the global community, who are often astounded at the astronomical financial rewards that top business leaders of temporarily or permanently failing U.S. companies receive without a blink, in a self-enclosed bubble of reciprocal board memberships and executive bonuses.

The gist of ethics in outsourcing is remembering as an individual (micro) to use your decision making power within the firm (molar) to represent workers who may not have a voice (macro). In times of extreme change, the informal power network that keeps large institutions running smoothly evaporates; most individuals "duck and cover" as events unfold almost daily.

The launch of an offshore program is often perceived as a crisis, especially in a poor job market; and the corporate structure is frequently ill-equipped to truly address it. Some of the potential costs of mismanagement during the difficult change period include deep and long-lasting negative impact on stakeholders such as key employees, loyal customers, community members, and current and future business partners. These stakeholders may resent the impact on the very communities that often provided financial incentives, at a cost, in the form of tax breaks or infrastructure investments. Oddly enough, some of the firms that spent millions of dollars to be perceived as outstanding community members suddenly abandon these efforts to embrace the offshore model. This can damage years, sometimes decades, of good-will investment in a matter of months, without any consideration of the effect on the business. Some firms react by completely clamping down on all communications—a strange form of denial that does not fool anyone, especially when the rumors hit the community and the first wave of employees is dismissed.

What is often the saddest part of this process is the difficulty of making pragmatic staffing decisions simply because of the lack of an appropriate decision-making organizational structure. The roles and responsibilities for key decisions are—overnight—out of the purview of the existing structure, and there is a sense of building not only the decision-making process on the fly, but also responsibilities, roles, and span of management control as the need arises.

Most human resource departments are not trained or equipped to address global staffing questions beyond relatively narrow legal compliance concerns. When I managed some of the early offshore programs, it was not unusual for me to bring together a group of people who literally never before sat together in a room. One such meeting was attended by security architects, IT standards experts, legal counsel, audit and compliance experts, and network designers—individuals who had never before needed to meet but had to do so quickly to create and evaluate global security requirements and oversight processes.

When decision making is about the difficult topic of people and job reduction, the old decision making structures no longer apply. This structure includes behind-the-scenes trading of resources, reviews, rewards, and salaries. There is no longer an appropriate formal or informal forum to review and discuss pressing ethical structural decisions. This often means concerns of general fairness and welfare simply go by the wayside. It is an ironic reality that the biggest underlying concern of any new or existing IT offshore program—the ethics as related to the firm's treatment of loyal, long-term IT workers—is almost never overtly addressed.

Ironically, this tendency towards full communication is just as true for those firms with generous worker soft landing provisions. I personally received a very generous payout of 2/3 of my yearly salary for a completely voluntary program to reduce managers at a large outsourcer. I had to sign an agreement that I would never disclose the generous contribution. This was particularly striking because I had very little seniority at the firm (less than 3 years). In another case, I was hired as a change management program lead for a very large West Coast organization that did not intend to dismiss staff. The executives decided that firm policy did not allow any formal communication whatsoever about the program. The result was a rapid and completely unnecessary exodus of top performers who were "spooked" when large numbers of offshore workers started arriving and the company issued no communications about their roles.

Now that we've looked at the context of IT culture in the face of new and existing offshore programs, let us review some of the conclusions in Chapter One on the nature of IT Outsourcing, and see if we can delve into the ethical questions behind them, as well as the early academic ethics research and debate.

6.2.1 Macro View: Follow the Money

Underlying the entire ethical structure of a corporation—the pink elephant in the room—are the differences in authority, power, and earnings across the organizational hierarchy. I suspect that later generations will find us as barbaric as we find the Middle Ages—instead of competing based upon physical strength, we conduct an intellectual competition. But today's competition for food and shelter is no less brutal than the time of our forebears. It is important to recognize that great disparities of income are indeed unethical. We are in the midst of a great debate about this in the United States: the fear of supporting laziness on one side and a commitment to fair play, especially in addressing childhood hunger and equal opportunity, on the other.

Citing DEC again, its culture was unique in the open acknowledgement of relative income differences and hierarchical classes of workers. Relatively uneducated workers in the factories and manufacturing line roles were acknowledged as having little control over the stability of their jobs. This made senior executives more accountable, not less, within the DEC culture and framework. These relatively lower paid, lower prestige workers (not a value judgment—just recognizing the line between the hourly wage factory workers and the salaried, usually college educated engineers) were culturally just as humanly important as their more highly remunerated counterparts in the political landscape of that was DEC.

It is difficult to describe the impact of an entire company acknowledging the value of each and every employee as equally important and deserving of job security. Each worker at DEC was culturally owed the deepest consideration for their basic right to have their financial well-being publically acknowledged and recognized. I have worked for many excellent managers who ensured that I as an individual felt valued within a large firm. But I was also aware that if and when they left the firm, or the market or the political landscape changed, my next manager might not have felt the same way about my performance or ability to contribute. The foundation of valuing employees at DEC did not preclude hard work or excellence. In many ways these were heightened as an expected part of employee performance. My feeling was of finally being in a place where the private world of American values was openly met in the business world. So much of American culture emphasizes equality among diversity, yet we spend so much time in work environments in which that is not acknowledged or even considered an appropriate conversational topic.

For me that key acknowledgement of equality was not only the healing of a very large rift between private and commercial life, but also created a much cleaner and clearer line of loyalty to the firm. In the typical business culture, there is the resentment related to unstated worker class distinctions—from the executive washroom, to the basement mail room, and everything in between. The stark reality is not all of job placements are based upon pure merit. Usually there are some gross inequities that give the most wizened political veterans pause. Since the hierarchy is clearly not a meritocracy—we see daily evidence that it is not always the best and brightest that move ahead—ultimately the hierarchy breeds a kind of underground contempt relating to the firm itself.

Having a visible and stated cultural expectation that DEC executives were not to use their power for self aggrandizement or ego gratification and were accountable for their business decisions based on a shared responsibility for all their workers engendered a deep loyalty that is hard to describe. That not every executive or manager was able or even wanted to live up to that cultural goal did not change the fact that this shared responsibility was their expected and valued organizational behavior. Their job was to protect and facilitate their workers' careers and contribution and through that ensure everyone's overall work and financial security.

Even if that "looking out" for workers only remained at the level of organizational intent, it was gratifying. And it was incredibly motivating for a young professional to try to contribute the absolute best for the good of the whole. The concept of equality was and remains radically unifying, without diluting the responsibility (perhaps enhancing it) for personal accountability, job performance, and creativity.

6.2.2 Our National Inconsistencies Color Ethical Discussions in Shades of Gray, not Black and White

Discussions of ethics are rarely straightforward and reflect our national inconsistencies. All dialogue takes place within the context of subtle, varying shades of gray. Interestingly, the open acknowledgement at DEC that some workers were dependent on the power of others, in other words an open acknowledgement of the financial and security implications of the usual corporate hierarchy, created an odd kind of clarity. The taboo was a topic for conversation, and everyone breathed a sigh of relief. The emperor had no clothes. It was okay to talk about it.

In my experience most professional workers view their relationship with their managers with an enormous, silent wariness. Across the various risks relative to making an income, the variables of the worker—manager relationship among the highest. There is little to no accountability—with the exception of relatively weak, legally enforced concerns such as racial discrimination—for the objectivity and fairness of employee evaluations. For most professional IT workers, and workers in general for that matter, there is an experience of absolute authority and control by their manager, a power relationship which is completely one sided, and Machiavelli's *The Prince* is utterly and completely relevant. [1] This is generally true no matter where the employee is in the hierarchy.

Stating that those in authority have an ethical responsibility to be not only objective in their measurements and assessments, but are to be held accountable, seems intuitively fair. This accountability extends to the breadth of the organizational span of control—the greater the control, the higher the level of accountability, for the decisions that create or undermine company security in terms of performance in the market place. If the power resides so completely in one party, so must the responsibility.

Ultimately, as one ascends the business hierarchy, the quality of business decisions essentially determines the robustness of the business itself, and its ability to provide a livelihood for all. Not only is there a managerial responsibility for objectivity, fairness, and balanced views across diverse employees, there is also the responsibility to steer the ship in the right direction. Because the power in the manager/worker relationship is so one-sided in the extreme, focuses of performance evaluation are entirely in reference to the worker. Ironically, in reality, it is executive level "performance review" that should be the focus of evaluation, because those are the decisions and performance that is the most impactful to overall job security within the context of overall firm success.

High level evaluations occur in the stock market, perhaps via various industry analysts, but these are not personal performance assessments. One weak link in the form of a misfit executive can drastically impact overall company performance. Again, oddly, today's large business culture is to spend endless hours, often at least twice a year, filling out detailed and relatively meaningless individual performance reviews. These reviews all-too-often apply irrelevant and outmoded performance decision criteria to individual worker performance metrics that have little bearing on either strategic goals or the marketplace. This pervasive focus on the trees means the forest can be burning. The stage is set to completely skip over key organizational decision-makers' performance relative to deployment of scarce resources, and the crafting and realizing of a successful competitive market strategy. While everyone is aware of employee rating, twice a year without fail, the performance of the company itself remains a mystery, pieced together via gossip and informal water cooler discussion.

A manufacturer must employ individuals responsible for executing detailed market analysis, melding together competition data, pricing models, customer demand, supply availability, and a host of other factors to determine feasibility, marketability, and profitability before a product is developed and launched. If even one of these functions is weak, it can impact the excellent work of the others. A product may have the right features mix, but if it is introduced at the wrong price or cannot meet demand and a competitor's second best becomes the available, de facto standard, the new product may fail. It is ironic that these critical executive business decisions and the individuals (or perhaps groups) who make them impact the financial security and success of all workers in the firm. Yet, they are rarely evaluated, lost in the noise known as the semiannual employee evaluation.

One of the unique aspects of DEC culture was that the open discussion of worker class distinctions also lifted the veil of silence that cloaks executive performance and accountability. Open discussion of the need to protect everyone's equal stake in a successful company ("our" collective financial security) resulted in tacit permission for everyone to weigh in on how the executives performed in protecting employee and firm interests. This open discussion also meant greater opportunity to fix an area gone wrong.

The corollary to this, of course, is that focus on individual worker performance in the context of denial of worker hierarchy fosters an environment of lower overall drive for performance because executive accountability to the general workforce is nonexistent and usually not even a sanctioned topic for conversation. In the more typical rigid business cultures, even discussing openly whether an executive blew a key market or other decision could be viewed as a kind of corporate disloyalty or "treason."

6.2.3 Ethics in IT Outsourcing at Macro Level

The central ethical issues in IT outsourcing at a macro level are (1) the transfer of corporate labor dollars overseas and (2) the resulting disenfranchisement of U.S.-based workers economically impacted by the transfer through job losses. If there is no organizational venue to safely discuss ethics, and the business culture is the typical one which incorporates a white-out of executive performance as well as their reciprocal responsibility to workers, the stage is set for ethical violations. These are often due to inattention or mere secrecy in the fast moving world of corporate decisions making. Confusion usually reigns regarding the following key questions : How did the firm get to the point where labor arbitrage is needed and necessary? Is this step required to keep up with competition and create funds just to stay afloat, a one-time adjustment due to an error in business strategy or execution, or simply the next new operational fad? Or is the news all good and the program involves globally fueled personnel growth without swap-out of jobs?

Unfortunately, most of the time these centrally important questions are left completely unanswered in any kind of program communications, and the fact they remain unanswered as the firm executes IT offshore outsourcing is the source of most of the unwanted employee attrition, and related customer, community and general dissatisfaction. What is the impact on the business culture if the questions remain unaddressed? Here's a sampling from my research.

Employee perspective — "Fred has been here 13 years, has always been a top-notch programmer, and now that he's just short of retirement they cut him loose like a stone. That is how they will treat me in 10 years. I should start looking now to see if there is a better alternative while I am still marketable; I can't trust this firm for the long term anymore."

Executive perspective — "I have always been responsible for all software engineering. Now I need to depend on a vendor I've met three times who lives half way around the world. The responsibility remains mine because my internal customer still sees me as in charge. But most of the programmers are no longer under my management. I am left with all the responsibility but little authority, the classic long-term recipe for managerial disaster."

Community perspective — "Our tax base is eroding and our home values plummeting because all of these lay-offs. This is straining our budget in a completely unexpected way and threatening many of our long-term, cherished community programs. We evidently cannot count on the same kind of business–community partnership that allowed us to provide so many advantages for this firm in the past. We need to redouble our efforts to bring new businesses into the community and look twice and three times at providing infrastructure, tax, and other support for this company in the future."

Business partner perspective — "While the company as a whole may emerge stronger financially from the offshore program, the way it has clamped down on communications so that all the managers and employees are running scared is going to impact the work culture very negatively. We may need to reevaluate the company as a business partner if this negativity bleeds into how customers are treated. That seems likely unless the firm starts communicating a positive vision of the future as well as its tactical cost-savings focus. I'm also concerned about the impact of key people leaving, especially those I have worked with for many years. Those that replace them may be less aligned with our partnership vision and goals."

Customer perspective — "I read how the firm is laying off so many people and essentially treated its workers unfairly. I need to assume that if it treats workers unfairly, it may treat me as a customer unfairly, and may even be riddled with ethical issues regarding the overall quality of its products and services like so many compromised firms I hear about daily. I need to rethink about where I buy such products and services, to see whether I can find a way not to buy from the firm again, if not right away, for the long term. I don't like doing business with unethical companies if I can avoid it, especially if I can find cost effective alternatives that still meet my needs. I'm going to be more open to alternatives and on the watch to see if my personal experience changes for the worse. I need to be ready to jump if necessary."

The lack of a formal organizational venue and mandate to consider and ameliorate this kind of cultural impact does not mean it does not exist. Even the negative "let's wait and see" concerns described above can quickly push long-term customer, employee, business partner, and community alignments onto very shaky ground and rapidly undermine years of careful relationship management and development. A business environment in which these concerns are palpable can create unstated but extremely pervasive uncertainty and paranoia that may in turn contribute to ethical violations that leave no one standing in the disenfranchised employee's corner. Examples of ethical violations that may ensue are:

1. Not investing in education, training, or other means of minimizing layoffs for long-term, loyal employees, even if these investments are minimal and quite pragmatic, contributing to the preservation of firm knowledge and minimizing risk in updating IT business process
2. Lumping employees together based upon arbitrary high level criteria, without distinction as to how and where they can be redeployed, when some can fit into unfilled new positions quite easily.

3. Pockets of unfair and illogical protectionism based upon political maneuvering within the context an essentially completely outmoded staffing value model.
4. Choosing U.S.-based offshore vendors that bring with them a large number of hidden costs, building a way for some executives to jump ship to these same firms. It is surprisingly easy to pad the cost structure on offshore programs because the savings are so enormous they can be easily lost in the shuffle. One example is charging extremely high out-of-pocket travel expenses for resources traveling from India to the United States for the months of knowledge transfer. Even the common practice of asking offshore vendors to implement, creating self-policing vendor management, so that SLA performance can be easily subverted, can lead to abuses.

There are many more kinds of molar ethical challenges, such as arbitrary decision-making criteria relating to which groups participate in the offshore program.

The main concern is that—the absence of an Ethics PMO which provides an ethical decision making framework, including overt ethical goals, organizational structure, roles, responsibilities, metrics, reporting and communications—the entire firm is at risk for alienating customers, employees including executives, business partners, and the community at large.

6.2.4 Egoless Decision Making as a Personal Framework

Egoless decision making can be utilized as a personal guiding framework for ethical behavior in a business context. Individuals can use this concept to validate whether they are acting to benefit and align with the business goal at hand. In times of shifting reporting structures, the underlying power relationships that comprise the workings of large firms are in flux, and even the most experienced and well-meaning individuals may be confused about what constitutes an ethical decision. The Ethics PMO discussed elsewhere in this chapter and volume can help provide a framework for this challenge. Navigating without such a framework makes it difficult to make fair and grounded decisions. The following personal questions can be used to develop initial ethical guidelines:

■ What is my perception of the business imperative behind the offshore program?
■ How fair and objective are the offshore job shifts? Are they consistent with what is happening in the industry as a whole?
■ In this context, what is my personal organizational span of control and power, and how do I choose to utilize it?

I had to make some difficult choices related to offshore programs. One was facing a board of directors for a large firm to tell them that the approach of shifting too much work to many onshore consultants from a favored long-term U.S. consulting firm was unfair to the long-term employees of the firm. To my surprise, they agreed, but at the time I felt my own job was on the line because I was the lone voice taking that position. I also felt it necessary to turn down a lucrative job representing a country developing offshore outsourcing capacity but known for many civil rights violations. These were some of my personal ethical lines in the sand. Clearly these were personal decisions that some would perceive as naïve and others would perceive as not going far enough.

6.2.5 "The Truth Will Out"

In our maniacally plugged-in, video-gone-wild world, unethical actions will be revealed. As I write this, a large bank with a formerly pristine reputation came under investigation by the Department of Justice for illegally profiling and targeting consumers unlikely to be able to repay home loans. In addition to paying almost $100 million in a civil suit fine without admitting wrongdoing, the media indicated that the bank would have a heavy, non-monetary price to pay. The legal challenges "add up to significant blows to the bank's once-pristine reputation." A community leader stated that his city's people "take great offense when institutions take advantage.... It's offensive behavior and we shouldn't tolerate it" [2]. As the business world is built on perceptions of trust and integrity, this type of damage is incalculable, even if such practices were accepted widely by other firms in the industry at the time. In what the company called unrelated news, it reported that its CFO retired with accolades.

The sense that ethical constructs are growing in importance is not only reflected in the negative impact to firms that fall short; it is also reflected in their choices of offshore business partners. As reported on the Globalization Today website [3], a straw poll of the International Association for Outsourcing Professionals (IAOP) taken at the Outsourcing World Summit showed dramatic increases in the focus on corporate social responsibility (Figure 6.1). Although not all ethical violations

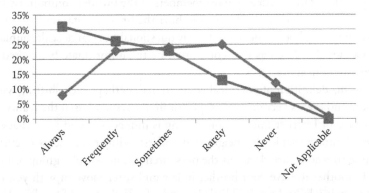

Figure 6.1 **Is corporate responsibility a factor in your outsourcing decisions? Results of straw poll conducted by International Association for Outsourcing Professionals. Diamonds = 2009. Squares = 2011.**

will "see the light of day," even in the Internet age, it appears that the level of ethical awareness and accountability is growing along with the depth of consequences for ethical violations.

In Chapter 7, we revisit the macro field of offshore outsourcing ethics and continue the discussions about several of hypotheses from Chapter 1.

6.3 Another Look at Business Ethics: Bound by Morality?

Perhaps this dialogue has revealed that the important question is not whether a corporation is a moral entity, but whether the individuals within it are held to a moral standard, and if so, who determines that standard. The wind shift of anger at the failure of regulatory agencies to ensure a clean and clear playing field in many of our industries—as more and more ethical failures come to light—suggests that at least part of this question has been answered.

The public and community hold corporations responsible for business decisions that violate a sense of ethical fair play. The individuals who lead them are held culpable in popular imagination and subjected to the potential public humiliation of senate and other formal inquiries along with the tangible and intangible costs of being branded unethical.

The second question—who or what determines what is unethical in the popular imagination—is always answered on a sliding scale, but this is not as difficult to identify as may appear. Without going into a lengthy philosophy discourse, an unethical corporate action may be defined as anything that an individual does on behalf of and with full knowledge and backing of corporate leadership that may be judged an unfair practice by most members of the broader community. In other words, any business practice that would hurt the firm's reputation if it was publically known would be considered ethically questionable. A large-scale, human reaction to a violation (such as that committed by the unfortunate bank cited above) confirms an ethical breach.

That this definition of unethical is situational, perhaps even shifting with time as society and events become more sophisticated, does not lessen the reality. Part of the potency of Internet information sharing is immediacy, and immediacy brings emotional impact that lends a heightened understanding to our sense of ethics. It is one thing to read an article about the outsourcing concerns of a group of IT workers; it is another to have your brother-in-law and sister move in with you because they lost their jobs and received little in return for their years of loyal work.

Clearly, a corporation should be governed to benefit its shareholders and owners, but that does not mean that the private governance of corporations is beyond the purview of human ethics. The availability or lack of "exit opportunities"—essentially a robust job market that enables workers to freely leave for jobs providing similar or better remuneration—does not give corporate executives a free ethical pass.

Rather, many companies follow the self-serving practice of focusing performance accountability downward on employees instead of upward on executive effectiveness in positioning the firm to win in the marketplace. This weakens the corporation as those most responsible for corporate performance are not held accountable for decisions except at the highest macro level of the market or analyst ratings. This postpones meaningful awareness and discussion until the damage is done and little remains but to bring in another leader while sustaining poor performance all the longer as the leadership shift ensues. Mutual leader and worker accountability and transparency appears to be a self-evident best practice that is strangely adopted only rarely, and as a voluntary part of business culture.

The foundation of any ethical business is objective accountability for business performance and results. It enhances the performance of a corporation of a whole and minimizes personal errors and inefficiencies arising from rank, political connection, nepotism, pre-conceived notions, or the myriad foibles to which all human institutions are subject, from neighborhood gatherings to large governments.

6.4 Ethics PMO Revisited: An Outsourcing Fable

As a new concept, the Ethics PMO case study must be theoretical, but that does not diminish its power. Here is an example of an offshore program with an effective, pervasive sense of ethical grounding.

A large tax and law firm, 48 HOUR TAX RETURNS, utilizes an online program to save its customers money by routinizing most of the tax analysis process. Its most successful competitor, TAX RETURNS NOW, just completed a similar program with additional advanced tax analysis features that present a threat to 48 HOUR. Automation of new tax analysis capabilities may lure away lucrative business customers who require these features. 48 HOUR currently charges additional fees for analysis services for businesses.

After some research, 48 HOUR decided that its one advantage over TAX RETURNS NOW was its IT process maturity. If TAX RETURNS NOW enabled a program to offshore 10% or 80 IT jobs, the savings could be re-invested into programming. TAX RETURNS NOW, although a very large U.S. firm, is privately held, so a long-drawn out debate about the action was not necessary. Of the 80 programmers, testers, and code maintenance professionals who were due to be offshored, TAX RETURNS NOW decided to reward them for their many years of work in developing the technical platform that had made the company so successful for so many years.

6.4.1 Implementation

An Ethics PMO was established by the two founders of 48 HOUR. The founders are brothers, one an accountant, one a tax lawyer. The firm had not yet experienced any kind of employee reductions in the 24 years since it was established. The brothers wanted to make sure that the friendly, professional, highly ethical reputation of the firm was maintained and that employees would continue to feel valued and appreciated. The first act was hiring a professional program manager to shepherd the Ethics PMO. The program manager's first move was to bring all of the 48 HOUR executives into a room to create and document their vision of ethics. In 48 HOUR's current business context, three principles agreed upon by the executive team:

- First, do no harm to relationships, including employee, business partners, and the community.
- Be aware of the short-and long-term impacts of all decisions and make all decisions within those contexts.
- Treat all individuals as you yourself want to be treated

Armed with these principles, the program manager facilitated a strategy statement that helped to communicate to all stakeholders the reasons behind the program. The key message was that the company was and would remain financially healthy. The offshore program was a pre-emptive strike to retain the 48 HOURS position as market leader. The statement included the three ethical principles above and noted that the firm would work as hard as possible to ensure that all employees whose jobs were moved offshore participated in a robust program that met their particular needs so that these ethical principles were maintained.

48 HOURS moved very swiftly to create a short list of offshore vendors. Offshore vendor decision and success criteria included the requirement of rapid U.S. growth to support hiring of displaced employees with the offshore vendor. Within a short time, to prevent the rumor mill from operating overtime, letters of intent were signed with two offshore vendors, each with the capacity to hire 40 people if needed.

Of the 80 IT workers, 20% (16) were eligible for generous early retirement packages that provided options for part-time work at 48 HOURS for 2 or 3 years along with full retirement benefits. Roughly half (8) of the retirement-eligible employees chose to remain part-time at 48 HOURS. These individuals represented the full-time equivalent of 4 people and they worked over the next few years to help orient the offshore team to the 48 HOURS culture.

Another 20% or 16 workers were happy to be hired by the new IT vendors, large consulting firms that would enable them to grow their skills. 48 HOURS arranged to use some of the savings from the program for a one-time salary payout. These employees were very pleased to shift to the new company and benefitted from more professional training, robust job opportunities, and a generous cash severance averaging 9 months' salary.

Not all employees were willing to shift to the offshore vendor, however, because the jobs required frequent travel and some employees had family commitments that did not support that lifestyle. 48 HOURS offered these employees extensive training opportunities. Thirty percent (24) employees chose to return to school for additional training. Most chose completely different fields, including nursing, medical technology, law, and accounting. Of the remaining 30%, 10% chose not to return to the workforce and accepted generous payouts equivalent to 1 1/2 years salary; and 20% used this same money to invest in their own businesses.

48 HOURS published an article to the broader community, outlining the ethical principles of the program and the measured satisfaction levels of former employees who participated in these various programs. All former employees rated the program as satisfactory, very satisfactory, or excellent. One individual was unable to successfully shift to the new vendor as an employee. From the start, his communication skills did not support his direct work with customers. A extended employee support program, designed to address the specific concerns of former employees struggling with workforce repatriation, included a counseling process where he was able to identify his problem. The employee was retained in the new company in a background role working only with other internal IT employees, and was ultimately very successful

As a result, 48 HOURS was able to report 100% satisfaction with the soft landing program at 3-month intervals across all stakeholders, including the community as a whole. Seeing that the community was not negatively impacted by falling hours prices or failing tax bases, the good reputation of the firm was not only preserved but enhanced, as the success of the program was publicized regularly.

The business strategy enabled by offshore savings was successful, and the additional funds were reinvested into the technology platform that was enhanced with new features and completely refreshed. The new technology platform was much more efficient for new code development and testing. Thus 48 HOURS not only matched but quickly outpaced the development of new tax features in their competitor's software. 48 HOURS established a vendor management PMO with a formally trained program manager to ensure that all business processes were appropriately revamped for a global team, and extensive training was conducted to support new roles and responsibilities within the new delivery framework. All in all, 48 HOURS emerged with its relationships and reputation intact, and a much more robust business footing.

6.4.2 Results: Answers to Burning Questions

The Ethics PMO created a structure in which the ethical strategy of the firm was far more solid than a piece of paper covered with value statements. The strategy included the reasons behind offshore outsourcing and the benefits that would accrue. In the context of a very strong, centrally and professionally managed ethical program, participants had robust choices fueled by generous investments in maintaining their goodwill. This was reflected in the community and the continued view of current and potential employees of 48 HOURS as an excellent place to work.

Employee perspective — "Fred has been here 13 years, has always been a top-notch programmer. Now that he's just short of retirement, he seems thrilled with his new option to retire at full benefits and stay on part time to help. I hope he stays on since he's such a good and knowledgeable resource. If this is how they will treat me in 10 years, I will be well satisfied. I wonder if I can bring my cousin in here sometime if there is an opening."

Executive perspective — "I have always been responsible for all software engineering. Now I need to depend on a vendor I've met three times who lives half way around the world. The responsibility remains mine because my internal customer still sees me as in charge although most of the programmers are no longer under my management. I am left with all the responsibility, but as a member of the vendor PMO and the Ethics PMO leadership committees, I also have the right level of authority to make this new model work. I'm nervous but all of the careful business process re-engineering and extensive new role training will help."

Community perspective — "I was concerned that our tax base would erode and our home values plummet if 48 HOURS had lay-offs. I should have known they would not have let me down—they never have. I feel even more confident now."

Business partner perspective — "I'm so impressed at how the company as a whole emerged stronger from this program. I'm going to tell my VP he is crazy to even consider anyone from TAX RETURNS NOW. Why align with second best?"

Customer perspective — "I read how other firms lay off so many people, but somehow 48 HOURS managed to lower costs, give me more of the business features I need, and keep everyone happy. If they are so careful to treat employees that well, I know that they care about people, and I can trust them to care about me. I feel even more confident about 48 HOURS' "people first" motto. I'm going to recommend the company to my entire office."

6.5 Summary

The challenges of implementing the offshore model—not an easy collective task—shed light on some of the less positive aspects of large U.S. businesses. One of these is the lack of accountability of executives as they implement the business strategy that ultimately holds up the corporate financial umbrella upon which all firm employees depend. Enabling a culture of accountability across all levels of an organization is a key component of a robust ethical framework that we will explore further in later chapters.

References

[1] Machiavelli, Niccolo. *The Prince,* translated by N.H. Thomson. Vol. XXXVI, Part 1. The Harvard Classics. New York: P.F. Collier & Son, 1909–1914; www.bartleby. com/36/1/

[2] Wells Fargo Target of Justice Department Probe; Agency Alleges Discriminatory Lending, Huff Post Business, July 26, 2011. http://www.huffingtonpost.com/2011/07/26/wells-fargo-justice-department-probe_n_910425.html

[3] Corporate Social Responsibility (CSR) Plays Role in Outsourcing Decisions, Straw Poll 2009. http://globalizationtoday.com/corporate-social-responsibility-csr-play-role-outsourcing-decisions-course-why/

[4] Principles of Socially Responsible Outsourcing: toward a Social Label for BPO and IT Services, Samasource Working Paper, May 2009. http://www.sourceoutpoverty.org/project-library

Appendix: Excerpt from Sama Code of Conduct

Samasource is a non-profit organization dedicated to bringing the benefit of outsourcing jobs to people living in poverty. Below is a small excerpt from its Code of Conduct. The full version can be found at http://www.sourceoutpoverty.org/project-library

- We pay fair and adequate wages, . . . spend at least 40% of annual revenue on employees.
- We . . . give workers representation in the decision-making process.
- We . . . minimize the environmental impact of our operation.
- We will submit to random, on-site verification . . . we are following this Code.

Chapter 7

Recalibrating the Reality

"Greed is good."

Gordon Gekko, *Wall Street*

7.1 The Reality of Outsourcing According to the American Public

As we return to the macro or broad economic view, let's look closely at the following four important touch points of public opinion.

I. In a dramatic shift over the last decade, Americans no longer believe we are the leading world economic power.

Figure 7.1 shows that public perception of the economic world leadership in the United States is shown to have dramatically shifted over the past 11 years. In 2000, only 10% of those polled believed China led the U.S. In 2011 that percentage increased to over 50%. In 2000, 65% of those polled believed the U.S. was the top economic power in the world; by 2011 that number had decreased to 32% [1].

II. Americans believe that outsourcing is hurting, not helping, the U.S. economy.

Figure 7.2 shows that over 60% of Americans believe that the economic expansion in China and India is "bad" for the U.S. economy. [2] Similarly, Figure 7.3 confirms that the public perceives that world free trade agreements such as NAFTA have harmed the U.S. economy in general. [3]

III. Not only does outsourcing hurt the U.S. economy in popular opinion, but almost half the U.S. population (48%) believes that free trade economic policies

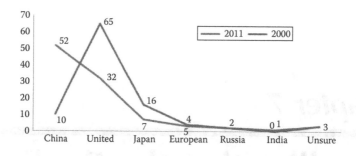

Figure 7.1 "Which one of the following do you think is the leading economic power in the world today: the United States, the European Union, Russia, China, Japan, or India?" Margin of error is ±3%. (*Source:* Gallup Poll conducted February 2011.)

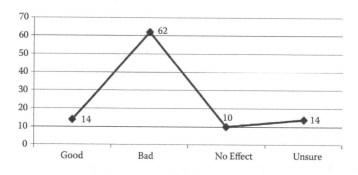

Figure 7.2 "Do you think the recent economic expansion in countries like China and India has been generally good for the U.S. economy, or bad for the U.S. economy, or had no effect on the U.S. economy?" Margin of error is ±3%. (*Source:* CBS News Poll conducted July 2008.)

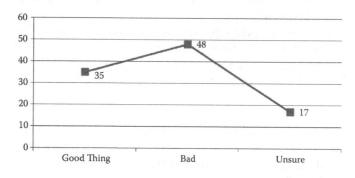

Figure 7.3 "In general, do you think that free trade agreements like NAFTA and the policies of the World Trade Organization have been a good thing or a bad thing for the United States?" Margin of error is ±3%. (*Source:* Pew Research Center survey conducted April 2008.)

have directly hurt them, their families, and friends. In a poll by the Pew Research Center conducted in April 2008, almost 50% of the U.S. public felt that free trade agreements probably hurt or definitely hurt the financial situations of their families (Figure 7.4) [4].

Now let's turn to the public perception of the etiology of offshore outsourcing (Figure 7.5).

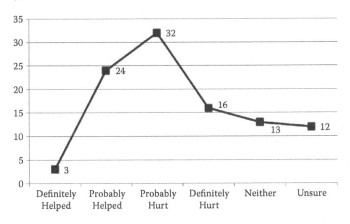

Figure 7.4 **"Do you think these free trade agreements have definitely helped, probably helped, probably hurt, or definitely hurt the financial situation of you and your family?"** (*Source:* **Pew Research Center survey conducted April 2008.**)

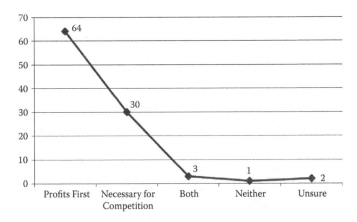

Figure 7.5 **"Some have said that outsourcing of jobs to workers in other countries is caused by investors and chief executives of companies who want profits and don't care where they come from, while others say that outsourcing of jobs to workers in other countries is sometimes necessary for American companies to compete. Which statement comes closer to your view?"** (*Source:* **Associated Press/IPSOS poll conducted May 2004.**)

IV. Most of the public (over 60%) attributed outsourcing to profit motives without reference to how those profits are achieved; only 30% believed that outsourcing was necessary for companies utilizing it to remain competitive [5]. In the same poll, 20% or 1 in 5 responders believed that someone they knew personally, a family member or acquaintance, lost their job within the past year due to outsourcing. [6]

Given the increase in outsourcing since 2004, it is safe to assume that this number has grown and underlines even more how personally customers and business partners feel about the impact of outsourcing [6].

In an interesting poll on public's perception of reasons behind outsourcing (Figure 7.6), the Americans ascribed the trend to the following drivers: lower wage structure overseas (80%); business driving for profit without any reference to where those profits originate (77%); lower standards for other countries in terms of worker safety and the environment (61%); consumer demand for inexpensive goods (56%); weak corporate leadership (42%); and overly strong labor unions (35%). The latter choice ostensibly driving labor costs too high in the U.S. by forcing businesses to look elsewhere for cheap labor. In other words, Americans perceive that lower

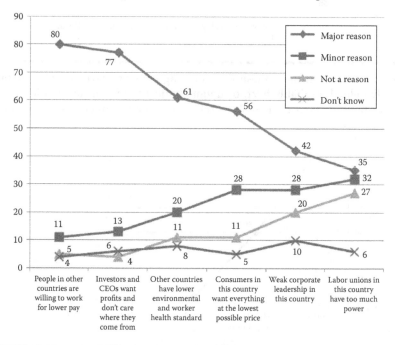

Figure 7.6 **"As I mention some possible reasons for the loss of American jobs to foreign competitors, please tell me if you think each is a major reason, a minor reason, or is not a reason for the loss of American jobs. What about (see options at bottom of figure)? Is this a major reason, a minor reason, or not a reason for the loss of American jobs to foreign competitors?" (*Source: Newsweek* poll conducted February 2004.)**

overseas wage structures (80%), unbridled profit seeking (77%), lower health and safety standards (61%), and consumer demand for low cost goods (56%)—were deemed major reasons for outsourcing. Slightly less than half or 42% perceived weak corporate leadership as a reason; only a third or 35% perceived strength of labor unions as a driver behind outsourced labor. Despite these concerns, when asked directly whether they would pay more for products and services that originated in the U.S. instead of purchasing similar, less expensive products from overseas, only slightly more than half or 55% would do so [7].

In sum, the data suggest that Americans are very concerned about worker job security, and a large number (1 in 5) experienced a job loss in their inner circles or among immediate acquaintances. The public generally does not trust the executive leaders of our large companies. Americans perceive executives as willing to compromise concern for the well-being of workers in the name of profit. This is expressed within a highly negative connotation, including executive willingness to barter ethical issues such as worker safety and environmental violations in pursuit of profit.

A good number of us (42%) see outsourcing as a necessary step because our corporate leadership is weak. Whether these large company executives are seen as weak in moral fiber, business savvy, or both is unclear. Clearly, every time a large firm announces, or even worse, starts unannounced layoffs that are later attributed to outsourcing, these are some of the negative conclusions of the consumer audience. Particularly concerning is that these negative characteristics are directly attributed to the company and its executive leadership. One can only conclude that while U.S. unemployment numbers are climbing or remain unacceptably high, the negative characteristics ascribed to these large firms and the executives that manage them are magnified.

At the end of the day, however, consumers in the U.S. vote for outsourcing daily—with their pocketbooks. Despite their strong economic misgivings and equally strong perceptions of financial concerns close to home, roughly half of us are not willing to pay more to keep outsourced goods and services based in the United States. Within this divided public opinion landscape, it is not surprising that the large U.S. firms implementing offshore outsourcing exhibit the same kind of deep ambivalence as is evidenced by our larger society. Each firm moves towards outsourcing as a difficult choice while at the same time feeling compromised and compromising.

7.2 Macro Offshore Case Study: The Function of the Chief Ethics Officer (CETO)

In this case study, the new role of the chief ethics officer (CETO) is serves a pivotal program function within the Fortune 100 firm. The role of the ethics officer is intimately tied to the strategy and operations of the business. There are five primary Ethics program goals that are the responsible of the CETO, each supported by a cluster of sub-goals.

7.2.1 Builds a Strong, Robust Business Based on Honest Growth, Solid Strategy, and Reasonable Shareholder and Profit Expectations

7.2.1.1 Ensure Clear Market Strategy and Executive Accountability

- Ensure a robust, healthy, growing firm by sponsoring the facilitation of a clearly articulated market strategy. This is generally achieved via professionally facilitated formal communications sessions scheduled on a regular basis, perhaps a quarterly 2-day think tank involving all C-Level executives.
- The direct tie between an updated or affirmed market strategy and the expenditure of firm resources includes establishing clear links between each firm-level strategic goal and the tactical measures of success for that goal for each executive. For example, the top strategic goals for the firm may be one of the following:
    1. Grow market share and presence in EMEA by additional 10% by end of year.
    2. Maintain current sales (do not lose ground) in flat U.S. market.
    3. Test and validate new ventures in Australia.
- Each executive has clearly marked metrics for their division associated with every individual strategic goal. Each strategic goal has a direct a sponsor in the division most heavily responsible for its success. Although overall ownership is allocated to the division most heavily aligned with the goal, however, all other divisions are also responsible for monitoring and achieving their metrics toward the goal.

To continue the above example, Facilities and Human Resources (HR) may need to add resources for goals #1 and #3, but would be expected to help create operational efficiencies to maintain low HR costs for goal #2.

7.2.1.2 Ensures Complete transparency to Employees Regarding Communications about Market Strategy and Progress of Strategy

- Each division reports quarterly to the entire employee staff—perhaps in writing, perhaps once a year in a meeting—upon the successful achievement of the metrics assigned to them for the strategic goals. If the targets are missed, the executive shares the plan to address the shortfall so that it doesn't happen again.
- There is always a person—a name and a face, in the form of a named executive—with clear responsibility for the achievement of metrics in support of each company's goal, and every single employee has the information provided to know and understand where his or her job fits in with those priorities.

7.2.1.3 Enforces balanced performance pressure on employees so that it remains within reasonable limits

■ The chief ethics officer (CETO) is responsible for ensuring, within a careful structure of clearly communicated expectations and accountability, that individual employee performance goals remain realistic. In particular, these goals do not put undue pressure upon employees to the extent that the firm's ethics are likely to be compromised.

■ This overtly means that there is not an unrealistic assumption that there is an endless increase in profit year over year at an exorbitant, unsustainable rate—the corporate short form of Bernie Madoff, and all that implies, in terms of ethical breach. Additional ethical goals such as a specific focus on fair treatment of economically challenged customers or clean and clear alignment with environmental precepts are carefully monitored.

7.2.1.4 Ensures employee performance reviews are based upon objective measures

■ It is the CETO's role to provide oversight to ensure that the performance goals are appropriately aligned with not only the quarterly market strategy but also the ethical structure of the firm. These individual employee performance goals are tied closely to employee recognition and rewards. Examples of these awards include the awarding of new career growth opportunities that support the development of highly marketable skills, favorable job performance reviews, promotions and employee recognition programs, and other items that represent drivers behind employee behavior. This underscores the need to structure the employee review and reward process to be as objective as possible. Multiple personal views (round robin performance reviews by a crowd of people doing each other's reviews reciprocally) do not necessarily translate into greater objectivity—achievement of on-time, on-budget projects, high customer satisfaction scores, etc., are to be weighted much more heavily.

7.2.2 Enables New Employee On-Boarding and Employee Skill Development as an Important Contribution to a Strong Ethical Culture

Every employee who joins the firm participates in a minimum 5-day orientation. The new employee is provided the latest employee communications including an update on marketing strategy and the most recent departmental or division performance metrics. As part of the on-boarding process, each individual is provided an overview of the organization—each division's location, function, executive(s), and current performance—as well as an equally in-depth briefing on the firm's products and services.

At the end of the new employee orientation or the annual 2-day refresher course required for all employees, each individual understands the organizational reporting structure, the market strategy, the current performance of the firm within that market strategy including any challenges, and where their particular role fits within that framework.

7.2.2.1 Sponsors the Development of Robust Corporate Ethics Collaterals Including an Employee Ethics Handbook, Behavior Guidelines and Training for All Employees

■ The focus of the training is to clarify the important ethical points for all employees, and enable them to practice these in learning situations without fear of retribution during the training process.
■ Some of the typical topics covered via this collateral include are entitled: Ethical Guidelines for Employees (part of the employee handbook), Ethics for New Managers, A Warm Welcome to our New Business Partners, and an Ethics Customer Interface Checklist and an anonymous Employee Ethics Hotline.

7.2.2.2 Actively Supports the dissemination high-quality, objective studies on the cost of ethical breaches in the industry and firm

The CETO increases awareness of the high cost of ethical violations by sharing the financial impact of ethical violations on industry competitors, and encouraging the development of solid research in this area across in the industry.

7.2.2.3 Supervises Periodic Ethical Audits of All Divisions to Ensure Alignment with Ethical Principles

It is the responsibility of the CETO to pro-actively monitor and address areas of the firm more likely to pose an ethical breach. These high risk teams may be comprised of underperforming divisions or employees, or newly formed divisions not yet fully acculturated to the deep commitment to ethical conduct in the context of solid business practices. Ethical audits may take the form of interviews, in-depth reviews of financial results, customer feedback solicitation and responses, and employee feedback. These audits are binding and there are serious individual and team consequences if breaches are identified. The goal is always to identify and eradicate the underlying cause of the ethical breach, which may be as simple as a hiring process without enough face to face interviews, or as complex as a rogue vice president determined to outshine his or her peers at any cost.

7.2.3 Actively Models Ethical Precepts, Represents Ethics in the Corporation, and Requires the Same of All Executives, Including the CEO

The CETO provides for well-publicized, robust cost-benefit and return on investment analysis for potential ethical breaches in support of the appropriate firm policies and communications. There is a deep need for the CETO to find a way to actively demonstrate the firm's commitment to its ethical structure, especially since many employees' prior firms would consider the role to be limited to putting a plaque of the corporate values on the wall. One way for the firm to embody ethics, for example, is to sponsor a yearly update in which the executive team speaks about the progress, commitment and new developments in their divisions.

7.2.4 Serves as a Whistle-Blower Escalation Point

The CETO "owns" the executive level interface with any employee who expresses concerns about ethical violations. The firm should maintain a well-publicized open door policy that allows any employee to meet with the CETO to share concerns about ethical conduct.

7.2.5 Works with Peer Senior Executives to Establish Guidelines for ethical Transparency and Frequency of reporting

- In concert with the chief financial officer, establishes rules for financial transparency that go far beyond the typical Generally Accepted Accounting Principles (GAAP).
- Similarly, in partnership with Human Resources, validates the robustness and quality of new hire processes and communications regarding the firm's culture and expectations.

7.2.6 Serves as Liaison to Other CETOs in Non-Competing Firms to Develop and Nurture Industry-Wide Ethical Best Practices

- The key function of the CETO is to promote the professionalism of ethics within the workplace, setting the example from the top.
- As such he or she directly participate as senior advisor on programs, such as offshore outsourcing, which often have a large and dramatic imprint on the ethics of the firm.

■ The CETO serves as communications focal point for resources outside of the firm to share the firm's strong commitment and active stance in promoting ethical behavior. The CETO contributes to the development of industry ethical practices by placing some of the firm's resources at the disposal of these associations.

7.2.7 Works with Academic Researchers to Sponsor and Benefit from Research on the Cost–Benefit Equation of Ethical Behavior

The CETO actively sponsors and participates in research formed for the advancement of ethical process and knowledge maturity. This information supports the understanding, management and development of ethical conduct within the industry.

In addition, the CETO overseas task forces that undertake to analyze and document in detail the cost of ethical breaches across large firms.

Some of the enabling business processes that must be in place to support these CETO responsibilities are listed below:

■ A robust, widely published strategy map clearly demarcating how the market strategy translates into specific company efforts and resource expenditures. This is a document that directly lists each component of the company strategy, including goals. For example, "Strategic Goal #1: via more competitive pricing, a new marketing campaign, and expanded product features targeted to that market, become market leader in southeast region by 2012 for product line Z."
■ The executive sponsor of this goal. For example, "This strategic goal is lead by Chris Smithson in marketing."
■ The specific measures of success by division. For example, "Marketing will design and deliver a campaign with robust objective measures of success, including positive customer levels of trial adoption of our products, no later than August 2011. The detailed marketing metrics for effort are to be published in July 15; the same level of detail for product development, marketing, test, customer support, etc."
■ The specific projects supporting these efforts. For example, marketing projects A1, A2, and A3 are directly supporting strategic goal #1; marketing projects B2 and B3 are indirectly supporting strategic goal #1; product engineering project A12 is directly supporting strategic goal #1, etc.
■ A dashboard that is published at least monthly and ideally updated daily and published weekly. This report is structured to highlight progress and current status (Red / Yellow / Green) by division for all projects as arranged by priority order of strategic goals.

■ A clear line of authority for CETO to provide oversight for ethical breaches across the organization. The oversight process is in alignment with the published ethical guidelines and principles. While these ethical guidelines are binding they are also understood to be a work in process, perhaps even relatively volatile at times, as the business evolves and additional industry revenue opportunities and associated regulations arise.

7.3 Utilizing Offshore Outsourcing to Address Gaps in Strategic Alignment across Business and IT

7.3.1 The Cost of Dampening the Strategic IT Voice and Partnership

Underlying many of the business processes related to the role of the CETO are some relatively radical assumptions vis-à-vis current business culture across large IT firms:

■ Executive performance accountability and transparency of accountability of across the firm.

■ Transfer of performance management out of the human resources division into strategic ethical oversight. In other words, performance management is to be updated and managed within an overtly ethical specialization and context including audit oversight under the office of the CETO.

■ Strong, consistent messaging on ethics, actively modeled by senior management and reinforced via formal and informal processes.

■ Clear ties of resource expenditure to strategic goals.

■ Transparency in the form of regularly updated metrics reporting to all employees on strategy, resource expenditures, and current status.

■ Minimization of group reciprocal feedback relating to job performance reviews; replacing it with emphasis on objective performance of projects relating to strategic goals.

Underlying these changes is the requirement that the CETO sits on an equal footing with other senior executives. As part of ensuring that the firm remains robust and oriented toward revenue growth, the CETO will also help to minimize organizational rogue silos that do not benefit the organization. Rogue silos are started by managers who choose to build their teams based on personal relationships and loyal to them (not the company). While to some extent these feelings of loyalty are needed and natural, they inevitably start to interfere with objective performance if they become more important than the ability to deliver the task at hand.

The untouchable senior leader who consistently undercuts performance because the values of loyalty to him take precedence over divisional performance is fairly common in large global companies. It is the job of the CETO to "bust" those empire-like pockets as they are essentially unethical. Building loyal teams is wonderful if they also perform, but performance must be paramount; otherwise the entire organization is at risk. It is unfair for a culture of nonperformance to be overlooked when the ultimate result could be the broad loss of jobs across the organization.

Another deeply cherished, well worn tradition that must go by the wayside in ethical firms is the finger pointing among divisions when efforts do not go well. Each division should have the opportunity to set its own metrics for monitoring in achievement of prioritized strategic goals. This should cut down the extraneous "noise," but it does not go far enough. The various arms of large organizations must be aligned behind the strategic goals. "Aligned" in this case means that the divisions (1) understand and interpret the goals in the same way; (2) understand the handshake of responsibilities across divisions in the same way; and (3) agree upon the values and benefits of the goals. In other words, if the benefits are pursued correctly, they will result in the desired outcomes.

These points of alignment within the large firm hierarchy mean, on a practical level, that the senior executives are in agreement as to their organizational goals value, meaning, process, and responsibilities, and that this agreement and understanding extend to the operational manager level. Operational level managers must work effectively across divisions; if they receive different directions from their leaders, they will find it impossible to execute and deliver as a team. This is the very, very important reason that many strategic efforts fail: operational resources that work at cross purposes or follow completely different playbooks without effective coordination.

This executive level alignment, so critically important, is rarely achieved, setting the stage for operational level resources to work the underlying differences out as best they can, resulting in the wasted time and escalation this implies. Yet, as difficult as this level of agreement is to achieve across very large organizations, agreement is also just the beginning.

7.3.2 High Performance Organizations

To become a truly high performance organization, a common understanding of not only goals and benefits is required, but also a deep and shared understanding on the process touch points across the organization.

To continue our example above, in which a new product is being both launched and marketed in an effort to take the lead in EMEA, there will need to be coordination and cooperation across several fronts, normally within distinct organizational divisions. Market research, product research and development, product design, marketing campaign development, manufacturing, sales, and product support may all be involved in achieving this goal.

A good to excellent organization enables each of these functional areas of expertise to work together via static due dates. The new product is researched, then handed "over the wall" to design. When design is completed, the product is handed over the wall to marketing and manufacturing, like a football handed down the field one pass at a time.

High performing organizations, however, have invested in building staff with a unique body of knowledge. These key resources understand how processes work in divisions other than their own and embody the meaning of a high performing organization if they perform their functions well.

A great deal of confusion surrounds the concept of the high performing organization. Much of the time high performance is interpreted as adopting the latest process du jour in the form of the hottest new IT or business delivery methodology, or quality certification.

While there is nothing wrong with these per se—I am a big proponent of robust methodologies—the irony is that sometimes these sophisticated process techniques actually backfire. They backfire because the real challenge to large firms is building an understanding across and within diverse groups that enables them to work together to achieve results. The high performing organization is not about attending a course, meeting more or less frequently, or any other pure process play. It is about building real bridges of mutual understanding so that the individuals that work together can be effective partners—they understand enough about each other's discipline to be able bring their own knowledge to bear in a way that enhances the whole. (see appendix at the end of this chapter) [12].

Most large organizations possess a hierarchy within a hierarchy. Engineering firms value engineers; marketing firms value sales and marketing personnel. Forcing all areas of a firm to bend to one particular group's discipline or minimizing the relevance and importance of the other functional roles and their contributions comes at a high cost. Stories abounded about DEC; the ultimate engineering firm, for example, Ken Olsen refused to sell internal tools to interested customers. The rumor was that Ken saw sales people as necessary but only to be tolerated. *DECTalk*, one of the internal tools at DEC, shared many features with a business we now know as eBay! Not only is it good business to cultivate an attitude of relative humility—anyone can come up with a good idea, and their role or designation should not be a barrier for that idea being realized—it is also great business savvy.

The best IT organizations have dedicated personnel who serve as liaisons to internal customers. Their sole purpose is to understand, from the inside perspective, how customers think, work, believe, and operate. Investing in a liaison means that the firm has the maturity to understand that there is no theoretical quick fix to achieve excellence or partnership. If there is a deep mutual understanding from the other's point of view, encompassing organizational, functional, and even areas of deep professional expertise, true creativity is enabled. Much of the role of the CETO is to ensure that not only are employees feeling valued, but that they are respecting and valuing each others' expertise, knowledge base, opinions and world view.

To take the next step and become a truly high performing organization, the following extremely difficult and elusive goal must be attained—individuals from diverse organizations, functional disciplines and expertise, all have a well-worn road map to follow so that they do not need to negotiate roles, responsibilities, approaches, metrics, accountability and all the other components of complex joint global delivery. They have been down this path before, and they know what to do. All that remains is applying the path to the specific effort at hand. This is the true function of methodology. Methodology simply means we don't need to build the road as we go down the road, and when we are talking global, complex, cross-division delivery, it can be extraordinarily complex to achieve. These deep partnerships are often centered in discreet individuals who have managed to build a level of mutual discipline understanding across the organization despite—not because of—the organizational structures and process. These valuable individuals usually take the knowledge with them when they leave, and often the fledgling partnerships fizzle as a result.

The value of a methodology is that it saves time—enabling team members to work from the same playbook despite differences in skills and background. The presence of organizational catalysts that speak across disciplines is often the first step towards achieving that understanding. If the task at hand is to build a marketing web site, for example, how wonderful it would be for the marketing experts to understand something about the technical processes and choices that go into building a world class website. In parallel, how useful it would also be if the technical web development team understood something about marketing. Only marketing experts understand the subtleties of motivating customers, and only technical web developers understand the complexities of utilizing different tools to enhance the customer web experience. Ideally, a true brainstorming ensues, a creativity born of the investment of mutual respect and knowledge.

In many similar projects that I have run, there are surprisingly few of these individuals, and they are almost never developed purposefully—some senior individual has figured out it will make them better at their job. This token competency-bridging individual spends a great deal of time translating from one half of the team to the other, because by the time a team member is on an important project in a major large firm, they represent a level of expertise that is usually narrowly immersed in that particular field's view. I have been in many meetings where individuals were unable to go beyond their discipline's jargon to truly communicate. It is the extremely rare large firm that can pull together a team from different functional disciplines and not have to start out with a large number of lengthy, gritty, time-consuming and inefficient sessions dedicated to answering the most basic of questions regarding "what do we do now" and "who is doing what"? Then starting that same negotiation process for the next team, and the next—these are the huge time sinks that create a performance drag, creating a long lag time for some firms, representing a very costly drag on all efforts.

Thus, in the name of building a robust business, the CETO is also responsible for building very deep inter-functional and inter-organizational relationships. Those that serve as liaisons should be omnipresent at all key meetings of their assigned organization, and should be a non-threatening presence to help facilitate their needs being met via other organizations. Investment in a robust set of cross-trained individuals can be one of the most pragmatic investments a large firm ever makes, as they can transcend boundaries to come up with truly creative solutions to old problems.

There is a particular difficulty, at times, in establishing partnerships such as these within the IT department and their internal customers. This may be because many of the large firms originally classified information technology as coming under the CFO's office—many still do—where technology is viewed and managed primarily as an expense. Depending upon the industry, this may be just old thinking and a lazy form of bias.

Based on my experience, it would be a fair statement to observe that most Fortune 100 firms are very challenged in the area of IT and business partnership. Much of the time, this is because the business—representing IT's internal customer—does not take the time to understand and value the contributions from the IT perspective. It is not unusual for large firms to have large numbers of "shadow IT" projects going, in which the business bypasses internal IT requests for resources and goes directly to external consultants for delivery. This adds many multiple layers of confusion as these resources have usually little to no shared grounding or understanding of the business context of their projects.

The real cost of a partnership wall between IT and their internal business counterparts is the lack of an IT technical voice at the table when the business strategy is under development. The technical arm can represent what is possible; the business arm can communicate what is needed. It is the creative and active melding of the two together that behind the elusive synergy of true business partnership creativity. To create a business strategy in a technical void is unwieldy and unnecessary. To create a technical strategy in a business void is an empty exercise. A robust partnership is the only ethical option in building equally robust businesses that enable long and happy work lives based upon market place success.

Let's turn now to our conclusions from Chapter 5 after this analysis, and test them against our new understanding.

7.4 Conclusions from Chapter 1: Macro Level Revisited

Our original macro level conclusions were:

Conclusion 5: Whether large firms (and the individuals who represent them) are prepared or not, the general public will judge them within a broader sense of ethics.

As discussed earlier, it is a puzzling feature of the culture of present-day U.S. business that we turn a strangely universal blind eye to the concept of executive performance accountability. The higher the level of the executive, the more shrouded in mystery the business decisions they influence, and the impact on the business. Most IT employees of large firms are forced to read between the lines like the general public, and often must actually look to the public financial reports and the general environment to take the business pulse of the company. Is the firm hiring? If so, what kind of roles? What kinds of new projects are receiving funding? These can provide clues to the mystery.

This employee knowledge gap on executive and company performance creates much anxiety, as workers correctly perceive they may be the last to know if the market shifts and their own company lands in trouble. It also has a much more pervasively negative effect, as individuals who are operationally responsible for day to day decisions on deployment of resources are running blind. Should my project accept a 2 week delay or should we hire more resources to stay on schedule? If the operational layer must operate within a complete absence of strategic information, they are operating in a day to day decision-making vacuum. If operational level decision makers are unaware of latest strategy and executive performance results in fulfilling that strategy, the mind boggles at the inefficiency that implies.

It is clear from the polls cited early in the chapter that the public ascribes negative ethical characteristics to large companies that utilize outsourcing and also questions the integrity and strength of their leaders. It is also true that there is a kind of guilty collusion in the large numbers of customers that patronize and intend to continue patronizing goods and services made less expensive via outsourcing. This love–hate relationship the U.S. public has with outsourcing is delicate. Firms that can, through judicious investment of a relatively small percentage of the returns accrued from offshore outsourcing, create significant cost savings along with significant good will by taking excellent care of their former employees are positioned to receive the best of both worlds.

Conclusion 6: Strategic workforce development—aligning skills development with market needs, opportunity, and global availability, may well be the next strategic IT imperative. Strategic workforce development is the art of positioning a firm to maximize the global value of IT and other human resources as they map to company strategy, and constitutes one of the more transparent measures of executive leadership benchmarking and performance. Unfortunately, most large U.S. firms are already struggling with internal business–IT partnerships without the additional complexities of global delivery and staffing. If a large disconnect in strategic partnership and collaboration exists without offshore outsourcing, it will only be exacerbated. On the other hand, offshore outsourcing represents an excellent opportunity to strengthen these critical relationships and alignments.

Let's take an example from my experience with a client in the consumer goods business, which had enjoyed market leadership due to several patents that were now due to expire. It was a profitable and lucrative U.S.-based business and clearly, the field would be crowded the moment the patent expired.

My entire experience with this particular client was one of extreme frustration, although I met their goals and left them more than satisfied with the implementation of their offshore program. My concern stemmed from their narrow view of the world—they were producing widget X, would continue to produce widget X, just cheaper than the competition.

They did not have the vision to utilize the remaining few years prior to the patent expiration to build upon their original discovery. One lucrative idea was to build a business providing marketing data associated with this widget, which was strongly associated with particular types of buying habits in other widgets, and other extremely valuable marketing data. As a result, they missed the opportunity to become a marketing data management company, with the many years of information they—and only they—possessed on their market. Unfortunately, I've watched their stock dwindle and their lay-offs increase over the years since expiration of the patent.

Now, had this firm been able to encompass this particular new vision (or something similarly bold and new), a new global staffing model could have supported them in rolling this out extremely cost-effectively. Instead of merely lowering the widget cost via the offshore program I delivered, they could have expanded their capability in marketing data sales and management via the inclusion of these capabilities via their chosen vendor.

Creating a vision in which data management may be strategically architected and marketed from the U.S., and carefully executed via a global staffing model, may have included very sophisticated algorithmic designs from offshore firms. These algorithms could be developed in a country such as Israel, well-known for hyper-intelligent data management. Such a global model may maximize the particular strengths of each global location by including database programming and testing in India. Infrastructure support and management of the data warehouse could reside in South America, where the time zone and flight time is highly compatible with the U.S. sales and data reporting efforts, while still accruing significant cost savings.

We will look more at the importance of strategic IT and business alignment in our macro offshore fable later in this chapter.

Conclusion 7: Change management, while invaluable in navigating the challenging waters of successful offshore program initiation, is not an effective model to evaluate the ethical implications—if any—of the change in question. Without an overt ethical mandate, formal change management, while recommended and helpful, would be extraordinarily challenged to be empowered enough to introduce an entire new vocabulary, level of accountability and communications regarding ethics. This is especially true in the chaos of an offshore implementation when more pressing tactical execution challenges may appear to be much more absorbing and important.

In Chapter 8, as we look at the future of ethics in IT Outsourcing, we develop an extended change management toolkit, with the hope and expectation that this will be incorporated into all major change management efforts.

An ethical toolkit should become part and parcel of protecting all firms and their executives and employees from the negative consequences of ethical violations.

Conclusion 8: Personal history, experience and observations are valid avenues for exploration in the realm of ethics and ethical conduct. Ultimately, although the three levels of ethics under research encompass the macro economy as a whole, the molar or corporation, and the micro or personal, it is ultimately individual human beings who make these choices.

Our methodology, comprised of a blending of academic research, analysis, direct social observation revealed by polling, and personal observation, can build a picture of a particular culture at a point in time.

Relevant research is cited and incorporated into these observations. Field observation can also help to identify gaps and to provide a context for learning and applying it, as well as helping to bridge the gap between practitioners and researchers.

It is ironic that the analysis of offshore outsourcing leads us directly to applying principles of objective measures of success, transparency, and alignment with true robust business growth for the firm. This in turn establishes the basis for creation of such a dynamically growing work environment that ethics violations resulting from widespread economic malaise are minimized.

7.5 Case Study: Industry Specific Commitment to Ethics—What Changes Would Accrue?

The industry-wide implications of placing Chief Ethics Officers within the context of an empowered Ethics PMO are many.

7.5.1 Productivity is Boosted

The emphasis on objective measures of productivity along with minimization of the drag represented by employees more valued for internal political reasons would bring a significant boost.

The open communications of company strategy would also boost productivity, as individuals would be much more empowered by their knowledge of where their efforts fit within company priorities. This clarity in turn would increase efficiency.

The environment of accountability, especially in the context of regular alignment and agreement of senior executives across divisions, would minimize expensive delays due to conflicting direction. Transparency of support and transparency of accountability leave little room for obfuscation, when in place, team members tend to be highly focused on meeting widely published goals.

7.5.2 Morale Gets a Lift

Enabling a culture in which accountability is not only from the worker, but also from the executive to the worker, reflects the reality that the decisions made by the manager impact the worker's fundamental job security. The wrong strategy can lead to massive job loss within the firm. It is a relief and a boost to morale to be able to acknowledge this truth openly. Accountability goes both ways, whether acknowledged or not; when the topic is no longer taboo, creativity and collaboration flows much more easily.

Setting the tone from the top that violations of ethics simply will not be tolerated makes everyone feel safer. Conversely, open season of ethical transgression, based on a false focus on short term profits and the belief that the world is too stupid to catch on, contribute to the feeling of living on borrowed time. The strong subliminal message of a workplace run by predators is that eventually they will turn to prey upon you and yours.

Human beings are flawed in their judgment and rarely capable of true dispassionate objectivity. Creating public metrics that are published widely encourages fairness and the morale that goes with the sense of positive reward for numbers-based, objective, successful contributions.

7.5.3 Industries Can Self-Police

The issue with losing public faith is that the public tends not to make fine distinctions. Many fine and ethically upstanding insurance companies and financial institutions are suffering in the aftermath of negative public opinion based on the activities of their not as ethically accountable peers. As ethical violations become more public, the resulting loss of faith impacts all businesses, and even the economy as a whole. In "The Impact of AIG Bailout on Investors," Christina Pomoni [8] wrote:

> The first immediate impact of the AIG bailout is evident on investor confidence. In spite of the increased consumer spending and household income...the AIG scandal overshadowed the markets....The U.S. economy and, consequently, the global economy, are affected by the governmental actions to help a corporate monster recover.

Sinha and Ahmad [9] also wrote about AIG:

> American International Group was saved by the American government. Same may not be true for other insurance companies. Thus, the insurers will have to be careful in future.... The insurance industry will have to be more realistic in future taking lessons from the debacle of AIG. *They should be careful while providing insurance and shall charge premium proportionate to the risk involved.*

It is not hard to imagine that, in retrospect, the insurance industry would love to be able to retroactively self-police AIG. Perhaps this can be a warning to the next industry's high visibility ethical meltdown. We discuss self-policing in detail in Chapter 8.

7.5.4 Creativity is Rampant

Opening the conversation to ensure accountability across the organization can serve as a great energizing force. The latest corporate fad in many large firms is to hide the organization chart from employees to minimize pirating of critical employees from competitors. Whether this strategy works to keep employees from leaving is questionable—if an employee leaves, it is not generally because the organizational chart has been pirated—but I know from personal experience that what this does achieve is to confuse everyone inside the organization.

I've been part of many unintentionally amusing conversations in which a new organizational change was reported although no one knew the old one had been in place. Announcing responsibility and accountability for strategic goals is simple but in these environments is strangely revolutionary.

Clear accountability means that individuals can share ideas. There is a clear mapping of how and why a project is important that validates the creativity and potential of every individual the entire organization. Not that everyone will be welcomed with an opinion, this is unrealistic, but it is a validating experience to become part of an organization that shares its goals openly as well as the progress on those goals. Leaderless groups by definition raise anxiety—unintentionally many organizations create such an atmosphere, outside of the small department to which the employee belongs. [10]

7.5.5 High Focus is Enabled

Clarity about the strategy and goals of the organization is the most powerful way to ensure that all employees are able to contribute to those goals. This simple statement again is quite radical; it is the rare organization that takes the time to detail to new employees the plan and approach to winning in the marketplace. Forced to piece this together over time, not only is much inefficiency created, but the employees live in a kind of constant uncertainty.

The business strategy must change with market changes; as a result, strategy changes may be frequent. Those that understand the strategy themselves may not be sure about who is responsible for realizing what component, or often, may not have the time or feel it is appropriate to share that information broadly within the company.

The cost of delegating work without a business context creates a kind of robotic disconnection with the value of the effort. Such disassociation with the value of the work ultimately means a loss of focus and other measures of excellence.

7.5.6 Jobs are Stabilized

There is a large difference between the firm that must implement IT outsourcing to keep afloat and one that maintains the kind of business environment that makes this a choice. These differences are palpable, and the creation of a work environment that maximizes profitability is essentially one and the same as the definition of the high performing organization. These organizations are not immune to downturns of the market, but for the factors under their control, they have maximized the value of the firm to both employees and shareholders.

In today's uncertain economic environment, growth and security related to the firm are the biggest value large firms can provide to employees. Clarity of goals enables employees to proactively identify and develop skills that are aligned with the strategy of the firm. It also enables employees to evaluate the relative importance of their efforts. Not everyone will be working on the top initiatives, but at least there is an acknowledgement of what the motivated employee can be working towards.

But the most important aspect of empowering the CETO is the support of the robustness of the business itself; not only aligning the work of the informed employees, but also cutting down the likelihood of internal groups that are focused more on political alignments than productivity and contributions. Minimizing the drag of these groups, which are easy to hide in large complex organizations, can boost the overall competitiveness of the firm greatly.

7.5.7 The Community is Nourished

Finally, a strong firm means the ability to remain an active partner within the social web that is the community. These contributions, which make a difference in the daily lives of workers, and which often provide a source of pride and loyalty for firm employees, are of course much more easily funded within an environment of business growth,

7.6 Summary

The great majority of Americans believe outsourcing hurts the economy, and many believe their own families' and friends' jobs have been directly impacted by outsourcing in a negative way. Despite the negative relationship in the public mind between supporting purchases from overseas and the loss of jobs, Americans are generally unwilling to forego the savings that purchasing outsourced goods and services represents. These are powerful marketplace drivers that are unlikely to change anytime soon. Thus it is the person in the mirror that is at least partly responsible for this seemingly unchangeable trend.

In another ironic twist, looking more deeply at the principles of robust ethical leadership within a large firm, we find that these principles are in many ways identical to those characterizing a high performance organization. A key enabler for these benefits, both material and ethical, is empowering a C-Level Chief Ethics Officer. The role of the CETO is to promulgate firm morale, productivity, creativity, focus, and stability through a robust ethical program implementation. We turn now the future of IT ethics in Chapter 8.

References

[1] Gallup Poll, February 2–5, 2011, International Trade/Global Economy Polling Report. http://www.pollingreport.com/trade.htm
[2] CBS News Poll, July 31–August 5, 2008, International Trade/Global Economy Polling report. http://www.pollingreport.com/trade.htm
[3] Pew Research Center/Council on Foreign Relations Survey, April 23–27, 2008, http://www.pollingreport.com/trade.htm
[4] Pew Research Center/Council on Foreign Relations Survey, April 23-27, 2008.
[5] Associated Press/IPSOS Poll, May 17–19, 2004. http://www.pollingreport.com/trade.htm
[6] *Newsweek* poll conducted by Princeton Survey Research Associates, February 19–20, 2004. http://www.pollingreport.com/trade.htm
[7] *Investor's Business Daily/Christian Science Monitor* poll conducted by TechnoMetrica Market Intelligence. May 8–13, 2002, http://www.pollingreport.com/trade.htm
[8] Christina Pomoni, The Impact of AIG Bailout on Investors, *Bukisa Business, Finance & Investing*, January 7, 2010. http://www.bukisa.com/articles/226441_impact-of-government-aig-bailout-on-investors
[9] S.K. Sinha and Zaid Ahmad, Global Financial Crisis with Special Reference to the Insurance Industry, *African Journal of Marketing Management*, 1(8), November 2009, 184–189. http://www.academicjournals.org/ajmm/PDF/Pdf2009/Nov/Sinha%20and%20Ahmad.pdf
[10] Anthony R. D'Augell, Changes in Self-Reported Anxiety during a Small Group Experience, *Journal of Counseling Psychology*, 2(3), May 1974, 202–205. http://www.sciencedirect.com/science/article/pii/S002201670762094X
[11] Alison Gray, What are the Characteristics of High Performance Teams in the Workplace? 2010. http://www.team-building-bonanza.com/teams-in-the-workplace.html

Appendix: Characteristics of High Performance Workplaces [11]

From "What are the Characteristics of High Performance Teams in the Workplace?", Team Building Bonanza.com, Alison Gray, 2010 [12] http://www.team-building-bonanza.com/teams-in-the-workplace.html

■ Well-defined roles for individual team members
■ Open and clear communication

- Effective decision making, ideally based upon comprehensive facts
- Balanced team participation, including valuing others ideas and opinions, and openness to new ways of working
- Valuing diversity, including diversity of background, thought processes and approaches to achieving the goals of the organization
- Managed conflict, emphasizing open and early communication of problems so they do not fester and become larger
- Positive atmosphere, supporting a climate of trust and openness
- Cooperative relationships across the team with open collaboration
- Participative leadership, where leaders are good role models

Chapter 8

The Future of IT Ethics

"Denial ain't just a river in Egypt."

Mark Twain

8.1 Building the Ethical Future

In our journey exploring ethics in IT outsourcing, we started with a look at our history, then academic research that specified three levels of ethical decision making: the macro (society), molar (corporate) and micro (personal). In particular, we looked in detail at the kind of fundamental change an empowered ethics PMO and empowered chief ethics officer (CETO) can effect.

To begin, let's ground the discussion in the present by reviewing the research in earlier chapters that identifies the following current trends. An extremely dramatic, precipitous drop in available U.S. labor is just around the corner but not yet felt in the marketplace.

- Dramatic and sharp declines in the U.S. labor force, oddly mirroring the rate of decline in the U.S. housing market in intensity, reaching full throttle from 2015 onwards (Chapter 2, Figures 2.1. and 2.2).
    - Very slow growth is forecast in "first world" labor markets, with simultaneous rapid population growth in very poor countries (Chapter 2, Figure 2.3).
    - Very large numbers of unemployed, disenfranchised workers rapidly breaking records for length of unemployment and sheer size U.S. workers

unemployed today are reflecting record numbers, growing in numbers more rapidly, and are unemployed for many more months (Chapter 2, Figure 2.4a).

- The skills mismatch between those seeking jobs and those seeking to fill jobs is at an all-time high (Chapter 2, Figure 2.4b).

■ Americans perceive companies that outsource as having poor leadership and chasing profit at any cost.

- Americans believe lower overseas wage structures (80%), unbridled profit seeking (77%), lower health and safety standards (61%), consumer demand for low cost goods (56%). and weak corporate leadership (42%) as major reasons for outsourcing (Chapter 7, Figure 7.5).

■ Popular opinion polls reveal Americans feel outsourcing is bad for the country as well as bad for themselves, their friends and their families. Despite this, they knowingly "vote" for outsourcing every day by purchasing lower cost goods and services made possible by the very concept they identify as hurting them and their country.

- One of five responders said they personally, a family member, or someone they knew lost a job because of outsourcing within the last year (Chapter 7, Reference [6]).
- Almost 50% of the U.S. public felt that free trade agreements probably hurt or definitely hurt the financial situations of their families (Chapter 7, Figure 7.4).
- When asked directly whether they would pay more for products and services that originated in the U.S. versus purchasing similar, less expensive products from overseas, only slightly more than half (55%) would do so (Chapter 7, Reference [8]).
- The primary cause of recent mass job losses is organizational change and increased productivity, not outsourcing. The total number of job losses due to outsourcing, though increasing, comprises a relatively low percentage of the total. Research shows that outsourcing—particularly moving work offshore—is uncommon in long-lasting large-scale layoffs and accounts for fairly few of the workers terminated in these actions (Chapter 4, Reference [1]).
- While secondary to job losses caused by productivity increases, the number of job losses related to offshore outsourcing is growing (Figure 2.10 and Figure 2.11a).

■ On the world stage, Americans perceive that the U.S. is rapidly losing ground as one of the top five economic powers. Depending upon the type of measure, traditional or non-traditional, that perception is invalidated or confirmed.

- In 2000, 65% of those polled believed the U.S. was the top economic power in the world; by 2011 that number had decreased to 32%. This represents is a very dramatic shift in a very short time. (Chapter 7, Reference [1]).

■ According to the traditional measures of relative national wealth, including the GNP, the U.S. remains at the top across all nations. Non-traditional measures, however, such as the Health Department Index (HDI), discussed in detail below, do not bear out that conclusion. On the world stage, recent research has established a direct tie between national GDP and quality of education. The United States ranks very low on the world scale in quality of education as compared to GNP.

- The quality of GDP (gross domestic product) is directly tied to the level of education of citizens (Chapter 2, reference [23]).The quality of U.S. education ranks very low as compared to the rest of the world (Chapter 2, Reference [17]).

■ Distribution of wealth in the U.S. is increasingly concentrated into the hands of the very few.
- The gap between the wealthy few and the many poor in the U.S. is reaching record levels (Chapter 2, Figure 2.21), increasing almost 20% between 1970 and 2008.
- Companies are reaping record profits with little reinvestment in hiring (stockpiling cash) (Chapter 2, Figure 2.20).
- Median CEO income increased 430% in the last 10 years compared to the average worker's wage income increase of 26%, and average corporate profit increases of 250% (Figure 1.18). The ratio of CEO pay to worker pay is at least 10 times (roughly) other nations (Chapter 2, Figure 2.17).
- The top 0.1% of Americans (about 152,000 people) showed increases in income of 385% between 1970 and 2009; the top 0.5% (about 610,000 people) showed overall increases in income of 141%; the top 1%, increases of 90%, and the top 5%, increases of 59%.
- During the same time period, the bottom 90% of Americans experienced negative (–1%) income changes between 1970 and 2009 (Chapter 2, Figure 2.21).

■ The number of hungry people increased dramatically between 2008 and 2009 (Chapter 2, Reference [32]).

Based upon this collated data, a picture emerges of our present course—and future course if we do not change. Outsourcing is here to stay. Americans hate the concept but love the bargains.

■ Driven more by other factors such as organizational restructuring and productivity gains, the number of jobs in the U.S. will remain smaller than the available labor force for the short term.
■ For the long term, geographic population statistics show a much smaller pool of available first world workers, including those in the U.S.
- Baby boomers aging to an average of 70+, along with the impact of significantly lower birth rates, will create a dramatic shock to a labor market grown accustomed to the long-term glut of available workers.

- Beginning around 2015 and rapidly accelerating, the currently scarce skill sets will be much more difficult to find. Firms will either need to train workers to take these roles or move elsewhere on the globe to fill these roles.

■ The already dramatic and extraordinary concentration of wealth in the United States is exacerbated by recent, vastly increased differences between CEO and worker pay. These differences are not mirrored elsewhere in the world and are not tied to company performance.

■ These trends portend a future similar to the Gilded Age. The great majority of workers remain at or near poverty, sharing a small percentage of the wealth. A very small number of extremely wealthy citizens living in heavily guarded enclaves, commanding over 80% of the total national wealth.

8.2 The Molar or Corporate Entity as a Driver of Ethical Change

This picture of the future, informed by the present, underscores the need for robust ethical constructs to be developed and enforced in large firms. The molar or corporate entity serves as the touchpoint between the macro broad economy and the micro personal realm. If large corporate cultures become ethically self-policing in recognition of the benefits that accrue, essentially powered by informed self-interest, a much more positive cycle of macro and molar ethics becomes possible.

We have evolved our definition of ethics in this volume as a result of our analytical journey. "Do the right thing" has been expanded to include the obvious truth that all workers are to be held accountable to objective, transparent measures of performance excellence—from the top down. This measure is in support of robust businesses that maximize a secure living for all employees. Enabling such a definition, and self-policing to that definition, is not so much of a stretch, even with the current business culture.

The need for robust, objective research on the true costs of corporate ethical compromise—validating important studies such as those conducted by David Sirota, Louis A. Mischkind and Michael Irwin (Chapter 5, Reference [3])—becomes evident. It is intuitive to believe companies cannot thrive without enthusiastic employees and loyal customers. At present there is much room between intuition and the definitive studies that confirm it.

8.3 Drivers of Future Ethical Change

Let's take a look at what the industry, here comprised of IT professionals, would require for meaningful definition and self-policing of a robust ethical construct. In order toachieve a workable set of guidelines for IT workers, the following items at a minimum are required:

- Global industry standards definition: what does ethics mean in the context of IT in general, and outsourcing in particular?
- Commitment to transparency of data sharing and information at an industry level.
- Global review board for enforcement, including reporting of violations, at an industry level.
- Sponsorship of robust academic and objective research on the real costs of corporate unethical behavior. This includes obtaining a solid base of data on the impacts of outsourcing on the U.S. economy as a whole, including communities and individuals.

IT outsourcing generally represents a small percentage (well under 30%) of a very large firm's IT organization—thus the requirement is for an international standard. If the outsourcing firm is founded in New York, with multiple workers located in India, China, and South America, all serving clients in Canada, the U.S., and Europe—creating a country-specific standard and source of ethical assessment is clearly far too narrow.

We will look at each of these requirements in detail below.

8.3.1 Definition of Global Outsourcing Industry Standards

The current global standards, including those in development by the International Association of Outsourcing Professionals (IAOP) are relatively young, reflecting the short history of the outsourcing industry as a whole (http://www.iaop.org/Download/Default.aspx?ID=374). They generally ignore the "pink elephant in the room"—the big question whether the outsourcing model per se is ethically challenged. As jobs literally move from one country to another despite the very fuzzy ethical and unanswered economic impact questions these movements incur, it is futile to pretend those questions do not exist.

Generic ethical standards that could apply to any professional group from accountants to bricklayers, such as those relating to professional conduct, measurable outcomes, and adherence to legal standards, are not sufficient here. The unique facets of outsourcing ethics require additional detail to achieve a meaningful ethical industry standard. A global statement of ethics within the context of IT outsourcing (see Appendix A at the end of this chapter) must, at a minimum, include the following:

- A definition of ethics that includes a prescriptive establishment of business principles that serve to make the firm grow in a robust way, but through ethical means.

- In addition to the obvious components of creation and support of a robust ethical culture from the top down, ethical alignment means creating a culture of objective performance accountability at all levels of the organization, as well as reasonable performance goals for employees who are not constantly pressured to bend the rules to keep their jobs.
- Open sharing of non-competitive data on the impact of IT outsourcing, to debunk the negative mythology (as research suggests), or finally, deal with it up front to address it, as a nation or as an industry.
- Promulgation of equal access to higher education across all income levels in the United States, to support our competitive standing as a nation including our national wealth as measured by GNP, and also to support the robust growth of U.S.-based firms through access to an educated labor force.

8.3.2 Commitment to Transparency of Data Sharing and Information at Industry Level

First and most important is a commitment by participating large firms to openly share non-competitive IT outsourcing program information, to build a database of reference material. So much disinformation and confusion surround the true impact of IT outsourcing that a genuine analysis would shine a light on the equivalent of the economic bogeyman. Perhaps the bogeyman is truly as bad as popular imagination makes it out to be, but to date the small amount of research data points to the opposite, and seems to suggest that outsourcing is actually a generator of economic well-being at the macro level. The conclusion of this volume based upon analysis of the compiled research—to the surprise of this author—is that it is unequal access to higher education in the United States, a direct result of the highly concentrated wealth in the hands of the very few, that is sending more and more jobs overseas. This creates a negative cycle that impacts even our future GNP.

There is evidence—although inconclusive—that the outsourcing of jobs actually produces greater wealth for the United States. Unfortunately, as measured by access to education, health care, and overall life expectancy per capita, the benefits of this wealth are experienced by fewer and fewer Americans. Note that this finding is not about quality of education and who or what is at fault if our educational system is not up to international standards. It is about simple access—of all the countries in the world, the United States rates very poorly in simply providing the average U.S. citizen the chance to participate in advanced education.

The kind of industry information that is desperately lacking includes historical metrics related to the recently implemented as well as long-standing IT outsourcing programs. This includes scope (type of IT outsourcing), cost (in categories to preserve confidentiality), description of program goals (financial and non-financial), percentage of goals achieved, and business impact. (Business impact would measure customer satisfaction, employee satisfaction, product and service quality, and the

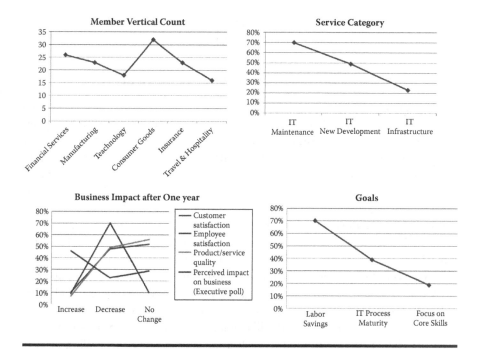

Figure 8.1   Example of IT industry ethics oversight report.

overall impact of program to the business (good / bad / neutral) as perceived by various stakeholders. These metrics are to be submitted anonymously and collected and reported only in aggregate across all companies—see Figure 8.1 for an example.

8.3.3 Global Review Board for Reporting of Violations and Enforcement

Self-policing of industry groups with robust power of censure appears to be an inevitable next step. Even before the recent vast array of ethical violations, the most serious of which threatened the economy of the country and even the world, it is clearly almost impossible for the government to keep up. This does not mean governmental regulation is not needed and important—think child labor laws—but the pace of change in business is such that new developments are so rapid and complex that it is difficult to achieve an understanding of how and where regulation can and should be applied, never mind getting them in place in time to be effective.

Pressures to align to industry peer ethical standards that have power to formally censure a particular practice, defined by the industry and to be publically called out when appropriate, are far more effective for the establishment of the "next new thing" in ethical violation. When the stakes reach the level of the economy itself, the future of business ethics—not just IT ethics—calls for a greater level of self-policing and intra-industry and government cooperation—for the well-being of everyone at all levels—macro, molar and micro.

8.3.4 Data-Driven Analysis of Economic Impacts

Solid research is needed at the macro, molar, and micro levels. We must understand who wins, who loses, and how to minimize the losses while maximizing the gains. At the macro level, some of the financial economic indexes can be mapped over time along with statistics on mass layoffs and announcements of large outsourcing programs. Traditional macro measures of economic welfare such as the Gross National Product (GNP), Gross Domestic Product (GDP), and Net National Income (NNI) are not sufficient. We must include other non-traditional, broad measures by country over time. Examples are the Human Development Index (HDI), the Index of Sustainable Economic Welfare (ISEW), the Genuine Progress Indicator (GPI), the Gross National Happiness (GNH) measure, and Sustainable National Income (SNI). We look more closely at the implications of these new indices later in this chapter.

Molar assessments such as aggregated earnings before interest and taxes (EBITA) over time (by industry), Altman Z-scores (published in 1968 by Edward Altman as a formula to predict the likelihood of bankruptcy within 24 months), the Zeta (1977) credit risk model, stock prices and ratings, and polling of public perception can be accumulated as they relate to discrete outsourcing industry events and metrics.

Finally the micro level should analyze the post-outsourcing program impact on individuals in 1-, 3-, and 5-year increments including statistics on income, job satisfaction, and views of their former employers.

8.4 Distribution of Income: Surprising Root Cause of Cycle of U.S. Job Loss

The GDP or Gross Domestic Product is a measure of the value of all goods and services produced within a country measured in U.S. dollars. As noted by the Central Intelligence Agency, it the "measure most economists prefer when looking at per capita welfare and when comparing living conditions or use of resources across countries" [1].

Challenges with the accuracy of measurement of the GDP are well documented, but the salient fact is that much of the GDP measures corporate wealth, and is not a general indicator of overall economic welfare for a typical citizen. Figure 8.2 shows the top 10 GDP levels by nation for 2010; Figure 8.3 shows the bottom 10. The U.S. is well within the top 5, running neck and neck with the European Union for the top spot in the world. The bottom 10 nations in GDP earn a fraction (about 10%) of the GDPs of the top two nations [1].

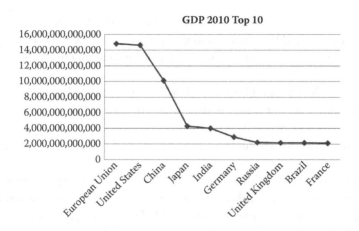

Figure 8.2   Gross Domestic Product (GDP) Top Ten for 2010. (*Source: World Fact Book,* Central Intelligence Agency.)

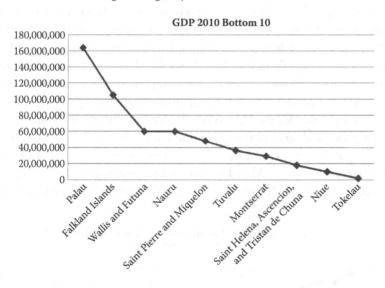

Figure 8.3   Gross Domestic Product (GDP) Bottom Ten for 2010. (*Source: World Fact Book,* Central Intelligence Agency.)

8.4.1 Beyond GDP:—Who Receives the Benefit is an Ethical Issue

If the GDP measures corporate wealth, not necessarily those of the citizens of a country, how is the actual average citizens' relative economic welfare measured?

One of the more interesting alternative indices is the United Nations Health Development Index (HDI) that measures social as well as economic development.

Each country is measured across three dimensions and four indicators as follows

■ The health dimension is measured by life expectancy at birth.
■ The education dimension is determined by two indicators (mean years of schooling and expected years of school).
■ Living standards are measured by gross national income per capita [2].

The HDI is only one of the indices that attempts to measure pure financial metrics but attempts to associate those financial metrics with factors that determine the impact of that wealth in terms of quality of life for the average citizen.

Figure 8.4 shows the relative growth over 30 years (1980 to 2010) in average HDI for the highest and lowest 10 countries. Despite the stellar and consistent GDP of the U.S., the perception that the U.S. is losing ground in quality of life for the average person, as noted in earlier research polls, is now validated. The United States is shown to be well under average in HDI growth rate for the world between 1980 and 2010, and at only 0.36% growth as compared with the world average of 1.05%.

The dip in the middle of the chart shows the U.S. is far closer to the bottom 10 than the highest 10—on a par with Kenya [2]. Figure 8.5 shows the same HDI growth rate information for 1980 through 2010 in table form [2]

How is it possible for the U.S. to be a leader in GDP (rated second in overall wealth of goods and services along with the European Union as of August 2011) to show so poorly in the HDI index? The HDI measures the quality of life for the average citizen based on health, education, and income, and ranked the U.S. 65th in the world. The answer lies in the distribution of income. Yes, the U.S. is one of

Average Annual HDI Growth Rate in % Top 10 and Lowest 10 Countries 1980–2010

Figure 8.4 Average Human Development Index Trend for Top Ten and Bottom Ten countries, 1980–2010. (*Source:* United Nations Development Programme.)

Country	2010 Rank	1980 to 2010 (%)	World Average, 1980 to 2010 (%)
Ten Highest			
Nepal	1	2.37	
China	2	1.96	
Bangladesh	3	1.99	
Benin	4	1.67	
Morocco	5	1.59	
India	6	1.61	
Tunisia	7	1.49	
Egypt	8	1.52	
Algeria	9	1.42	
Pakistan	10	1.52	
United States	65	0.36	1.05
Ten Lowest			
Togo	86	0.70	
Kenya	87	0.50	
Central African Republic	88	0.58	
Côte d'Ivoire	89	0.42	
Chad	90	0.19	
Lesotho	91	0.24	
Zambia	92	0.11	
Liberia	93	0.05	
Congo	94	−0.37	
Zimbabwe	95	−1.81	

Figure 8.5 Average Annual HDI Growth Rates for Top Ten and Bottom Ten countries, 1980–2010 showing U.S. placement and world average. (*Source:* United Nations Development Programme.)

the top two holders of wealth in the world, but the actual benefit of our high levels of gross income is not felt by all citizens equally.

Distribution of income in the United States may be unfortunately lopsided, but how does that impact the ethics of IT outsourcing? The implications of the HDI are quite significant. The HDI paints a picture of, extremely limited access to higher education provided to the average U.S. citizen, due to lack of income and relative cost of education.

As documented above, national wealth is reduced significantly over time with a poor HDI. Research confirms that the overall GNP of a nation is reduced by limiting access to quality education to a relatively wealthy few. If we do not provide all our citizens access to higher education, we cannot compete in the world market over time. If the country with the highest skills, lowest cost human resource pool "wins" in the labor marketplace, we are poised to lose—big time. [Figures 1.11 and 1.13]

A completely under-the-radar problematical trend, that is nonetheless quite real, is the skills mismatch gap. This gap describes the widening gulf between the increasing numbers of the unemployed and the number of unfilled U.S. jobs. Many jobs go unfilled due to lack of qualified, educated candidates, and represent the jobs that the ever-increasing numbers of American unemployed are not able to fill due to lack of requisite skills and experience, based in higher education.

As less of our population is able to build these highly desirable skills due to limited educational access, global firms will move these high level, well-paying jobs to other first-world countries. A noticeable trend in my own professional life is the increasing numbers of senior managers of very large U.S. companies who now reside in the European Union, with all of the implications that brings for building out their own organizations within the same geographical base.

These trends in turn portend a negative cycle, to wit—the less our income is distributed, the lower our access to education, the greater the numbers of both high and low paying jobs are moved elsewhere. This decreases our national wealth over-all, and increases the concentration of wealth in the hands of even fewer Americans, in a self-perpetuating negative cycle of more and more U.S. jobs moving overseas.

8.4.2 Our Dramatic Income Distribution Inequality

Even professional economists are surprised at the extent of income inequality in the United States. In a telling study (Norton & Ariely, 2010), most Americans believed that the distribution of income looked something like left side of Figure 8.6, when in reality it actually looks like the right. [3]

Part of the difficulty in communicating this surprising reality is that it is difficult to comprehend the depth of the wealth distribution gap. Most charts cannot accurately depict the bottom 40% because their relative percentage of wealth ownership is so small that it cannot to fit to scale when depicting percent of the concentration of wealth by the top 20% . While some charts define wealth differently, leading to small differences in percentages here and there, the primary and incredibly wide gaps of wealth ownership remain constant across all research.

The facts depicted in Figure 8.6 inform that the top 20% of Americans own 95% of the wealth—in popular imagination, the top 20% of Americans are estimated to own 60% of the wealth, not 85%. In actuality, 99% of the wealth is owned by the top 60% wealthy Americans, although it is by far concentrated in the hands of the top 20%. Most Americans, however, have the misconception that the bottom 20% share about 3–4% of the wealth.

Surprisingly, this study found that even professional economists subscribed to this myth. In reality, the bottom 20% of Americans own only about 0.7% of the wealth—a number so small it cannot fit on the scale.

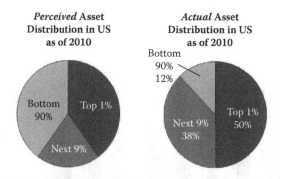

Figure 8.6 Comparison of perceived and actual distribution of wealth in the U.S., 2010. (Based upon data from M.I. Norton and D. Ariely, *Building a Better America One Wealth Quintile at a Time*. With permission.)

It is important to note that these figures are extremely conservative; when defining wealth as ownership of assets such as real estate and stock, the distribution is such that the top 10% of the population owns 95% of the wealth [3]. The figures become even more lopsided if we delve into the details of wealth distribution and asset ownership within the top 20% (Figure 8.7) [4]. Income is not as concentrated as wealth (Figure 8.8), as shown by an analysis of income from 1982 to 2006 [5]. The trend, however, is still to concentrate income in the top 20%, reducing income in the bottom 80%. Looking more closely at the distribution of income across the top 1, 5, 10, and 20%, even back in 1992, 80% of Americans shared only 32% of the income (Figure 8.9) [5].

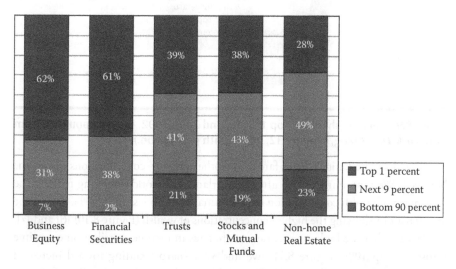

Figure 8.7 Wealth and asset distributions across top 10% of Americans.

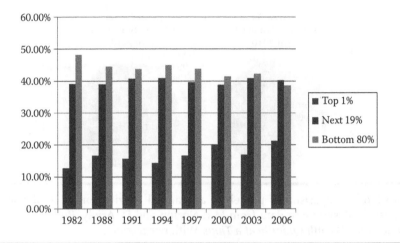

Figure 8.8   U.S. annual income trends, 1982–2006. (Based upon data from *New York Times* blog, January 12, 2011. With permission.)

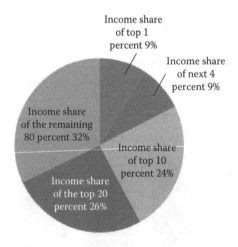

Figure 8.9   Income shares of Top 1, 5, 10, and 20%, 1992. (Based upon data from *New York Times* blog, January 12, 2011. With permission.)

How does the United States fare across other nations' concentrations of wealth? Not well. We rank number two after Switzerland, the world's banking nation. The percentage of wealth concentration drops dramatically, to less than 50%, within the top 10 nations showing the highest concentrations of wealth (Figure 8.10) [6] and [7].

Again, when we look more closely at changes in income distribution over time across the top 10% (Figure 8.11), we find very sharp trending toward increased income concentration between 1993 and 2008, echoing the inequality of the so-called Gilded Age between 1918 and 1928 [8]. It is no wonder that the current

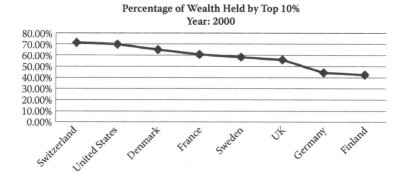

Figure 8.10   Wealth concentrations in top ten countries, 2000. (*Source:* Uni-Wider World Institute for Development Economics Research.)

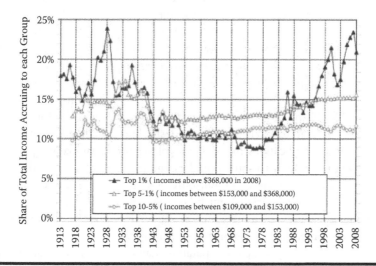

Figure 8.11   Changes in U.S. Income distribution over time. (*Source:* Uni-Wider World Institute for Development Economics Research.)

economic climate is referenced as the Great Recession. Levels of income inequality have not been this dramatic since the Great Depression.

Why are these relatively esoteric economic calculations of general well being relevant to the future of IT ethics? Data-driven assessments of the impact of IT outsourcing have little meaning within the context of broadly misunderstood economic indicators. When we see the GDP, it appears all is well; it is only when we look at alternative indexes that the reality of what we personally see and experience is validated. Intuitively, Americans know that it is harder to afford a good education, stay healthy, and make ends meet today in 2012 than it was in 1980. Indexes such as the HDI at least try to reveal our collective experience in attempting to have income meet the basic needs of education, health care, and covering the monthly bills. What is important is to create a body of knowledge that establishes the impact of outsourcing on these macro indicators.

It is not hard to conclude that over the 30 years from 1980 to 2010, outsourcing enhanced the GDP (corporate wealth), but negatively impacted HDI (economic wellbeing of U.S. citizens based on health, education, and income). This is because the impact to U.S.-based IT workers is not the same across the board. Those that are able to develop new skills marketable in the post-outsourcing world may even prosper. Others—the unfortunate 10% with outdated skills— may become part of the chronically unemployed or underemployed. However, it would be helpful to focus these initial findings into a more definitive analysis by tracking trends of mass layoffs and other data to GDP and HDI over time via robust, well-funded research.

If indeed the HDI is minimized, the challenge is to work on awareness for all citizens about the price that we all pay for short-lived, poorly educated, and unhealthy citizens. The underlying costs of supporting a consistently shrinking HDI are many. Ultimately, we will need to decide the kind of country and people we want to become and the values we want to represent. Will we use our enormous collective wealth to provide equal—or at least more equal—access to educational opportunities for the one in five children and one in seven persons who live in poverty in the U.S.? Improving access to education brings more wealth for all.

The commitment to open research and sharing of industry data has both molar and macro implications in the intangible realm of company reputation. It is imperative that large firms start to understand the complex and subtle relationship between announcement of IT outsourcing-related layoffs and customer loyalty. Clearly, price point is driving much U.S. purchasing. However, given a choice between equal products, customers such as the wealthy boomer consumers prefer to align with a company that demonstrates social conscience [9].

Just how much is a company reputation damaged when IT outsourcing is announced? What kind of difference is made when a company invests in a soft landing and publicizes its investments in former employees and the communities in which they live? These are critical questions that perhaps do not lend themselves to purely objective scientific assessment methodology, but can be explored within the context of a large chartered international organization willing to share anonymous, summary level information and data over the long term with similar large organizations.

8.5 Ethical Implications of Findings on Distribution of Wealth

A compelling explication of economic human rights can be found in a book by Lisa Dodson titled the *Moral Underground: How Ordinary Americans Subvert an Unfair*

Economy [10]. Filled with stories about how ordinary heroes bend the rules to do the right thing—Ms. Dodson's heroes find a way to help feed hungry children, steer poor dying patients into medical studies, or avoid docking the pay of a single working mother living in poverty, at home with a very sick child. Dodson's Economic Bill of Rights (my terminology) is based upon these five principles:

- Work provides a livable wage.
- People with families have equal opportunities for professional advancement.
- All children are protected and valued.
- Poverty creates illness and disease, thus undermining society as a whole.
- Education is a national priority to develop every citizen's potential.

8.5.1 Support of Economic Bill of Rights

If moving jobs overseas is the pink elephant in the room, any kind of economic bill of rights becomes a lightning rod, dividing Americans in their core beliefs about the causes of poverty. The line is drawn between those who believe that poverty is self-inflicted (reflective of character deficiencies such as lack of personal work ethic) versus those who perceive poverty as a systemic, structural part of society that could easily entrap any U.S. citizen.

Underlying these divergent beliefs is the uncomfortable truth, difficult for generous and helpful Americans to acknowledge, that daily we look the other way in ensuring the wellbeing of our most vulnerable of citizens—the incredibly high number of children in the U.S. and the world living in poverty. There the verbal static and debate lessen—we are not so concerned, with children, as to whether they "earned" it or not. If poverty status is reflective of personal character and work ethic, or other personal characteristics open to judgment, it is clear that these judgments do not apply to these innocents. How is it that the richest country in the world routinely does not feed its hungry children? Is the hungry two-year-old son of the single mother, the same mother who must routinely choose between food and heat, to be held to a character test?

8.5.2 Pulling it All Together: Ethics of the Personal as Informed by the Ethics of the Molar and Macro

In Chapter 5, we discussed culpability and the need to establish a personal line in the sand. We must face this culpability. Thus it is, for every IT offshore program that is executed without a view to providing fair play, for every middle and senior manager making the politically expedient instead of the right decision, we must face ourselves [11]. There is the chance that the innocent suffer as a result of that action or inaction. This is the so-called worst-case scenario, and this reality is the one that must inform that line in the sand.

As I write this book, 20% (1 in 5) of children in the U.S. children live in poverty [11].

It is these underlying truths that lead many of members of Lisa Dodson's moral underground to bend or break the rules in the name of ethics and fairness. These truths also lead me, as a vice president and offshore program manager, to look in the faces of the members of my board of directors and tell them exactly what they did not want to hear, and later turn down a lucrative opportunity to represent the offshore interests of a country with many ethics violations. That I would have never met with the individuals hurt by my cooperation does not lessen the impact of my decisions. Am I culpable or responsible for the plight of poverty in general? No. Am I responsible for looking the other way when I could help, perhaps significantly? I believe the answer must be yes.

Why reference the line in the sand? We started this volume with vague concepts of how IT outsourcing impacts the economy at large, the corporation, and the individual. We are now in a position to help that individual make informed decisions, referencing the research that has lead us on this journey of understanding.

One of the foundational concepts of effective business negotiations is to enter the deal-making process understanding the limits beyond which you will not negotiate, in other words, the edge of what you will accept. The ultimate negotiation power, it appears, is to be able to walk away from the table, and thinking this through ahead of time provides the clarity to do so when the moment is upon us. It is clear that IT offshore outsourcing presents the kind of ethical dilemmas that require all working professionals to identify their own line in the sand—beyond which they cannot cross. One way to evaluate that line is within the context of extremes. Corporations may not be moral entities, but the thought that any company would allow its products and services to benefit and promote the extreme evil represented by Nazi Germany puts this question in a different relief. That extreme example clarifies that corporations clearly do not exist within an ethical vacuum. Where and when they focus their energy imposes a level of ethical accountability beyond the balance sheet.

Similarly, the extreme example of the potential impact of our actions on the most vulnerable can help us draw our own negotiation line in the sand when making decisions regarding how we utilize our influence in the murky waters of IT offshore decision making. Whether we recognize it or not, when our actions have the potential to impact the most vulnerable—such as children of the poor or about to become poor—the concept of where we draw our personal line may come into sharper relief. Unfortunately, the face of the unemployed—in prior times generally acknowledged to be going through "tough times" but able to survive until the next job, perhaps with some compromises—is rapidly at risk of turning into the next face of poverty. A recent study from the Bureau of Labor Statistics [11] stated the following in regards to collection of long durations of unemployment, which prior to 2011 had been capped at 2 years:

...An unprecedented rise in the number of persons with very long durations of unemployment during the recent labor market downturn. Nearly 11 percent of unemployed persons had been [for] 2 years or more.... [Thus, we] have updated the CPS instrument to accept reported unemployment durations of up to 5 years.

8.6 Summary: Change Management for an Ethical Future

The future is ours to build. Most Americans sense we are at a critical juncture. Key to building a positive future is enabling broader access for all members of American society to higher education to enable our workforce to compete in the global marketplace.

Interestingly, careful collation and analysis of current research trends show that outsourcing, despite popular opinion, may actually be bringing greater wealth to the United States. In some sense, the focus on outsourcing is obscuring a more dangerous trend that should serve as the greatest concern for most Americans. This is the documented narrowing of access to higher education for an increasing number of Americans. This lack of access to education is based upon shrinking income and the relatively high cost of higher education. As our workforce becomes less educated, Americans becomes less able to compete, more jobs go overseas, establishing a negative cycle that is contributing to today's "Great Recession" with increasing numbers of unemployed, and unemployed for longer.

If the United States is unable to unlock the death grip represented by our high concentration of wealth, our collective wealth will be lessened, and our quality of life continue to deteriorate.

In this volume, we discussed three levels of ethical decision making: personal or micro, corporate or molar, and society as whole or macro. It is the corporation that can take the driver's seat to both embody and enforce a new ethical construct across society and individuals. Appendix E outlines a fledgling international charter for ethics, with a strong emphasis on creating robust internal corporate accountability via an Ethics PMO managed by a chief ethics officer, as well as sponsorship of extensive objective research on the cost benefit of these investments. These are the mechanisms by which true "change management" can occur within the context of each industry and each corporation, perhaps eventually emulating the positive cultures at companies such as DEC (Appendix B).

It is my sincere hope that we create a future based upon these and similar robust ethical principles, to build a better work world for ourselves, and for those who come after us in this great nation that is the United States of America.

References

[1] Central Intelligence Agency, *The World Factbook.* Accessed August 28, 2011. https://www.cia.gov/li brary/publications/the-world-factbook/docs/whatsnew.html

[2] United Nations Development Programme. *Human Development Index Trends, 1980–2010.* Last update January 31, 2011. http://data.un.org/DocumentData.aspx?q=HDI&id=229

[3] Michael I. Norton and Dan Ariely. *Building a Better America One Wealth Quintile at a Time.* Perspectives on Psychological Science Series, Downloaded from pps.sagepub.com February 3, 2011. http://www.people.hbs.edu/mnorton/norton%20ariely%20in%20press.pdf

[4] G. William Domhoff,. Wealth, Income, and Power. Who Rules America: Power in America, September 2005, Updated July 2011. http://sociology.ucsc.edu/whorules america/power/wealth.html

[5] Paul Krugman, Why Does Inequality Make the Rich Feel Poorer? *New York Times* Blog, January 12, 2011. http://krugman.blogs.nytimes.com/2011/01/12/why-does-inequality-make-the-rich-feel-poorer

[6] Edward N. Wolff, Recent Trends in Household Wealth in the United States. Rising Debt and the Middle-Class Squeeze: An Update to 2007. Working Paper 589, Levy Economics Institute of Bard College, March, 2010. http://www.levyinstitute.org/pubs/wp_598a.pdf

[7] James B. Davies, Susanna Sandström, Anthony Shorrocks, and Edward N. Wolff, The World Distribution of Household Wealth, Uni-Wider World Institute for Development Economics Research, February 2008. http://ideas.repec.org/a/ecj/econjl/v121y2011i551p223-254.html

[8] Emmanuel Saez, Striking it Richer: The Evolution of Top Incomes in the United States. *Pathways Magazine.* Stanford Center for the Study of Poverty and Inequality, Winter 2008, p. 6. http://elsa.berkeley.edu/~saez/saez-UStopincomes-2008.pdf

[9] Martin von Meyer-Gossner, For Boomers Optimism and Social Conscience of Brands is Key, Strategy Web, April 18, 2001. http://www.thestrategyweb.com/study-for-boomers-optimism-and-social-conscience-of-brands-is-key

[10] Lisa Dodson, *The Moral Underground: How Ordinary Americans Subvert an Unfair Economy.* New York: New Press. 2009. http://thenewpress.com/index.php?option=com_title&task=view_title&metaproductid=1778

[11] Judy Molland, *One in Five American Children Now Living In Poverty.* The Human Rights Cause, Annie E. Casey Foundation. 2011. http://www.care2.com/causes/1-in-5-american-children-now-living-in-poverty.html

[12] U.S. Bureau of Labor Statistics, Labor Force Statistics from the Current Population Survey: Changes to Data Collected on Unemployment Duration. Last modified July 8, 2011. http://www.bls.gov/cps/duration.htm

[13] Reesa Abrams and Steven Heiser, *A Study in Corporate Cultures. Digital Equipment Corporation, The Reality: HeroSpeak,* Digital Equipment Corporation, 1988.

[14] Reesa Abrams, *A Study in Corporate Cultures. Digital Equipment Corporation, The Myth: A Cultural Operating Manual,* Digital Equipment Corporation, 1988. http://decconnection.org/ReesaAbrams-DIGITAL.pdf

Appendix A: Proposed International Charter of IT Outsourcing Ethics (iCIOE)

- Purpose: The goal of the iCIOE is to promulgate ethical and informed decision making in IT outsourcing based upon objective research and shared information to create an ethical body of IT Outsourcing knowledge (eBIOK).
- Ethical and informed decision making means supporting the economic growth of the firm through ethical means, via the following ethical business principles:
  - Creation of a culture of accountability and transparency for firm performance at all levels of the organization.
  - Commitment to enabling a high performance organization.
  - Ensuring job performance measures are directly tied to the strategic goals of the firm.
  - Creating a culture of meritocracy in which there is an open understanding of business strategy and technical support of that strategy, encouraging open and creative dialogue at all levels of the organization in which all functional disciplines are encouraged to participate.
  - Ensuring each employee has realistic performance goals that do not create a work environment in which deception must be practiced in order to be successful.
  - Cultivation of an ethical work culture in which senior executives are required to model and support the highest standards, including protection of scarce natural resources and the economic and physical health of employees and customers.
- Method: Each member company agrees to share in the collective sharing, analysis and reporting of anonymous ethics information relating to IT outsourcing, including financial information at a high level. In addition, each member agrees to financially sponsor global research, and publish the findings without prejudice.
- Member information collected, analyzed and published shall include:
  - Measures of customer satisfaction prior, during, and after IT outsourcing.
  - Financial goals and achievement of those goals after program implementation at macro level.
    - What was the planned versus actual ROI of the IT outsourcing program?
    - At regular intervals of 6 months, 1 year, 3 years and 5 years, what is the percent achieved of year over year savings from the program?
    - What were the high level original goals for the cost savings from the program (stock dividends, investment in infrastructure, R&D, company purchases, etc.)? What percent was diverted elsewhere and where?
    - Measures of employee satisfaction prior, during and post IT outsourcing.
    - Measures of community impact.

- Unemployment rate by country as related to major IT outsourcing announcements.
- Measures of goods and services quality.
- Public perceptions of the vertical industry as related to number of large outsourcing announcements year over year.
- GNP and other macroeconomic (stock index) measures for major purchasers and providers of IT outsourcing services. While none of these necessarily would be able to establish cause and effect, clearly, since so many factors impact GNP or stock price, it will be interesting to determine a relationship over time for the following broad economic indicators:
  - Analysis of aggregate stock prices of vertical industries as related to number of large outsourcing announcements for that industry by country.
  - Analysis of aggregate EBITA by vertical industry as related to number of large outsourcing agreements for that industry by country.
  - Tracking of changes in GNP for purchasers and providers year over year as related to large outsourcing announcements for that country.
  - HDI and other alternative methods for analyzing economic wellbeing.
- Commitment to minimizing negative impacts for long-term loyal company workers.
  - Cultivating awareness and supporting objectivity regarding the underlying decision making processes for worker releases.
  - Ensuring that a percentage of savings from the program is re-invested to create an economical soft landing for impacted workers commensurate with the realistic events of the economy. Pragmatically, this means a different program at a different level of funding and options at 4.0 % unemployment than at over 10% unemployment.
  - Monitoring and measuring the success of the safe landing program with a commitment to meet metrics such as 90% of impacted employees re-integrated into the workforce at equal or better levels of income within 1 year.
- Commitment to maintaining the community social contract—the defacto understanding that the corporation was a member of the community, building little league fields and sponsoring those teams, and other activities overtly contributing to the betterment of all who lived there.
- Sponsor an active ethical oversight body.
  - The function of the oversight body is to monitor and comment upon IT outsourcing customers and providers.
  - The goal of the oversight body is not to levy fines but to review and censure firms that overtly violate the ethical guidelines outlined in this document. An important component is to underscore to the community that these violations are not sanctioned by other firms.

- The oversight body reviews newspapers and other sources of information for information about compliance with ethical guidelines. These include providing livable base wages for workers, adhering to minimum standards of health for work environments, and robust programs to help those who lost their jobs due to IT outsourcing that match the level of viable economic alternatives for those workers.

■ Economic Ethical Guidelines
  - All workers earn a livable wage.
  - All workers work in a healthy environment.
  - All long-term loyal workers who are displaced via IT outsourcing receive robust soft economic landing suite of benefits. These benefits are designed to successfully realize the overall goal of 90% repatriated in to the workforce within 1 year. If this is not feasible, they receive economic benefits equivalent to 1.5 to 2 years of salary to minimize their long-term financial commitments and enable them to live indefinitely on lower wages.
  - Community programs will be evaluated and supported.

■ Members are strongly encouraged to establish a formal chief ethics officer position to represent them in this body, actively participate in supporting further industry research, and establish an atmosphere of accountability and transparency of business goals for the firm.
  - Members will participate in annual ethics forum panel discussions.
  - Members will sponsor community transparency and accountability in communications, including measurements of soft landing programs for displaced workers.

Appendix B: Creativity Unleashed: Another Look at Digital Equipment Corporation

I was fortunate to be an employee of Digital for the greater part of a decade, and that experience left an indelible impression. One of those impressions that grew stronger over the years was a work culture that expected each leader to express a personal commitment to the economic welfare of every employee (not all lived up to that expectation, of course) and possess a strong personal code of ethics.

In the course of writing this book, I was in contact with Reesa Abrams, the co-author of *A Study in Corporate Cultures. Digital Equipment Corporation, The Reality: HeroSpeak* [13] and *A Study in Corporate Cultures. Digital Equipment Corporation, The Myth: A Cultural Operating Manual* [14]. Reesa Abrams worked at DEC for over 20 years and was tasked with researching and documenting DEC's culture for on-boarding of new employees. These are her experiences as recorded in an interview in August 2011.

Reesa was born and raised in the Deep South. As a result of participation in a program for gifted and talented students she was offered work at the University of Texas in Austin. Her class brought up Node 4 on the Internet, and she then joined NASA on the Apollo 8 and 10 Programs in Houston. After a stint in New York at IBM, she moved to New Mexico with her husband, where she worked at the University of New Mexico and studied cultural anthropology and technology. She was teaching a course there when her supervisor relocated to Massachusetts and recruited her to work at DEC.

Reesa moved to Maine and started work for Bill Johnson, then head of DEC's engineering group. DEC provided Reesa a PDP-11 for her personal use at home—a very unusual step then; the computer was valued at $200,000! Reesa's assessment of the unique DEC culture included the following key points:

■ Engineering driven: DEC took on the culture of nearby engineering schools such as MIT. The culture at MIT is very entrepreneurial, with a heavy emphasis on intellectual meritocracy and equality. Anyone who had a good idea was welcomed; no one was to be left out of the creative process.

■ Job self-definition: It was not atypical for very smart and accomplished employees to leave within the first 3 to 4 months due to the very high level of self initiation required to be successful. Employees were expected to spend a few months soaking in the atmosphere, then devising projects and their roles, and sell both the projects and themselves (in the roles) to their entire teams. For those used to relatively passive roles in typical hierarchical cultures, this requirement to self-define and "sell" was a culture gap sometimes impossible to bridge.

■ Heavily matrixed organization: The only way that projects moved forward was with everyone on board. Often this meant more time negotiating a project than executing it. The highly agreement oriented, consultative requirement meant a very high value was placed on each individual's opinion without regard to rank. DEC was both a meritocracy and an "ideaocracy." Those with the best ideas won.

■ The freak in me speaks to the freak in you: the underlying value, never really published, was that DEC was instrumental in helping build the Internet; it did not simply sell computers. DEC had an overt awareness of how the Internet would change global interactions and computing. It maintained strong, long-term relationships with many educational institutions including MIT, Columbia, Harvard, UCLA, Stanford, Texas, and University of North Carolina. The collective best of the brilliant minds of the day worked to create an Internet by which information could be broadly shared, and secrets difficult to keep—an underground pipeline of information flow in which the engineering culture of equality, connectivity, and intellectual meritocracy could be delivered to the world.

Early on, the engineering staff at DEC, including Reesa, trained with Deming in Japan on lean manufacturing. As part of that effort, Reesa's group developed the following core values of the DEC culture including ownership, clarity, trust, honesty, respect, and informed decision making. Reesa later spent years as DEC's liaison to Stanford University where she often served as a catalyst. She played a role in creating and funding the space grant college fund, a privately funded program on over 50 U.S. campuses dedicated to helping students learn about the science involved in the space program.

According to Reesa, the uniqueness of DEC was the feeling of coming home for many. She said, "We were there because we had to be there—it was our passion."

The following excerpt from her publication entitled *A Study in Corporate Cultures. Digital Equipment Corporation, the Myth: A Cultural Operating Manual* defines and explains the culture:

1. Definition of Culture

The pattern of basic assumptions that a given group has invented, discovered, or developed in learning to cope with its problems of external adaptation and internal integration, that has worked well enough to be considered valid, and therefore, to be taught to new members as the correct way to perceive, think, and feel in relation to those problems.

2. Purpose of Culture Studies

The goal of the Digital Culture Research Project is to get people to realize that it is their responsibility to understand the culture—to get involved—to work the network—to sign up—to get committed—to make Digital work—to make Digital successful.

3. Assumptions

Following [are . . .] some assumptions that support the DEC culture. Remembering these can often make clear why Digital does business a certain way. These are not necessarily all the assumptions about the company. They are limited to beliefs about people, relationships, and business at the operating level. They were adapted from the works of Scorzoni, Dyer, and Schein.

A. We Are All One Family

Digital is a company where appropriate subcultural differences are encouraged, failure among members is tolerated to some extent, promotions are from within the company, people are encouraged to express their feelings and give candid feedback when approached, all doors are open, informality and working through people (instead of memos) is encouraged, and verbal commitments are to be kept.

B. People Are Creative, Hard Working, Self-Governing, and Can Learn

People are encouraged to learn from experience, follow do-it-yourself careers, learn by the sink-or-swim method with some support, be self starters, create jobs that are greater than formal job descriptions, push at the system from the bottom up, respect the differences of others, find ways to enjoy work, take ownership, and do the right thing.

C. Truth and Quality Come from Multiple Viewpoints: Free Enterprise

People are all working at Digital to help the company produce good products and services and thus make money for the company. Individuals in the process of governing themselves have different ideas about how to proceed. Some people view this as conflict. Indeed there is some conflict. The basic idea is that we are all in this business to win. That requires buy-in from key areas, selling ideas to get support, confronting ideas that are not considered good for the final outcome, taking risks, tolerating mistakes (but not big ones), and accepting that this is a political world. Top management feels that they are not smart enough to know every detail. Top management is able to sort out ideas.

D. Survival Equals Responsiveness to Changing Environment

Working at Digital is fast-paced and involves constant reorganizations. The matrix is the basis of management. Things need to happen if you are to succeed, you will be judged by the results you obtain, and you are expected to build and work within teams. Proposals are to be clear and brief and there are turf issues to be worked through the management layers. To find success you have to solve cross-functional problems and time-to-market problems as well as produce.

Index